The Moral Status of Combatants

This book develops a new contractualist foundation for just war theory, which defends the traditional view of the moral equality of combatants and associated egalitarian moral norms.

Traditionally it has been viewed that combatants on both sides of a war have the same right to fight, irrespective of the justice of their cause, and both sides must observe the same restrictions on the use of force, especially prohibitions on targeting noncombatants. Revisionist philosophers have argued that combatants on the unjust side of a war have no right to fight, that pro-war civilians on the unjust side might be targetable, and that lawful combatants on the unjust side might in principle be liable to prosecution for their participation on the unjust side. This book seeks to undercut the revisionist project and defend the traditional view of the moral equality of combatants. It does so by showing how revisionist philosophers fail to build a strong foundation for their arguments and misunderstand that there is a moral difference between collective military violence and a collection of individually unjustified violent actions. Finally, the book develops a theory defending the traditional view of military ethics based on a universal duty of all people to support just institutions.

This book will be of much interest to students of just war theory, ethics philosophy, and war studies.

Michael Skerker is an Associate Professor in the Leadership, Ethics, and Law Department at the US Naval Academy. The views in this book are the author's alone and do not necessarily reflect those of the US Naval Academy, the Department of the Navy, or any branch of the US Government.

Series Editors: War, Conflict and Ethics

Michael L. Gross, *University of Haifa*, and James Pattison, *University of Manchester*

Ethical judgments are relevant to all phases of protracted violent conflict and inter-state war. Before, during, and after the tumult, martial forces are guided, in part, by their sense of morality for assessing whether an action is (morally) right or wrong, an event has good and/or bad consequences, and an individual (or group) is inherently virtuous or evil. This new book series focuses on the morality of decisions by military and political leaders to engage in violence and the normative underpinnings of military strategy and tactics in the prosecution of the war.

Just War Thinkers
From Cicero to the 21st Century
Edited by Daniel R. Brunstetter and Cian O'Driscoll

Contemporary Just War
Theory and Practice
Tamar Meisels

Just American Wars
Ethical Dilemmas in U.S. Military History
Eric Patterson

Ethics and Military Strategy in the 21st Century
Moving Beyond Clausewitz
George Clauswitz

The Moral Status of Combatants
A New Theory of Just War
Michael Skerker

For more information about this series, please visit: www.routledge.com/War-Conflict-and-Ethics/book-series/WCE

The Moral Status of Combatants

A New Theory of Just War

Michael Skerker

LONDON AND NEW YORK

First published 2020
by Routledge
2 Park Square, Milton Park, Abingdon, Oxon OX14 4RN

and by Routledge
52 Vanderbilt Avenue, New York, NY 10017

Routledge is an imprint of the Taylor & Francis Group, an informa business

© 2020 Michael Skerker

The right of Michael Skerker to be identified as author of this work has been asserted by him in accordance with sections 77 and 78 of the Copyright, Designs and Patents Act 1988.

All rights reserved. No part of this book may be reprinted or reproduced or utilized in any form or by any electronic, mechanical, or other means, now known or hereafter invented, including photocopying and recording, or in any information storage or retrieval system, without permission in writing from the publishers.

Trademark notice: Product or corporate names may be trademarks or registered trademarks, and are used only for identification and explanation without intent to infringe.

British Library Cataloguing-in-Publication Data
A catalogue record for this book is available from the British Library

Library of Congress Cataloging-in-Publication Data
Names: Skerker, Michael, author.
Title: The moral status of combatants : a new theory of just war / Michael Skerker.
Description: Abingdon, Oxon ; New York : Routledge, [2020] |
Series: War, conflict and ethics | Includes bibliographical references and index.
Identifiers: LCCN 2020009765 (print) | LCCN 2020009766 (ebook) |
ISBN 9780367247140 (hardback) | ISBN 9780429284045 (ebook)
Subjects: LCSH: Just war doctrine. | War–Moral and ethical aspects. |
War (Philosophy)
Classification: LCC U22 .S56 2020 (print) | LCC U22 (ebook) |
DDC 172/.42–dc23
LC record available at https://lccn.loc.gov/2020009765
LC ebook record available at https://lccn.loc.gov/2020009766

ISBN: 978-0-367-24714-0 (hbk)

ISBN: 978-0-367-52108-0 (pbk)

ISBN: 978-0-429-28404-5 (ebk)

Typeset in Times New Roman
by Wearset Ltd, Boldon, Tyne and Wear

For Cristina and Seneca

Contents

Acknowledgments   viii

PART I
Revisionist just war theory   1

1   Introduction: the challenge of revisionist just war theory   3

2   Reductive individualists' theories of liability   23

PART II
The foundations of the moral equality of combatants   53

3   The culpability standard of liability   55

4   Responsibility, justification, and liability in war   74

PART III
The moral equality of combatants   117

5   The foundations of military norms   119

6   Military norms   138

7   The moral equality of combatants   172

Index   200

Acknowledgments

Thank you to the following scholars for commenting on parts of this book: Adam Betz, Helen Frowe, James Pattison, Nikki Coleman, Stephen Coleman, David Luban, Adam Henschke, David Whetham, Yitzhak Benbaji, Heather Roff, Whitley Kaufman, Ed Barrett, Mitt Regan, Michael Robillard, Chris Eberle, Marcus Hedahl, Bradley Strawser, and anonymous reviewers at *Ethical Theory and Moral Practice* and the University of Chicago Press. Thank you to the series editors of this book, James Pattison and Michael Gross, and the acquisitions editor, Andrew Humphrys.

For technical information and insights into military service, thanks to LCDR Bill Kuebler (USN), LT Randall Leonard (USN), LT Zachary Prager (USN), LCDR Chris Kimball (USN), MAJ Ian Fishbeck (USA), Col Ed Barrett (USAF), Capt Justin Farrar (USMC), Capt Mosi Smith (USMC), Capt Joshua Girton (USMC), LtCol Dan Healey (USMC), LT Chad Bayse (USN), CDR Adan Cruz (USN), CDR Mark Maglin (USN), CAPT Wes Huey (USN), CDR Bill Lawrence (USN), LCDR Mike Rak (USN), CDR Dave Shopler (USN), LT Perry Hepworth (USN), CAPT Rick Rubel (USN-Ret.), CDR Kevin Haney (USN-Ret.), CAPT Glenn Gottschalk (USN-Ret.), CAPT Mark Adamschick (USN-Ret.), LtGen John Sattler (USMC-Ret.), LT Trevor Thomson (USN), CPT Michael Robillard (USA), LCDR Laurie Coffey (USN), CAPT John McGrath (USN), CAPT Greg Chapman (USN), CAPT Roger Isom (USN), CAPT Glenn Kuffel (USN), LtCol Rafford Coleman (USMC), RADM Alan Baker (USN-Ret.), SOC Daniel Luna (USN), LT Andrew Hiller (USN), CAPT Doug Rau (USN-Ret.), LCDR Danielle Litchford (USN), LCDR Mike Good (USN), LtGen John Sattler (USMC-Ret.), Capt Aaron Maclean (USMC), Capt Charlton Howard (USMC, NCIS), Glenn Carle (CIA-Ret.), Barry McManus (CIA-Ret.), Chris Inglis (NSA), and Steve Ward (USA, CIA).

The views in this book are my own and do not necessarily reflect those of the US Naval Academy, the Department of the Navy, or any branch of the US government.

Part I

Revisionist just war theory

1 Introduction

The challenge of revisionist just war theory

Philosophers have engaged in moral reflection about war since ancient times. This book presents an argument about how such reflection should proceed. The central reference point for this argument will be the moral status of combatants, particularly the moral status of combatants participating in unjust wars.

According to the ancient tradition known in the West as *jus ad bellum* (justice of war), in order to be just, wars have to be declared by a legitimate authority, acting with a right intention, in prosecution of a just cause. The war must be the last resort to correct some profound injustice, consequent to a proportionality calculation in which the overall good accomplished by the war outweighs the damage done by the war, where the prosecuting state or political entity has a reasonable hope of success. Some formulations also include an intention or ability to fight the war using just means.

The consensus for the last three to four centuries in the Western just war tradition is that all combatants obeying the laws and customs of war are moral equals, no matter whether their political entity is prosecuting a just or an unjust war.[1] This designation has a restricted meaning. Combatants on opposite sides of the war may be morally unequal in the sense that one group's political entity may have a just cause for war and the other may lack a just cause for war. In this way, two lawyers may be morally unequal in the sense that one acts in the interests of a guilty client and the other, an innocent client.[2] The combatants themselves may be unequal in terms of their courage, patience, honesty, and the like. In the same arena of personal character, there is no moral equality between combatants who commit war crimes like perfidy, rape, or the deliberate targeting of noncombatants, and those who refrain from such actions.

The moral equality of combatants employs a restricted sense of morality regarding privileges and liabilities. The traditionalist view in the just war tradition is that during wartime, combatants on either side of a war are equally permitted to kill their enemies anywhere and at any time except when they have surrendered or are incapacitated. They are also equally morally and legally liable to be attacked at any time except following their surrender or incapacitation. This standard for the use of violence is markedly different than conventional justifications of self- or other-defense in civilian contexts. Unlike civilians in standard cases of self- or other-defense, combatants can be killed when they are

4   *Revisionist just war theory*

performing justified actions, such as defending themselves or their communities against unjust attack. They can be killed even if they are not a direct threat to the invaders, due to their incompetence, retreat, non-lethal specializations, or their distance from adversaries. Contrary to standard justifications of violence in civilian contexts, in war, corporate liabilities and privileges are universally afforded to (at least) all conventional combatants involved in the war, irrespective of their individual personal qualities, permitting lethal violence regardless of its ultimate political purpose. Neither side's combatants—neither German nor Polish, Israeli nor Syrian, American nor Iraqi—wrong the other's by engaging in, contributing to, or directing lethal violence. Whether combatants fight for an unjust or just cause, the argument is that they are neither consistently in the epistemic position to judge nor endowed with the professional authority to make determinations about the justice of the war. Since they are obliged by voluntary oaths of service or bonds of conscription to obey the orders of their superiors, the culpability for the collective action combatants execute is borne almost exclusively by the political leaders who have the knowledge and authority to make monumental foreign policy decisions. Combatants can only be justly punished for violating the norms of *jus in bello* (just warfighting) and the laws expressive of those norms.

This convention of combatant moral equality has come in for renewed attention in recent years, especially since the Iraq War of 2003. The convention, and its most prominent twentieth-century advocate, Michael Walzer, have been exposed to sustained, systemic critiques by "revisionist" philosophers. In broad terms, these theorists argue that combatants should not enjoy moral blamelessness and even legal immunity for fighting in unjust wars. This follows because combatants are responsible, to varying degrees, for judging the justice of wars in which they might serve and for refusing to serve in unjust wars. Failing that, some or all the actions the service member performs contributing to the main strategic thrust of that war are unjustified, making these service personnel individually and unilaterally liable to the defensive violence of the just side.

As the revisionists and many others use the term, liability to defensive harm is the condition of being targetable with harm without being morally wronged when that harm accomplishes some good, usually averting an unjust threat or harm. Liable parties may be targeted by people who are unjustly harmed or threatened by the liable party or by agents acting on behalf of the wronged party. The liable party is liable to a level of harm that is proportionate to the harm she is inflicting or threatening and that is necessary for the defender or a third party to use in order to halt the unjust harm or threat. The liable party no longer retains a right of self-defense and so is not permitted to defend herself or counter-attack against the non-liable party's proportionate defensive violence nor ask for defensive help by a third party.

Revisionists argue that a combatant fighting for an unjust cause has no right to kill enemy combatants who are merely defending themselves and their homeland. Like all people, combatants incur liability to defensive violence when they are responsible (in some form or another) for an unjust threat without justification that makes it necessary and proportionate for a non-liable defender to resort to violent self- or other-defense. A threat is called unjust because of what it might do to the non-liable defender; it is unjustified if the agent lacks strong moral reasons for carrying out the action. Generally speaking, justified violent action, such as that performed by the non-liable defender, does not incur liability to defensive violence. So combatants defending themselves and their citizens from an unjust attack no more incur liability than a person defending herself or a friend against a mugger. What is more, the defender's non-liability coupled with the unjust party's liability denies permission to the unjust party to fight in counter-attack, despite the fact that the defender's violence physically threatens the unjust party. Just as a mugger is not granted permission to fight back against his victim and call it "self-defense," neither is the unjust army newly permitted to fight once enemy personnel begin to defend themselves (McMahan 2009: 14).

Further, since ordinary service members are responsible for judging the justice of the wars to which they might be deployed, the traditional post-Westphalian distinction between *jus in bello* (justice in war, or just warfighting) and *jus ad bellum* (justice of war) fails to demarcate separate moral responsibilities for most service members and political leaders, respectively. ("Service personnel" are members of the military. "Combatants" are people who can be permissibly attacked in wartime. Combatants might include service personnel, members of organized sub-state militant groups, intelligence agency personnel, and civilians who attack combatants. I will refer to "service personnel" rather than "combatants" when discussing military members in peace-time and especially in the fraught moment when they receive deployment orders and have to decide what to do about their pending combatancy status—deploy or refuse, resign, desert, etc.) Revisionists typically argue that no service member should feel obligated by professional duty to deploy to a war simply because he was so ordered. He cannot foist responsibility for the war on his political leaders. Depending on his personal responsibility, measured in various ways, the unjust combatant may be a culpable attacker, an innocent threat, or a partially innocent threat (like an attacker who wrongly thinks his life is endangered by his victim). In theory, some combatants deserve to be punished in *post-bellum* war crime trials for participating in unjust wars, even if they did nothing to violate the traditional rules of just warfighting.

Finally, revisionists typically argue that the key principles of *jus in bello*, discrimination and proportionality, are wrongly formulated by traditionalist just war theorists. Per discrimination, the combatant/noncombatant distinction does not correspond to groups of people liable to, and immune from, being killed, respectively. Regarding proportionality, the unjust side's tactical goals do not count as "goods" that can be balanced against evils in a proportionality calculation (where one can proceed with an otherwise-permissible action if the good effects outweigh the bad effects). Regarding discrimination, military personnel on the just side of war are non-liable to violence, for the reason just mentioned, and some noncombatants on the unjust side may be even more liable than their military's combatants for demanding, supporting, or for formally launching the

6 *Revisionist just war theory*

war. As an example of the problem with proportionality, imagine a conscientious Wehrmacht officer in 1939 who only orders attacks on Polish military targets in cases where the military benefits for the German side are proportionate to the harm done to Polish civilians. He still fails to perform morally right actions because the Wehrmacht's tactical goals do not count as goods in a proportionality calculation. Nothing done to further the unjust aims of the war can be a "good" (Tadros 2012: 259–277, 2014: 42–77; Bazargan 2013: 177–195, 2014: 114–136; Strawser 2013; Bomann-Larsen 2004: 142–160; Norman 1995; Frowe 2014, 2011: 530–546, 2015: 1–16; Fabre 2009: 36–63, 2012, 2014: 90–114; Gross 2010; Garren 2007: 8–11; Lichtenberg 2008: 112–130; McPherson 2004: 485–506; Rodin 2002, 2011: 74–110, 2008: 44–68; Coady 2008: 153–175; Øverland 2006: 455–475; Mapel 2004: 81–86; McMahan 1994a: 252–290, 1994b: 193–221, 2004: 75–80, 2005a: 386–405, 2005b: 1–21, 2006a: 377–393, 2006b: 13–17, 2007: 50–59, 2008a: 19–43, 2008b: 227–244, 2009, 2011: 544–559, 2014a: 428–453, 2014b: 104–137, 2014c: 115–156).

If legally implemented, revisionist ideas would upset centuries-old laws of war, exposing civilians to direct targeting by combatants, inviting service personnel to refuse deployment orders based on their personal assessment of the war's justice, making deterrence and war-planning difficult since leaders could not legally compel service personnel to deploy, and exposing all combatants on the unjust side of the war to prosecution following the war.[3] Despite the radicalism of their claims and the destabilizing potential of their arguments, revisionist just war theory today is arguably the dominant school of thought among analytic philosophers with an interest in war.

The revisionists articulate an intuitively powerful argument. It might strike some readers as counter-intuitive that grandpa had no more or less a right to fight the Nazis than the Nazis had to fight him. It seems very strange to say that soldiers fighting for an aggressive, genocidal regime have the same right to kill their enemy as troops defending their democratic countries from invasion. Yet a reader familiar with conventional just war theory, coming from a legal, international relations, or political science background, may be surprised by the revisionists' conclusions and methods. As some revisionists acknowledge, their conclusions are impractical, counter-intuitive, and unsettling to readers accustomed to reverential discussion of military personnel and military service.

How do the revisionists reach their conclusions? Let us start with the position revisionists reject. Advocates of the moral equality of combatants and associated egalitarian *jus in bello* norms (i.e., norms extended in equal measure to both sides) say that the morality of a war, specifically, the morality of deciding to wage or continue to wage a war, is independent of the morality of fighting the war, except in cases where the widespread use of unjust tactics makes the entire war unjust. Combatants' liability to being targeted with proportionate and necessary amounts of violence has nothing to do with the collective goals they pursue. Instead, their liability depends on the material threat they directly or (even very) indirectly pose to adversary combatants. Their liability to punishment is linked only to violations of *jus in bello* that are directly in their control or, consequent

Introduction 7

to their unlawful orders, affected by most of the standard conditions of culpability countenanced by criminal law.

By contrast, the thesis uniting revisionists is that liability to being targeted with defensive harm and, potentially, *ex post facto* punishment is not independent of the ends combatants promote with their actions (or even their mere presence in the armed forces).[4] They are liable to varying degrees of harm if they are responsible (in some specified way) for contributing to an unjust threat without justification. In many cases, there will have to be an unusually strong moral reason to justify imposing an unjust threat on innocent people, such as risking "collateral" (foreseen, but unintentional) killing of civilians while targeting a vital military target in a just war (McMahan 2005a: 400). Typically, one is unjustified in imposing an unjust threat.

Combatants are not liable to harm if their violent actions or violence-supporting actions are justified, on the revisionist line. This standard applies to all combatants involved in a war and so even combatants on the just side unjustifiably participating in an unjust intermediate aim like a massacre of noncombatants are liable to defensive violence. By the same token, combatants on the unjust side are perhaps non-liable if they are currently pursuing an intermediate just aim like rendering aid to refugees.[5] These are atypical cases, qualifications to the revisionists' main point. Revisionists are in a position to make a very powerful argument in the more typical scenario where most combatants are contributing to the main strategic thrust of a war. To express this argument, let us first note that our conventional reference to a war like "the Russo-Japanese War" is really a combined reference to two wars, e.g., Russia's war against Japan and Japan's war against Russia (Bazargan 2011: 514). In many cases, both sides are fighting unjust wars (such as in the Russo-Japanese War, where both sides had imperial designs on Korea). Yet in wars where one political entity is fighting an unjust war and its adversary is fighting a just war, the revisionist theorist knows *a priori* that the number of non-liable personnel on the just side will vastly outnumber those on the unjust side. All the adult, sane[6] personnel contributing to the main strategic thrust of the unjust side are liable to defensive harm to varying degrees since their actions are unjustified and all the personnel pursuing the main strategic thrust of the just war are non-liable to harm because their contributory actions are justified. Call this the revisionists' "asymmetry thesis." This thesis denies the doctrine of the moral equality of combatants. There can be neither equality of permissions to engage in violence nor of liabilities to suffer violence between two people or groups when one is justified in acting and the other is unjustified.

This book seeks to defend traditional just war thinking in content and method. In Part I, I will challenge the revisionist project by arguing that the asymmetry thesis is not adequately defended by most revisionists. In Part II, I will argue that the thesis *cannot* be defended because it is not necessarily the case that most adult, sane service personnel on the unjust side of a war are performing unjustified, liability-incurring actions by virtue of their contributions to the main strategic thrust of an unjust war (i.e., excluding atypical missions like

8 *Revisionist just war theory*

protecting refugees in an unjust war or massacring POWs in a just war). The macro injustice of a war is not present in the majority of the individual contributing actions in the sense of providing agents strong moral reasons to halt action. Part II will also explain how combatants on opposite sides of the war, say, two mechanics, can be performing the same action from a normative point of view, distinct from the morally unequal ends they promote. Part III will then explain how both actors can be objectively justified in performing these actions. I will develop a contractualist account of battlefield permissions that can justify the actions of opposing combatants under certain conditions. This account will support the moral equality of combatants, traditional egalitarian military norms, and the traditional immunity of noncombatants to intentional harm.

I Clarifications regarding revisionism

Two qualifications need to be made now regarding differences among revisionists before I can outline my argument in greater detail. This section is necessarily technical. The majority of revisionists hold that military actions, along with all other complex collective actions, should be reducible for the purposes of analysis, critique, and prescription to simple individual actions. Most revisionists, and those I will focus on in Part I, might be called reductive individualists. The distinction between individualism and reductionism is not fully developed in the literature,[7] so I will try to be clear here in how I will use the terms. Individualism might be further divided into descriptive and evaluative individualism (Lazar 2017: 40). Descriptive individualists think that only individuals act in war or other collective activities; there is no philosophically meaningful way in which states, militaries, or navies "act." Another way of putting this point is that collective actions like wars are reducible to component individual actions without moral remainder. There are no irreducible collective actions that can be normatively considered apart from the collective's members' individual contributory actions. This fact would seem to make it unlikely that certain classes of collective activity could have uniquely applicable moral rules. It follows, then, that most, if not all, descriptive individualists are also evaluative individualists. They see the individual as the sole focus of moral reflection and accountability. Members of groups do not get special privileges unavailable to non-group members.

Reductivists hold that there is only a single moral domain, without any special applications for the behaviors of certain groups. Therefore, the same moral principles pertaining to individual civilians in self- or other-defense scenarios or other plausible justifications of individual violence pertain to combatants in war. Characteristically, most reductive individualists use thought experiments involving civilian self-defense scenarios to model claims about military ethics. Clarifying the definition of reductivism is important because many traditionalist scholars who defend the moral equality of combatants could be considered reductivists if the term means that all justified action, in and out of groups, "is justified *at root* by precisely the same properties" (Lazar 2017: 40, emphasis added). Some traditionalist scholars who think institutions are important in the moral life argue that institutional agents like government actors should follow institutional norms that are institutionally mediated or institutionally affected expressions of ordinary morality. Since reductive individualists typically juxtapose their work with traditionalists like these who allow combatants to adhere to different norms concerning violence in war, I will use a vaguer definition of reductivism than the "at root" definition to refer to the relevant revisionists. Call this vaguer definition "unmediated reductivism"; it excludes mediation of moral principles by institutions. Adherents of this kind of reductivism argue that service personnel must follow the same norms for violence as civilians and would be contrasted with "exceptionalists," who argue for unique military norms, be they *sui generis* or derived in some mediated way from foundational moral principles (see Frowe 2015: 1).

Not all revisionists are reductive individualists. There is at least one prominent revisionist who uses a collectivist approach. There are also traditionalist just war thinkers who use individualist or reductivist approaches. These permutations will be addressed in Part II.

This book in part is an argument about how theorists should engage in just war theory. I am going to argue in this book that descriptive individualism is a problem for just war theory for it fails to address the existence of collective entities that are more than an aggregate of the individuals therein as well as the existence of irreducibly corporate actions that are more than the mere sum of contributory individual actions. In addition to reductive individualists, some individualist traditionalists will also be subject to this critique in Part II. The descriptive individualists' denial of unique collectives can lead to *evaluative* individualism and reductivism. Evaluative individualism is a problem for just war theory because militaries and certain kinds of political entities *are* properly governed by their own norms and members of those institutions should adhere to those norms under certain circumstances.

Reductivism is a problem in just war theory for two reasons. First, the moral content of a war does not necessarily reduce down to all or most of the strategically significant contributing actions of combatants marking them with the same moral content. A war is not simply an aggregation of individual actions with a particular moral valence. It follows, then, that moral prescriptions worked out in reference to civilian individual self- and other-defense scenarios will not necessarily be relevant to combatants in war. Second, reductivists wrongly assume that there cannot be special moral rules for members of certain groups like militaries. I will argue that properly constituted military norms are institutionally mediated expressions of the same fundamental moral principles that govern civilian life. In sum, then, I will be defending an exceptionalist, collectivist (descriptive and evaluative) approach to just war theory in this book.

The following *possible* distinction between reductive individualists is important to highlight in order to defend my way of characterizing the general reductive individualist position. One has to engage in interpretation whenever one presents another scholar's views; sometimes that interpretation involves

10 *Revisionist just war theory*

critique, as one excludes implausible readings of the text (e.g., "surely, s/he cannot mean *that*"). I am not entirely clear if the following is a difference in substance or exposition, but I will be avoiding one of two following reductive individualist formulations that seems inconsistent with other reductive individualist commitments.

In presenting the asymmetry thesis, some reductive individualists characterize the injustice of a war as, in a sense, infecting the contributory actions of individual combatants and some reductive individualists present unjust wars as being the aggregate of unjustified individual actions. As examples of the first characterization, consider these selections from Cecile Fabre and Lene Bomann-Larsen, respectively.

> Taken together, my account of defensive rights and the account of the right to wage and kill in wars of collective self-defence which it underpins imply that whether combatants may … kill enemy combatants (in large part) depends on the moral status of their war *ad bellum* in general and whether it has a just cause in particular.… [I]f an act of aggression as carried out by A's army against the territorial integrity and sovereignty of community V is morally wrong, then its constitutive elements are wrong as well, and combatants$_A$ are therefore committing a wrongdoing. If it is morally wrong for A's army to cross over the border into V's territory, it is morally wrong for combatants$_A$ to do precisely that.
>
> (Fabre 2012: 70–71; see also Rodin 2002: 173)

> If we further accept that for a self-defensive counterattack to be justified, the initial attacker must be engaged in an "objectively unjust proceeding" (Anscombe), and if this is relevant also in war, an inequality between just and unjust belligerents is generated in terms of the objective justice (*ad bellum*) of the war they fight. And the injustice on the macro-level will then be repeated on the micro-level in every encounter between individual soldiers and fractions of armies.
>
> (Bomann-Larsen 2004: 149, quoting Anscombe 1981: 53)

This picture of the relationship between unjust wars and unjustified contributory actions is surely correct phenomenologically. A state's leadership declares war. Troops are deployed in massive numbers to a particular place and then clash with adversary troops. Under certain conditions, related to the leadership's goals and options as well as the facts on the ground, one group is fighting a just war and the other is fighting an unjust war. The theorist can analyze the situation once these conditions obtain and conclude that most or all of the troops are performing unjustified individual actions since they are responsible (in one way or another) for materially contributing to the main strategic thrust of the unjust war. The theorist can further take into account mitigating circumstances such as a combatant's youth, ignorance, compulsion, minor material contributions, etc. to reduce the baseline level of liability to

Introduction 11

defensive harm or the moral worth of halting him (for the purpose of proportionality calculation).[8]

Other reductive individualists seem to build their individualist analysis into their description of war. The presupposition seems to be that the martial context does not matter, because in the end, the individual is the relevant moral unit and responsible for an individual unjustified action. With respect to individual permissions and liabilities, a war differs from a mugging, a riot, a duel, or a gang fight only in terms of scale.

> First imagine a case in which a person uses violence in self-defense; then imagine a case in which two people engage in self-defense against a threat they jointly face. Continue to imagine further cases in which increasing numbers of people act with increasing coordination to defend both themselves and each other against a common threat ... What you are imagining is a spectrum of cases that begins with acts of individual self-defense and, as the threats become more complex and extensive, the threatened individuals more numerous, and their defensive action more integrated, eventually reaches cases involving a scale of violence that is constitutive of war.
>
> (McMahan 2004: 75)

Whereas in this quotation, McMahan seems to conceptualize an unjust war as a complex aggregate of unjustified individual actions, Frowe doubts the utility of even talking about unjust or unjustified wars as opposed to unjustified individual actions and clusters of unjustified individual actions.[9] In war, some people in a given military perform justified actions, and some, unjustified actions. We will expect to see far more unjustified actions in the military that is conventionally considered to be fighting an unjust war, but as there are no collective entities with their own standards of collective moral action, reductive individualists would be better to just focus on individual actions.[10]

By juxtaposing what at least are different ways of expressing the asymmetry thesis, I do not mean to draw an overly stark distinction between descriptive and evaluative modes of reflection, but I think that reductive individualists get the mix of description and evaluation wrong, especially in the formulations favored by Frowe and McMahan. I will argue in Part II that military actions are irreducibly corporate actions, meaning that the moral character of military action is not necessarily present in the individual actions of combatants contributing to a war's main strategic aim. This argument applies to all reductive individualists (and individualist and reductive traditionalists), yet the more resolutely individualist analysis is wrong by reductive individualists' own lights if, like Frowe, the theorist's revisionist arguments are in reference to unjust wars that could be unjust due to multiple derogations from the *jus ad bellum* checklist and not merely because they lack a just cause (as is the principal focus of McMahan's work). If we are taking into account multiple *ad bellum* criteria (e.g., just cause, last resort, proportionality, etc.), wars cannot be made unjust because they are an aggregate of lawful but unjustified actions (possibly outweighing a lesser

12 *Revisionist just war theory*

number of justified actions). Lawful, counter-combatant individual battlefield actions cannot be deemed justified or unjustified based on their proximate effects alone without appeal to the war they advance.

Imagine that combatant A1 kills someone on the enemy force, B1, and a combatant on that side, B2, kills A2, a compatriot of A1. Assume that the lethal physical behaviors are identical (each attacker fires one round from a rifle), each action was necessary for the shooter to defend himself and proportional to the lethal threat his target posed to him or his compatriots, each agent believes with an equal amount of subjective (or evidence-relative) justification that his country's cause is just, and each agent acts without any personal animus toward his enemy, but merely because he is following orders. Why is A1's lethal action justified and B2's lethal action unjustified? Some traditionalists defend the idea of the moral equality of combatants by focusing on the mutual threat posed by adversary combatants, their identical epistemic and intentional states, and their equal non-culpability for starting the war. Reductive individualists like Fabre, Bomann-Larsen, and Rodin can counter that there may be a moral asymmetry between what otherwise *look like* symmetrical actions because B2's action helps prosecute an unjust war or at least an unjust aim less expansive than the war itself while his victim A2's rights are intact (neither waived nor forfeited) because he is active on the just side or is contributing to a just aim less expansive than the war itself. B2 has a duty not to act violently while A2 has a right to defend himself and other innocent people. Yet according to Frowe and McMahan (or at least according to how they express themselves), it seems we can focus tightly on B2's action and determine that it is unjustified because it is an attack on someone whose rights are intact, without reference to the collective action B2's action advances. McMahan writes that there is a "just cause for war only when those attacked have made themselves liable to be warred upon" (McMahan 2005b: 8). One is justified in acting in self-defense if it is necessary and proportionate to use a certain level of force against a target who has made himself liable to harm by being responsible for the relevant unjust threat without justification. If many people have made themselves liable in such a way, the defensive response may be war. A war or subsidiary collective action (e.g., an assault on a particular town) could be called unjust because it is an aggregate of unjustified actions. Similarly, Frowe argues there is no distinction between *jus ad bellum* and *jus in bello* in part because the two standards assess the same objects. When politicians are considering the prospective justice of an imminent war, they are really speculating ahead of time about all the justified and unjustified actions that would potentially be performed in the war in aggregate (Frowe 2015: 7).

This argument is unsound. The collective action of war is not made unjust simply by the aggregation of thousands of individual unjustified actions.[11] An unjust war is not, for example, simply a case of thousands of people deciding on their own to commit murder or assist a murder and all setting out to do so in the same general time and place. This is my substantive view, but it seems that even by a reductive individualist like Frowe's own lights, a combatant cannot

Introduction   13

individually, or by teaming up with others, make a war unjust through *lawful counter-combatant* lethal actions (i.e., excluding war crimes like the murder of civilians or use of chemical weapons).[12] If a reductive individualist wants to say that collective actions have no true existence—they are merely a semantic short-hand for what is actually an aggregation of individual actions—then even their own rules for applying the term "unjust" to the semantic construction "war" are not met by aggregating thousands of individual unjustified actions.

What leads to this reading of the relevant group of reductive individualists? With a few caveats and subtractions, the reductive individualists accept the *jus ad bellum* checklist to determine if wars are just or unjust.[13] The reductive individualists' strongest case for arguing that the aggregation of individual unjusti-fied actions makes a war unjust (or at least makes it appropriate to call it unjust) at a particular moment[14] is that many combatants on the unjust side of a war are objectively contributing individual actions that further the unjust cause of the war. This may be why McMahan limits his argument in favor of the asymmetry thesis to wars made unjust by their cause (McMahan 2009: 6).[15] (That said, whether or not this material contribution makes the individual actions unjustified depends on the McMahan's account of liability, discussed below.)

Moving on to the other *ad bellum* criteria (I will discuss them all for the sake of thoroughness, though some reductive individualists reject legiti-mate authority and right intention), we see that a single combatant does not have the legitimate authority (compared to his president, king, or parliament) to make the collective action of which he is a part just through *his* declaration of war.[16] *His* intentions are also not germane to the justice of the war. The last-resort criterion has to do with statecraft—sanctions, diplomacy, etc.—not whether a combatant has attempted to flee or capture his foe before electing, as a last resort, to use lethal force.[17] One might argue that policymakers con-sidering reasonable hope of success and proportionality have to prospectively imagine an aggregation of all their troops' chances of success and proportion-ality calculations in each of their tactical engagements—such that a war is pro-portionate if all the anticipated tactical engagements are proportionate unto themselves (Frowe 2015: 6)—but this is not the case. Rather, when con-sidering hope of success and proportionality, policymakers have to consider opportunity costs of different possible strategies, whereas combatants assess reasonable hope of success and proportionality within the context of the strategy their leaders actually chose. Consider the following.

> State A has been asked by its ally, B, to come to its aid after B was unjustly invaded by C. A's policymakers consider if the prospective war is propor-tional and has a reasonable hope of success given two different strategies, one engaging C's forces in the north of B and one engaging C's forces in the south. The generals think either strategy will force C's forces into retreat from B if the initial attack is successful. In considering proportionality and the likelihood of success, policymakers compare prospective benefits to harms, including all combatant and noncombatant casualties, infrastructure

14 *Revisionist just war theory*

damage, and economic disruption in the north *or* the south *plus* the opportunity cost of not initially engaging the enemy in the south or the north (leaving the enemy free to continue killing B's troops and noncombatants there).

When a combatant from A makes a calculation about proportionality or likelihood of success regarding a particular attack on an enemy position in the south or the north (wherever A's military is deployed), he can factor in the harm an unrestrained enemy would do in this specific location as a cost to his inaction, but cannot include the harm the unrestrained enemy is doing in the region of the country where A's military is not deployed and where combatants A can have no effect. Yet this harm was part of policymakers' *pre-bellum* proportionality and likelihood-of-success calculations as an opportunity cost of their eventual decision. Thus, wars are not just or unjust merely by virtue of being an aggregation of all the justified and unjustified individual actions performed in one military versus the other. So the first of the two above-mentioned reductive individualist formulations is correct if the scholar thinks multiple derogations from the *ad bellum* list can make a war unjust. Wars are unjust on the collective level in the sense that the factors making the war unjust at a particular stage are only present in a context where political leaders are making decisions against particular geopolitical realities and considering or conducting the coordination of thousands of troops acting under centralized command. Reductive individualists then assume that the contributory actions supporting the main strategic thrust of this war are unjustified. I will refer to this formulation in discussing the reductive individualists' views, below.

If the differences in formulations referenced above are merely differences in exposition rather than substance, than it seems to me that there is an inconsistency in the views of those reductive individualists who accept that wars are unjust given multiple derogations from the *ad bellum* list, but also claim that unjust wars are simply an aggregation of individual unjustified actions. McMahan is not inconsistent in this way, but at any rate, I will make a substantive argument against his aggregation view and the views of any others who subscribe to this view in Part II.

II Liability for unjust threats; project outline

Revisionists argue that there are no moral grounds to extend an equal set of permissions and liabilities to the majority of combatants on unjust and just sides of a war because one set of combatants is mostly liable to defensive violence and the other is mostly non-liable. Merely posing a threat to someone does not make one liable to defensive violence. One only becomes liable to defensive violence when one is responsible (in one sense or another) for unjustifiably posing an unjust threat. Again, this means that the threat of harm is to a non-liable person and the actor lacks a strong moral reason for posing the threat.

Introduction 15

The revisionists' asymmetry thesis depends on a normative connection between a combatant's contributions and the collective action or end he materially advances. This follows because in many cases, combatants on both sides of a war are engaged in the same *in bello*-compliant behaviors under identical epistemic and intentional conditions. The combatants on both sides intend to complete discrete actions that, as far as they reasonably believe, are in service of a just war. The moral asymmetry between combatants cannot, then, come from a comparison of their actions at that level. Rather, the moral asymmetry between the two political entities' efforts is manifest at the macro level. Barring some overriding moral consideration,[18] a combatant's action is unjustified if it is meaningfully connected with an unjust threat such as manifest in the unjust war or unjust aim within a war. As McMahan writes, "there can be no justification for violence or killing in pursuit of unjust aims" (McMahan 2004: 79).

As we will see in Chapter 2, many reductive individualists are quite brief in their discussion of the connection between unjust collective actions and unjustified contributory actions.[19] No doubt this is because it is intuitive that a person's action is unjustified in some way if she contributes to an unjust collective action or end. For example, Smith's purchase of duct tape, ski masks, and pepper spray is unjustified if she means to give these items to a crew of bank robbers in order to facilitate a robbery. She ought not to help the robbers in this way; the merchant should refuse the sale if he knows the purpose and others would be permitted to take proportionate measures to halt her purchase or transfer of the items. Yet let us consider examples in which individuals are individually responsible (in some way) for furthering unjust collective actions or outcomes that will complicate the intuitive connection between individual actions and unjust outcomes. We will start with domestic examples before considering less-familiar military examples. As we will see, there are military analogs to all of the following.

- An assembly line worker moves a box full of aspirin down a conveyer belt. He does not know the pills have been poisoned.
- A waitress brings a hearty breakfast to a group of policemen she regularly serves, reasonably believing they will perform many justified actions that day. They later engage in an unjustified shooting.
- An engineer contributes to the development of a computer chip for her company. She knows the chips will be bought by hundreds of other companies for use in different projects, but she does not know that a rogue regime will years later use the chips to build illegal chemical munitions.
- Under threat of torture, a group of prisoners fight in "gladiatorial games" against other prisoners for the amusement of sadistic guards.

Smith is culpable for an unjustified action if she knows what her purchases will be used for, shares that end, and is free to assist or refuse to assist the robbers. She is their accomplice. Yet what if people lack some of those elements of culpability? In the above examples, individuals are engaged in responsible action that causally advances an unjust threat. By responsible

16 *Revisionist just war theory*

action, it is meant that they are in control of their actions; they are not hypnotized, psychotic, drugged, or "objectified" by being hurled at someone. Yet, in order of the four examples, the above individuals lack knowledge and intentionality with respect to that action (and would not reasonably expect any unjust threat to evolve), reasonably believe that they are enabling justified actions, generate a socially acceptable level of risk that intervening agents might misuse their work product, or act under duress. If, through some fanciful turn of events, it was necessary and proportionate for potential victims of the unjust threats in these examples to save themselves by directing lethal violence at the causally responsible, but non-culpable, parties, would they be permitted to do so on account of the non-culpable agents' liability to defensive violence? Obviously, this would be a highly counter-intuitive result in the first three cases since, on a common-sense view, the agents do not seem connected to the unjust threat in a way that should make themselves liable to defensive violence. While the coerced prisoners are directly posing an unjust threat, their non-culpability and extreme duress also suggest that a complicated argument is required to fully justify their opponents' violence. Yet different accounts of what makes a person liable, drawing on different potential elements of responsibility like causal efficacy, avoidability, knowledge, intention, and motive, could deem some, all, or none of the above agents liable to defensive violence. It is not even clear that all four actors are performing unjustified actions. While the factory worker objectively ought not to be moving the box down the conveyor belt (he would presumably remove the box from the line if he knew it contained poison), there may only be weak reasons for the waitress or chip designer to desist from their actions given the attenuated causal connection and intervening agents between their actions and eventual unjust outcomes. These weak reasons may not be sufficient to deem the action unjustified.

Military examples make clear that the intuitive connection between unjustified actions and unjust collective actions or ends is far more complex than in the case of Smith, the culpable robbery accomplice. Traditionalist critics have raised the following questions. What if combatants have no idea about the strategic ends their minute contributions advance? What if they reasonably believe the unjust ends they advance are just? What if they disagree with or are unsure about the strategic ends, but understand that states need functioning militaries to fight just wars and those militaries rely on obedient members to function? What if the combatants are conscripts marched to the front at gunpoint? None of these combatants are culpable for the unjust war like Smith is for the robbery. In order to redeem the asymmetry thesis, one first needs an account of justification connecting the strong moral reasons related to the collective action of the war to the contributory actions within the war. Second, one needs a standard of liability less exacting than culpability to deem combatants responsible for an unjust threat and liable to other service members' defensive violence.

Reductive individualists do not have an account explaining why contributions to unjust ends are unjustified—seemingly taking it as a given. Most reductive individualists draw on one of three minimal accounts of liability for unjustified

Introduction 17

action that have such minimal requirements that most sane, adult participants in an unjust war are liable to defensive violence to varying degrees provided they causally advance the unjust war in some way.

In the next chapter, I aim to undercut the asymmetry thesis by arguing that the reductive individualists' three main accounts of liability are deeply problematic. Without a viable account of liability, the asymmetry thesis, and all the other dependent claims of revisionist just war theory, are without foundation.

Chapter 3 in Part II (consisting of Chapters 3 and 4) largely finishes the critique against extant revisionist arguments for the asymmetry thesis by showing how a culpability standard of liability can meet the challenges reductive individualists set for any potential alternatives to their minimal standards of liability. If the asymmetry thesis is largely undefended by *extant* theories, Chapter 4 goes further and shows that the asymmetry thesis cannot be defended by any emergent theory. Certain kinds of collective actions, including military actions, *can be unjust without most of their members' constituent individual actions being unjustified.* The causal attenuation, intervening agents, indeterminacy of the outcomes, and other structural features of the relevant kind of group actor can mean that different sets of moral reasons for commission or omission apply to the contributory action and to the resultant collective actions. It follows, then, that a theorist cannot claim that most or all contributory actions to collective unjust actions or outcomes are unjustified simply because they advance those unjust actions or outcomes. That said, a culpable orientation toward the unjust ends of the group's actions can mean the contributory actions are unjustified for the culpable actor since there are strong moral reasons for not knowingly and intentionally advancing unjust ends. Yet a theorist is not in a position to claim *a priori* that a strategic number of combatants on the unjust side have that culpable orientation. Crucially, these arguments in Part II show how the moral equality of combatants is even possible.

The reason the asymmetry thesis is unsupportable is also the reason individualist and reductivist approaches to just war theorizing, be they in service of revisionist or traditionalist arguments, will not work. Military actions are irreducibly corporate actions, collective actions that are greater than a mere aggregate of their contributory actions. Individualist approaches miss the existence of these types of actions and the unique type of collectives that produce them. Reductivist approaches basing their theorizing on civilian self-defense scenarios will not necessarily be normatively relevant to military cases since the moral content of the collective action is not contained in combatants' individual contributory actions. Finally, Chapter 4 will employ this action theory and the culpability standard of liability (defended in Chapter 3) to defend the traditional assignment of *jus in bello* considerations to combatants and *jus ad bellum* to political leaders.

Part III of this book (Chapters 5 to 7) develops a contractualist foundation for just war theory and defends the traditional egalitarian construals of military norms as well as the moral equality of combatants under certain conditions. Chapter 5 defends a view of professional morality that sees professions as social

18 *Revisionist just war theory*

instruments for the delivery of morally important goods like security, health, and education. The associated view of professional morality views it as the application of collective responsibilities in institutional contexts, directed toward the efficient delivery of morally important goods. Thus, professionals should sometimes behave differently than non-professionals—not because they are inhabiting different moral spheres, but because they are acting on different expressions of the same moral principles. Properly constituted professional norms in vital professions are moral norms—institutionally mediated expressions of collective moral responsibilities. I use a hypothetical consent model to delineate the contours of these norms, incorporating respect for the rights of all affected parties into the duties of professionals. Chapter 6 articulates the military norms, including obedience, that are institutionally mediated expressions of the collective moral responsibility to deliver security to a society.

Chapter 7 argues that moral equality follows if the military is a necessary institution in just societies and military service is incompatible with selective conscientious objection (SCO), a putative right to refuse service in particular wars. By contrast, moral inequality would follow if militaries were designed to give service personnel detailed knowledge about the collective actions they further and to permit service members' resignation at will. At present, service members on both sides of many conventional conflicts are in the same position of serving in a necessary institution that is authorized to use violence, and that is factually dependent on the general obedience of its members to function. Personnel on both sides of a conflict are justified in obeying deployment orders from their legitimate authorities and fighting in those conflicts. Each side has permission from the other to participate in a fallible process that is the only way to protect their states (in the event that SCO is untenable), a moral duty to obey all lawful orders, including deployment orders, and positive moral reasons for obeying regardless of the moral status of the war.

Finally, a note about how to read this book. I will be focusing on the philosophical literature on just war theory in this book but intend it also for scholars in theology, law, international relations, and political science. One chooses a writing style with trepidation when working in a field well-attended by specialists but also of interest to a more general audience. This is all the more pressing in this case given the methodological differences between most revisionists and traditionalists. The latter tend to be impatient with the former's fantastical thought experiments, but merely presenting my traditionalist proposal without a consideration of revisionism would be to ignore the major debate in the field. On the other hand, extensive technical disputes with revisionists may turn off traditionalists who typically focus on applied military ethics. I will have to beg patience from both sides. The formats of Chapters 2 and 3 are more like that of a revisionist text and the latter chapters are more like a traditionalist text. There will be times where I have to dip into more technical side-discussions, though I am going to try to address commonalities between revisionists and traditionalists in the main text in a way that does not presuppose familiarity with their

Introduction 19

arguments and largely leave internal critiques about specific authors to the footnotes. Readers less interested in a discussion of different models of liability may wish to skip Chapters 2 and 3 and move on to Chapter 4. Readers who are simply interested in my constructive theory of just war rather than its conceptual underpinnings can go right to Part III.

Notes

1 The "regular war" strain of the just war tradition that promotes this equality extends back to Roman times and is defended by Christian canon lawyers throughout the middle ages. It exists alongside the Christian theological strain of the just war tradition, which grappled with the tension between soldiers' default obligation to obey their lords and their personal duty to refrain from participating in unjust collective action. Francisco de Vitoria (1492–1546) is a crucial transitional figure in the march toward the modern consensus. While positing the traditional theological position that soldiers may not fight in wars they believe to be unjust, he sympathetically presents the regular war view that soldiers may obey their princes if the war does not seem obviously unjust, (2010: Q2.2). Vitoria actually imposes such light epistemic duties on soldiers he creates an opening for both theologians and jurists to increasingly adopt the regular war paradigm in the post-Westphalian period. Revisionists who have highlighted their arguments' continuity with the pre-modern just war tradition neglect the canonist strain of the tradition, e.g., Fabre (2012: 73).
2 Jeff McMahan avers to this sense of inequality after conceding that mutual consent between service personnel could give them permission to fight one another (2008a: 19–43). This equality of cause is not the sense of equality characterizing the post-Westphalian consensus.
3 Some revisionists disagree whether their revisions to the morality of war should be legally implemented; cf. McMahan (2008a) and Rodin (2008).
4 McMahan allows that service personnel serving in a military that will shortly be sent on an unjust war are liable to preventative attack despite the fact that they have not, as of yet, done anything wrong (2009: 183–184).
5 McMahan parts company with most of his colleagues in arguing that even the service member on the unjust side pursuing an intermediate just aim could still be liable since he will likely revert to unjust aims when finishing his just mission (2005b: 21; cf. Tadros 2016: 8; Bazargan 2011: 522).
6 Some revisionists allow that mentally ill combatants are not liable for their actions.
7 For example, compare the different usage between Frowe (2015: 1–16) and Lazar (2017: 37–54).
8 Dill and Shue read the reductive individualists, including McMahan, in this manner (2012).
9 McMahan takes an allied but less extreme view in stressing that deeming a war as a whole "just" or "unjust" is inexact as a war may have just or unjust phases.
10 Frowe (2015: 11). Several other revisionists stress what Bazargan calls the "moral heterogeneity" of war, limiting the usefulness of deeming a whole war just or unjust (2011; Tadros 2016; McMahan 2005b: 20).
11 This dynamic *is* afoot in group action formed by informal, *ad hoc* groups united by a common goal, e.g., riots, lynchings, or pogroms, discussed in Chapter 4. Lazar and Rodin argue that wars of national defense against purely political aggression (where the non-genocidal invader will not kill anyone if the defenders surrender) are not aggregates of many cases of individual self-defense (Lazar 2014; Rodin 2002: 127).
12 Combatants could make, say, an otherwise-just war unjust by frequently performing atrocities.

20 *Revisionist just war theory*

13 Legitimate authority and right intention are typically excluded (Fabre 2014; McMahan 2005b; Frowe 2015: 3–6).
14 Or, with Frowe, that these individual actions are sufficient to reject the moral equality of combatants, without worrying about whether we call the war just or unjust.
15 I am not aware if McMahan anywhere pursues the tantalizing statement he makes here that there may be moral equality between combatants who fight a just war on one side and those who fight for a just cause in a war that is unnecessary or disproportionate.
16 Fabre rejects the traditional construal of legitimate authority, because she thinks ordinary citizens can declare war (2008). Yet her view is not that every service member on the battlefield has declared war so that their individual authority adds up to a kind of mega-authority.
17 Lazar makes a similar point regarding necessity (2012: 30–31).
18 For example, Bazargan, a collectivist revisionist, suggests that one could be justified in participating in an unjust war if the war aims to serially accomplish an unjust aim and then a more important just aim (2011: 522).
19 An unjust war, one failing the *ad bellum* checklist, can be justified if it contributes to a greater good such that it is an all-things-considered best action. I will restrict my discussion to unjust war and unjustified contributory actions since this is the basic, and more common, relationship.

References

Anscombe, G.E.M. (1981) "War and Murder," in *Collected Papers* III, Oxford: Blackwell Press.

Bazargan, S. (2011) "The Permissibility of Aiding and Abetting Unjust Wars," *Journal of Moral Philosophy*, 8: 513–529.

Bazargan, S. (2013) "Complicitous Liability in War," *Philosophical Studies*, 165: 177–195.

Bazargan, S. (2014) "Killing Minimally Responsible Threats," *Ethics*, 125: 114–136.

Bomann-Larsen, L. (2004) "Licence to Kill? The Question of Just vs. Unjust Combatants," *Journal of Military Ethics*, 3(2): 142–160.

Coady, C.A.J. (2008) "The Status of Combatants," in Rodin, D. and Shue, H. (eds), *Just and Unjust Warriors*, Oxford: Oxford University Press.

Vitoria, F. de (2010) *On the Laws of War and Peace* in Pagden, A. and Lawrence, J. (eds), *Political Writings*, Cambridge: Cambridge University Press.

Dill J. and Shue H. (2012) "Limiting the Killing in War," *Ethics and International Affairs*, 26(3): 311–333.

Fabre, C. (2008) "Cosmopolitanism, Just War Theory, and Legitimate Authority," *International Affairs*, 84(5): 963–976.

Fabre, C. (2009) "Guns, Food, and Liability to Attack in War," *Ethics*, 120: 36–63.

Fabre, C. (2012) *Cosmopolitan War*, Oxford: Oxford University Press.

Fabre, C. (2014) "Cosmopolitanism and Wars of Self-Defence," in Fabre, C. and Lazar, S. (eds), *The Morality of Defensive War*, Oxford: Oxford University Press.

Frowe, H. (2011) "Self-Defence and the Principle of Non-Combatant Immunity," *Journal of Moral Philosophy*, 8: 530–546.

Frowe, H. (2014) *Defensive Killing*, Oxford: Oxford University Press.

Frowe, H. (2015) "Reductive Individualism and the Just War Framework," *Legal Philosophy between State and Transnationalism Seminar Series*, 46: 1–16.

Introduction 21

Garren, D. (2007) "Soldiers, Slaves, and the Liberal State," *Philosophy and Public Policy Quarterly*, 27(1–2): 8–11.

Gross, M. (2010) *Moral Dilemmas of Modern War*, Cambridge: Cambridge University Press.

Lazar, S. (2012) "Necessity in Self-Defense and War," *Philosophy and Public Affairs*, 40(1): 3–44.

Lazar, S. (2014) "National Defence, Self-Defence, and the Problem of Political Aggression," in Fabre, C. and Lazar, S. (eds), *The Morality of Defensive War*, Oxford: Oxford University Press.

Lazar, S. (2017) "Just War Theory: Revisionists vs. Traditionalists," *Annual Review of Political Science*, 20: 37–54.

Lichtenberg, J. (2008) "How to Judge Soldiers Whose Cause is Unjust," in Rodin, D. and Shue, H. (eds), *Just and Unjust Warriors*, Oxford: Oxford University Press.

Mapel, D. (2004) "Innocent Attackers and Rights of Self Defense," *Ethics and International Affairs*, 18(1): 81–86.

McMahan, J. (1994a) "Self-Defense and the Problem of the Innocent Attacker," *Ethics*, 104(2): 252–290.

McMahan, J. (1994b) "Innocence, Self-Defense, and Killing in War," *Journal of Political Philosophy*, 2(3): 193–221.

McMahan, J. (2004) "War as Self-Defense," *Ethics and International Affairs*, 18(1): 75–80.

McMahan, J. (2005a) "The Basis of Moral Liability to Defensive Killing," *Philosophical Issues*, 15: 386–405.

McMahan, J. (2005b) "Just Cause for War," *Ethics and International Affairs*, 19(3): 1–21.

McMahan, J. (2006a) "On the Moral Equality of Combatants," *Journal of Political Philosophy*, 14(4): 377–393.

McMahan, J. (2006b) "Liability and Collective Identity," *Philosophia*, 34: 13–17.

McMahan, J. (2007) "Collectivist Defenses of the Moral Equality of Combatants," *Journal of Military Ethics*, 6(1): 50–59.

McMahan, J. (2008a) "The Morality of War and the Law of War," in Rodin, D. and Shue, H. (eds), *Just and Unjust Warriors*, Oxford: Oxford University Press.

McMahan, J. (2008b) "Debate: Justification and Liability in War," *Journal of Political Philosophy*, 16(2): 227–244.

McMahan, J. (2009) *Killing in War*, Oxford: Clarendon Press.

McMahan, J. (2011) "Who is Morally Liable to be Killed in War," *Analysis*, 71(3): 544–559.

McMahan, J. (2014a) "Proportionality and Just Cause: A Comment on Kamm," *Journal of Moral Philosophy*, 11: 428–453.

McMahan, J. (2014b) "Self-Defense Against Justified Threateners," in Frowe, H. and Lang, G. (eds), *How We Fight*, Oxford: Oxford University Press.

McMahan, J. (2014c) "What Rights May be Defended by War?" in Fabre, C. and Lazar, S. (eds), *The Morality of Defensive War*, Oxford: Oxford University Press.

McPherson, L. (2004) "Innocence and Responsibility in War," *Canadian Journal of Philosophy*, 34(4): 485–506.

Norman, R. (1995) *Ethics, Killing and War*, Cambridge: Cambridge University.

Øverland, G. (2006) "Killing Soldiers," *Ethics and International Affairs*, 20: 455–475.

Rodin, D. (2002) *War and Self-Defense*, Oxford: Clarendon Press.

Rodin, D. (2008) "The Moral Inequality of Soldiers: Why *jus in bello* Asymmetry is Half Right," in Rodin, D. and Shue, H. (eds), *Just and Unjust Warriors*, Oxford: Oxford University Press.

22 *Revisionist just war theory*

Rodin, D. (2011) "Justifying Harm," *Ethics*, 122(1): 74–110.

Strawser, B. (2013) "Revisionist Just War Theory and the Real World: A Cautiously Optimistic Proposal," in Allhoff, F., Henschke, A., and Evans, N. (eds), *Routledge Handbook of Ethics and War: Just War in the 21st Century*, New York: Routledge.

Tadros, V. (2012) "Duty and Liability," *Utilitas*, 24(2): 259–277.

Tadros, V. (2014) "Orwell's Battle with Brittain: Vicarious Liability for Unjust Aggression," *Philosophy and Public Affairs*, 42(1): 42–77.

Tadros, V. (2016) "Unjust Wars Worth Fighting For," *Journal of Practical Ethics*, 4(1): 52–78.

2 Reductive individualists' theories of liability

I introduced the asymmetry thesis in a military context in the last chapter. Due to the reductive individualists' reductivist commitments, the thesis will apply to all facets of life, including civilian contexts. One's contributory action to an unjust collective threat is unjustified absent very strong and atypical justifying reasons. Provided a theory of liability with a specific threshold of responsibility, one may be liable to a defensive response or punishment on account of this action. When this unjustified action occurs in an adversarial context, one's opponents contributing to the main strategic thrust of a just collective action will be justified and, therefore, non-liable to any kind of defensive action or sanction. The asymmetry thesis may seem intuitive to a lot of readers, so I would like to transition into this chapter's discussion of the different liability accounts central to the thesis by showing the asymmetry thesis's counter-intuitive implications in a more familiar civilian setting. A problem with the reductive individualists' approach to non-military collective action will indicate a problem with their approach to war.

Diplomacy

Diplomats from neighboring states Alphaville and Bravostan are negotiating a treaty regarding a disputed border. Alphaville claims that Bravostan illegally occupies a swath of Alphaville territory. The territory has been administered by Bravostan for 40 years, but its ownership has recently become contentious since the discovery of valuable mineral deposits there. The states are disinclined to go to war over the issue.

The case is complicated; the diplomatic teams have to work through bilateral treaties and armistices of various vintages. The stakes are high. Not only does Bravostan currently benefit from mineral extraction; the 60% of ethnic Bravosis who live in the disputed territory would join an under-class of minority Bravosis in Alphaville, a country where Bravosi discrimination is enshrined in law. Yet Alphaville diplomats feel that Bravosis and the other peoples in the disputed region would be better off living in Alphaville even as second-class citizens.

24 *Revisionist just war theory*

> Bravostan is a much poorer country than Alphaville and has an authoritarian government intolerant of dissent. Opposition politicians, journalists, and human rights activists are violently repressed.
>
> Most of the diplomats are not privy to the whole portfolio of treaties but are instead assigned discrete jobs pursuant to their state's case, such as researching international law on a relevant topic. The diplomats who negotiate with the other side's diplomats in pursuit of a deal engage in hard-nosed strategic behavior: overstating their position, arguing, blustering, feigning ignorance, etc. Just the same, most of the diplomats do not bear any ill will against their opposite numbers. Most of them are focused on performing in a technically proficient manner in the discrete area they have been assigned and understand their efforts to be more in service of their state than directed against the personnel from the other ministry.

This case does not involve the stakes of war, but notice the formal similarities: obscure claims of justice, adversarial collective action, the absence of a central authority to judge the case, epistemic limits of participants, and a displacement of participants' personal animus in favor of professional dedication. Given the reductive individualists' reductivism, the asymmetry thesis should indicate that the Bravosi diplomats are performing unjustified actions and are liable in some cases to violent responses.

Assume Bravostan really is guilty of willfully and illegally occupying Alphaville territory. It is stealing Alphaville's natural resources, violating its sovereignty, and terrorizing politically active persons (who would otherwise be Alphaville citizens). Do the diplomats working for Bravostan lack a moral right to engage in diplomacy? Are they wronging the diplomats and other citizens of Alphaville? Most importantly, for our purposes, would it be just if each Bravosi diplomat was personally blamed, professionally sanctioned, or prosecuted for participating in an unjust enterprise (perhaps to different extents depending on their involvement)? After all, Bravosi diplomacy, if successful, would enable further unjust Bravosi activity. We might further ask if mining companies in Alphaville could sue the Bravosi diplomats since their success would spell a great loss of potential revenue for the companies. Also, could political dissidents in the disputed territory kidnap, blackmail, or kill the diplomats in pre-emptive self-defense, given that the diplomats' success would entail further repression of the dissidents?

Applying the asymmetry thesis to the diplomatic case would appear to prompt affirmative answers to these questions. The Bravosi diplomats should not be working on their unjust case. They are wronging the Alphaville diplomats and the citizens they represent. The injustice of the macro action—one team of diplomats attempting to enshrine their state's unjust holdings via treaty—means all the associated micro actions furthering the macro action, including all the actions of the Bravosi team, are *pro tanto* unjustified. The diplomats lack strong overriding moral reasons for furthering these unjust collective actions. The

Reductive individualists' theories of liability 25

Bravosi diplomats are therefore morally liable to proportionate personal sanctions and defensive measures for their unjust actions.

It would seem that Bravosi diplomats should not have taken up the negotiation or should have resigned if not given the option of refusing to participate. Yet how was a diplomat to know at the start of negotiations which side was in the right? The case was very complicated and most of the diplomats did not have access to the entire portfolio. Even the senior diplomats with a more privileged perspective might not have sufficiently understood all the technical nuances to judge the justice of either complaint at the start of negotiations. As negotiations proceed and some diplomats become better acquainted with the details of the case, what threshold of certainty do they have to reach before resigning, particularly when resignation breaches their professional obligations to their state?

It would also seem that Bravostan should be without diplomatic support in this matter. It should simply withdraw from the disputed territory and not try to legally enshrine its territorial holdings. As the revisionists make clear in their discussions of war, the morally correct action may not always be practical or even knowable for a given actor. Yet this analysis produces a problem even on the objective level. On the one hand, Bravostan should not have diplomatic representation in this matter, but on the other hand, Bravostan requires diplomatic representation to prevent Alphaville's diplomats from pressing for an unjust settlement (or Alphaville officials creating an unjust situation on the ground in the event that Bravosi authorities simply withdraw).

The diplomatic example is obviously different to military cases because the diplomats are not killing one another, but the foregoing assessment of the Bravosi diplomats' liabilities and duties would seem to follow if we apply the asymmetry thesis to non-military, adversarial collective action. Reductivism indicates that we must apply this thesis universally. I take it that the following conclusions from this discussion are counter-intuitive: a state engaged in unjust actions should not have diplomatic representation; its diplomats lack a right to serve their states in this matter; and one group of diplomats is not only wronging the other, but is liable to lawsuits and pre-emptive defensive killing. The counter-intuitive result of applying the asymmetry thesis to the diplomatic example suggests a problem for the reductive individualist project. The reductive individualists take as basic the idea that contributory actions to unjust collective actions are unjustified absent atypical overriding justifying reasons—micro actions are tainted with the same immorality as the macro action. Under certain circumstances, the contributor is liable for those contributions, whereas her adversary in an adversarial collective activity, contributing to the main thrust of a just collective action, is not. None of the reductive individualists' conclusions regarding service members' *ad bellum* responsibilities, belligerent privileges and liabilities, vulnerability to *post-bellum* prosecution—nor the revisions to the discrimination and proportionality principles—can stand without the asymmetry thesis. The counter-intuitive result of the application of the asymmetry thesis to a diplomatic example with

26 *Revisionist just war theory*

obvious parallels to war suggests there is something deeply wrong with the reductive individualist project. At the very least, these scholars need an argument detailing the relationship between unjust collective actions and unjustified contributory actions nuanced enough to show the difference between military and diplomatic cases.

Herein lies the difficulty. The asymmetry thesis assumes contributions to unjust collective actions and ends are unjustified (absent overriding reasons) and depends on an account of liability deeming most or all contributors liable to some degree for these contributions. The more robust the liability standard, the fewer participants are liable for an unjustified action; the less demanding the standard, the more participants are individually liable. One would expect very robust accounts of these connections between contributory and collective actions given the revisionary conclusions of the reductive individualists' work. Yet many reductive individualists do not offer a detailed account. No scholar offers a detailed enough argument to distinguish the application of the asymmetry thesis from military to non-military cases.

Chapter 4 will show how collective military actions can be unjust without most contributory actions being unjustified. This chapter will focus on reductive individualists' standards of liability. Most reductive individualists draw on one of three standards: the "agent-responsibility" account (Seth Lazar's term) associated with Jeff McMahan and Michael Otsuka, the "unjust threat" account first associated with Judith Thomson, and the "objectively unjust proceeding" account first associated with G.E.M. Anscombe.[1] Frowe articulates an important hybrid theory drawing on McMahan's and Anscombe's work. I will argue in this chapter that the asymmetry thesis is without a foundation because all these single accounts of liability fail. The unjust threat account is deeply problematic on its own, the objectively unjust proceedings approach yields highly counter-intuitive results, and the agent-responsibility account collapses into an account of mere causal responsibility. Frowe's tripartite account is partly vulnerable to the latter two critiques, but also has a feature that will have to be challenged with a positive defense of combatant equality (in Part III).

I am not taking the route of some traditionalist philosophers by showing revisionist conclusions are impractical for epistemic reasons (Shue 2008; Walzer 2006), unrealistically demanding (Benbaji 2009; Lazar 2012), grotesque in its implications (Lazar 2010; Statman 2014; Benbaji and Statman 2019: 14), or counter-intuitive. The reflective equilibrium most of the relevant scholars use— wherein theory is meant to accommodate considered intuitions about complex thought experiments—makes it difficult for critics to find internal contradictions in their arguments. Clever philosophers can contrive even more outlandish thought experiments triggering an even finer intuition that some people allegedly feel circumvent the critic's point. With respect to critiques regarding counter-intuitiveness, reductive individualists tend to be forthright that their work is highly revisionary, and therefore counter-intuitive. With respect to practicality critiques, some revisionists allow their work concerns the "deep morality" of war, which may or may not be able to be practically reflected in law. So in lieu

Reductive individualists' theories of liability   27

of engaging their conclusions *seriatim*, I will try to undercut the entire reductive individualist project by showing the commonly shared asymmetry thesis is without an adequate foundation.

I Reductive individualists' foundational arguments for the asymmetry thesis

Revisionists often explain how the injustice of a war makes combatants on the unjust side liable to their enemies' defensive violence in a sentence or two. Lene Bomann-Larsen's previously cited quotation is illustrative.

> If we further accept that for a self-defensive counterattack to be justified, the initial attacker must be engaged in an "objectively unjust proceeding" (Anscombe), and if this is relevant also in war, an inequality between just and unjust belligerents is generated in terms of the objective justice (*ad bellum*) of the war they fight. And the injustice on the macro-level will then be repeated on the micro-level in every encounter between individual soldiers and fractions of armies.
>
> (Bomann-Larsen 2004: 149, quoting Anscombe 1981: 53)

Note, the connection between micro and macro levels is assumed in the first sentence, presented in the conditional mood in a way anticipating the reader's assent. Bomann-Larsen begins with a fundamental assumption about the borders of morality: what is unjust on an interpersonal level is unjust when something analogous happens between states. Then, having asserted that the macro-level action is unjust, Bomann-Larsen asserts the practical, corrupting effect of the macro-level injustice on micro-level actions without argument. The content of the assumption can be expressed with the analogy: a liter of salt water contains 1,000 milliliters of salt water. A milliliter of salt water is just as salty as the liter. Now, let us first note that while this presentation may be accurate, it is surely a terse and question-begging presentation of a complex phenomenon.

We can find further examples of brevity about the foundation of the asymmetry thesis among other reductive individualists. To mention a few examples, Fabre briefly refers to the same self-defense comparison made by Bomann-Larsen. Combatants on the unjust side are liable to defensive violence by force of an analogy with an individual engaged in unjustifiable violence against an innocent person (Fabre 2009: 47). Lionel McPherson takes it for granted that the same kind of liability accruing to individual unjust actions accrues to participation in unjust collective actions. The burden, he writes, is on the conventional just war theorist to explain why war is not covered by the common moral assessment of interpersonal violence (2004: 491). David Mapel appeals to Anscombe's argument to assert personnel on the unjust side have no right to defend themselves (2004: 84). Gerhard Øverland states that combatant moral equality is implausible, without giving a supporting argument (2006: 457),

28 *Revisionist just war theory*

though cites approvingly Richard Norman (1995), Jeff McMahan (2009), and David Mapel (2004). (The three have different foundational arguments.)

The usual brevity of reductive individualists' discussions of combatants' basic liability makes it difficult to accurately categorize all of the scholars, but Fabre, Mapel, and Bomann-Larsen judge individual liability to accrue to combatants on the unjust side because they are engaged in an objectively unjust collective action. McMahan argues that people have to be morally responsible for posing an objectively unjust threat, with moral responsibility being defined very minimally as the actor's having the capacity for responsible action when he began an action or causal sequence eventually terminating in an unjust threat—a threat that the actor knew was possible. Bradley Strawser and David Rodin endorse Jeff McMahan's approach. McPherson and Frowe adopt a hybrid of Anscombe's and McMahan's approaches.[2] Other revisionists may fall into one or the other camp. We can now turn to critiques, having partly clarified some of the reductive individualists' foundational commitments.

II The "objectively unjust proceeding" approach

i Critique of the objectively unjust proceeding approach

Mapel and Bomann-Larsen's argument, based on Anscombe's work, deems one liable to defensive violence if one is engaged in an "objectively unjust proceeding" the defender has a right to make his concern. The attacker is liable to defensive violence regardless of his level of responsibility for the objectively unjust proceeding. Many have argued that this objective view, as well as a closely allied one articulated by Thomson (1991)[3] and endorsed by Fabre (2014: 101), is problematic. Many feel that Anscombe's view problematically implies that people whose rights would be infringed by an agent's *justified* threatening action cannot permissibly defend themselves or others—since their halting an objectively justified action would itself be objectively unjustified (McMahan 1994: 108).[4] An example would be civilians living near a military target taking up arms to defend themselves when that target is about to be attacked by a bomber pilot fighting for the just side of a war (McMahan 1994: 274–275).

Anscombe's objective liability standard also shares a problem with Thomson's objective liability standard; Thomson's version states that a person posing an objectively unjust threat (regardless of the threatening person's intentionality, responsibility, or agency) to an innocent person is liable to defensive violence because he must not violate an innocent person's right not to be killed. I agree with the critique of Thomson's theory advanced by several thinkers—rights can only be violated by morally responsible agents (Rodin 2002: 86; McMahan 2009: 33–35; Otsuka 1994: 90; Zohar 1993).[5] Morally responsible agents are agents with the minimal levels of rationality, self-awareness, and self-control necessary for understanding and exercising duties to respect others' rights. It is the failure to exercise one's duty to respect someone's right that violates the

Reductive individualists' theories of liability 29

right. Liability, then, does not accrue simply because one's physical motions pose a physical threat to someone else. "[T]he threat we respond to must be *his* threat rather than simply a threat of the world at large which happens to manifest itself through his body" (Rodin 2002: 88). Asserting that merely physically posing a threat to an innocent person violates his rights, regardless of moral responsibility for the threat putatively generating the rights violation, leads to the absurd implication that a falling stone could violate people's rights (Rodin 2002: 85–87; Otsuka 1994: 80).

Liability can only accrue to agents who are acting as morally responsible agents when they pose the threat if liability follows from unjustified threats. So people posing unjust threats to others after being hypnotized, drugged, or thrown from windows do not incur liability to defensive violence. This critique is most germane to Thomson since she invokes the language of rights, but the critique also makes Anscombe's account of liability less promising. The indifference of Anscombe's theory to the level of responsibility of the attacker creates a counter-intuitively long list of threats who are liable to defensive harm. On her theory, non-culpable and/or non-responsible threats are liable to defensive harms because the sufficient criterion for liability is physically performing or participating in an objectively unjustified action. All of the following parties would therefore be liable to defensive harm when they (or their bodies) posed objectively unjust threats: fetuses stuck in their mothers' birth canals, toddlers brandishing guns, brainwashed child-soldiers, agitated mentally ill people, drugged and hypnotized people, people clambering aboard crowded lifeboats, asymptomatic plague carriers, and victims of defenestration, duress, trickery, and reasonable mistakes.

Recall, the definition of liability to violence many use is that it is permissible for certain others to violently engage the liable party, the liable party is not wronged by necessary and proportionate violence, and the liable party acts wrongly if she tries to defend herself. Third parties may not intervene to save her either. Many scholars argue that the above parties meet *some* of the criteria of liability. For example, some argue that it may be permissible to violently engage the above parties but also acknowledge that the non-culpable parties are wronged or that they may defend themselves.[6] While some scholars argue for the full liability of some of these threats, few are willing to deem all of them liable in the full sense of liability. To me, the breadth of liable targets makes the objectively unjust proceedings approach implausible. The approach does not seem just for the non-culpable but objectively unjust threat, who, in all the above cases, is a victim too. The question of how this innocent threat *should* be treated seems to elicit different intuitive responses likely having to do with deep, pre-theoretical convictions about human dignity and what people fundamentally owe one another. For example, some might find it grotesque to assert that a shipwreck survivor clambering aboard an overloaded lifeboat is not morally wronged and has no right to defend herself when the passengers start to beat her and claw at her face to keep her from boarding. Others find these assertions obviously correct; the woman makes herself liable to defensive violence.

30 *Revisionist just war theory*

Scholars engaging in the reflective equilibrium method can sometimes accept a proposed theory contradicting an intuitive response to one of many test cases. Yet counter-intuitive results to many cases suggest an error in the theory. I would suggest we search for a theory that does not seem so implausible to some and require proponents to make such strenuous and strained defenses to cover the long list of putatively liable targets.

Unless one is willing to accept the very broad list of liable parties (or modify the definition of liability), one must accept that objectively unjust proceeding is not a sufficient criterion for liability to defensive liability. It is, then, not enough to assert combatants are liable because they are engaged in objectively unjust proceeding by furthering the main strategic thrust of the unjust war or contributing to an unjust mission through their physical actions. Questions about combatants' moral responsibility, if not also their culpability, at the time of their enlistment or during combat have to be addressed.

I will address some objections before discussing moral responsibility. A general defense of the objectively unjust proceeding approach and its near variations puts the burden on critics to show that a prohibition on killing innocent threats does not require the potential victim to rescue the innocent threat at the cost of his life (Frowe 2014: 66). This is not as robust a challenge as it might seem at first. First, scholars using the reflective equilibrium method disagree as to whether it is intuitive that one may omit saving an innocent person if rescue requires one's death. Second, if all people are inherently morally equal, then no one, not even an innocent pedestrian endangered by a defenestrated man, is ultimately all that special (Zohar 2004: 750–751). One cannot kill innocent people just because one's own innocent life is at stake.

Another defense of the objectively unjust proceeding approach points out that limiting a right of self-defense to potential victims being threatened by responsible or culpable parties means that third parties could not defend someone menaced by a psychotic, and so non-responsible, attacker. Instead, the third party would have to side with the psychotic attacker if the victim attempted to violently defend herself (Fabre 2012: 59). This maneuver offers a powerful reason to think there must be some connection between objectively unjust proceeding and liability. Yet the above list of non-culpable persons deemed liable on this thesis also seems implausible. A response will have to wait until the next chapter, where I will propose a way of justifying the potential victim's self-defense against most non-culpable threats or a bystander's defense of another even while maintaining culpability as a standard of liability. Thus, I can meet the above two objections and permit the intuitively indicated cases of defense without endorsing the objectively unjust proceeding approach.

Finally, it should be noted that an Anscombian argument will not suffice to deem all, or even a strategically significant number, of personnel on the unjust side of a war liable to defensive violence. This follows because Anscombe's argument about objectively unjust proceeding sufficient to trigger liability to defensive violence is usually understood to refer to directly posing objectively unjust lethal threats. Yet most combatants are not directly engaged in "kinetic" (i.e., violent)

Reductive individualists' theories of liability 31

activities. In order for revisionists to have a theory of liability sufficiently broad to justify effective prosecution of a war against an unjust military force (which would usually entail targeting more than just the combatants involved in kinetic action), the theory would need to argue that participating in the unjust war effort in nearly any way will make one liable to defensive violence.[7] The revisionist would have to move beyond objectively unjust proceedings to include the actors' subjective states, including their participatory intentions to contribute to collective action or to be a member of the military or the like.

ii A hybrid approach to liability

Frowe develops a more specific version of the objectively unjust proceeding approach that should be separately addressed because of elements guarding it from the preceding critiques. Regarding the first critique mentioned above, Frowe might approach McMahan's justified bomber thought experiment in a way that removes its sting in a military context. Recall, some express concern that the objectively unjust proceeding approach counter-intuitively implies noncombatants cannot defend themselves against a justified airstrike. Frowe thinks most adult noncombatants on the unjust side of the war are liable to proportionate defensive violence anyway (Frowe 2014: chapter 6). Regarding the second critique, unlike Thomson, Frowe focuses on the victim's defensive rights to justify defensive violence rather than the threatening party's lack of a right to kill the victim (Frowe 2014: 64). She can therefore avoid critiques regarding the innocent threat's inability to violate duties when it comes to her own justification of defensive violence aimed at direct threats. Frowe can also partly dodge the force of the third critique because she can accept that most of the non-culpable threatening parties listed above are non-liable, but nonetheless targetable by the defender due to two reasons unrelated to liability (see below). Finally, regarding the last critique, Frowe's three different standards for permitting defensive violence against unjust threats provide sufficient grounds for targeting the whole of the enemy force.

Frowe has three arguments for permitting an innocent person to engage in proportionate defensive violence. First, direct threats to innocent people may be met with proportionate force no matter the threatening party's level of agency or responsibility (Frowe 2014: 64). Direct lethal threats are people whose movements, actions, or presence will kill the victim unless the direct threat is stopped. Second, indirect threats and indirect causes of threats to innocent people can be met with proportionate force if the threatening parties are morally responsible for the fact that they pose a threat, meaning that the threatening parties had a reasonable opportunity to avoid posing the threat and intentionally failed to avail themselves of that opportunity (Frowe 2014: 72–73). Indirect threats are people whose movements, actions, or presence contributes to threats on the victim's life, but who will not themselves kill the victim (Frowe 2014: 32). Indirect causes of threats are people who casually contribute to a direct threat (Frowe 2014: 84). Third, these two parties can even be targeted without being wronged

32 *Revisionist just war theory*

even if they are non-liable since they have an unmet duty to not pose unjust threats to innocent people (Frowe 2014: 83).

If successful, Frowe's theory would provide reductive individualists ample grounds for deeming service members on the unjust side unilaterally targetable with lethal force. The justification for targeting active kinetic actors would be similar to the justification proposed by the objectively unjust proceeding advocates. Since *in bello*-compliant combatants on the just side are, by hypothesis, doing nothing wrong, threats posed to them by their antagonists are unjust threats. The direct threat that combatants on the unjust side pose to combatants on the just side makes the threatening personnel targetable regardless of their moral responsibility for the threat. A portion of kinetic actors will be classified as indirect threats because not actively engaged in direct action when the just side contemplates targeting them, but instead occupying flanking or defensive positions. Support personnel can be classified as indirect causes of threats insofar as they make the kinetic actors' actions possible. These latter two groups are liable to proportionate defensive force if they had a reasonable opportunity to avoid posing the unjust threat and intentionally failed to avail themselves of that opportunity. Personnel posing an indirect unjust threat even when they are subjectively justified in believing their cause is just will still often be liable since Frowe thinks only meeting the highest subjective epistemic threshold can make the poser of an unjust threat non-liable (Frowe 2014: 83). Thus, Frowe deems a wider group of personnel liable than do Anscombe, Thomson, or their followers, as these scholars are chiefly concerned with direct threats. Finally, even rare non-liable service members on the unjust side can be defensively harmed without being wronged since they have an unmet duty not to unjustly cause harm to others.

As an aside, Frowe's argument justifying proportionate violent defense against all direct threats may fail as a general theory since it would explain the permissions it grants to defenders in reference to the duties of even non duty-holding people. Drawing on Frances Kamm and Victor Tadros, Frowe argues that the fact that a direct threat will kill an innocent victim is morally significant even without liability because everyone has a duty to refrain from harming innocent people. Even if the direct threat is unable to act on her duty in the moment when she poses a threat, the innocent threatened person can force her to accept the level of harm she would be morally required to absorb in order to avoid causing harm to an innocent person (Frowe 2014: 67). This duty explains why even a non-liable direct threat is not wronged by being defensively harmed (Frowe 2014: 87).

Yet it seems wrong to say that all direct threats have a duty not to impose harm on innocents. I would contend that a toddler is not yet a duty-holder, a senior citizen with dementia is no longer a duty-holder, and an adult with severe intellectual disabilities has never been a duty-holder. All could be direct threats, for example, if they were thrown down a well at an innocent person. According to Frowe's argument, all direct threats, including these non-duty-holders, could be forced to comply with their duties, an apparent self-contradiction. It is extremely counter-intuitive that these non-duty-holders could be treated *as if* they were duty-holders—perhaps on account of their species membership—because then babies could be punted about and physically manipulated in all sorts of ways to make them comply with the duties they would have if they were adults.

The relationship Frowe wishes to draw between the duty not to impose harm and the innocent party's permission to defensively harm direct threats is not clear to me. Is the innocent party only permitted to defend herself if the direct threat is not being wronged, or is she permitted to defend herself because of her own rights—and we should simply be comforted to know that the direct threat is not wronged? If there is a dependency relationship, then the preceding argument about non-duty-holders would seem to show that it is not the case that all direct threats may be defensively harmed. This result would undercut Frowe's claim to be advancing a general theory about direct threats, as opposed to a theory about duty-holding direct threats. In the more likely event that the argument about a direct threat's duties to refrain from harm is gratuitous to the permission to defensively harm them, then it would be the case that non-liable, non-duty-holding direct threats would be wronged by the innocent party's defensive violence. They should be able to defend themselves if they are being wronged. This result complicates Frowe's theory by identifying an unacknowledged right (like Fabre acknowledges) for some direct threats to fight back.

Frowe's theory may be further weakened if only limited to duty-holders since it is not clear why temporarily immobile direct threats like a defenestrated person should be considered a duty-holder with respect to the duty not to harm. She is a duty-holder in the general sense that she still has the faculties necessary to be a duty-holder, but not with respect to the duty not to harm. She could be held to her duty to refrain from actions still in her power, like slander. Yet if she is unarmed—and so cannot pre-emptively kill the victim who is perhaps preparing to defensively kill her—her duty not to impose harm is nominal.

I will not pursue this argument further here since even the argument's restriction to duty-holding direct threats would suffice to justify defensive violence against adult, sane combatants engaged in kinetic activities on the unjust side. Further, all adult, sane combatants—including the vast majority who are not engaged in kinetic activity—are also targetable by the just side, regardless of their liability, to be prevented from violating their duty not to cause harm to innocent people.

I do not have an internal argument to make against these, her first and third arguments, and so will need to challenge the arguments' applicability to war. I need to challenge the overall idea that some inter-state wars involve a group of unjust actors attacking a group of innocent actors by making a positive argument in favor of combatant moral equality. My approach with other reductive individualists is to argue that combatants on the unjust side are not individually, unilaterally liable to defensive violence on account of their participation in a collective unjust action because they are not committing individual unjustified actions. However, since the above-mentioned two arguments of Frowe's do not

34 *Revisionist just war theory*

depend on the actors being liable, I will need to argue that combatants on the just side are not innocent in the relevant sense (wronged by being harmed) to rebut her arguments. If combatants on the just side are not innocent in the relevant sense, then they do not have a unilateral right to defend themselves against direct threats nor impose a cost the threatening parties are obliged to absorb on account of failing to meet a duty to avoid threatening innocents. This external challenge, based in a positive defense of the moral equality of combatants, will come in Part III.

Applying Frowe's second argument to the military—the argument about moral responsibility—we can see that virtually all indirect threats and indirect causes of threats in the military would be unilaterally liable to proportionate violence from the just side since the justice of a war is not the sort of thing about which many could have a liability-neutralizing amount of evidence. According to Frowe, a person choosing to pose a threat to someone must have very good evidence that he lacks a reasonable opportunity to avoid posing that threat in order to avoid liability if it turns out that he is actually unjustly threatening an innocent person. A paradigm scenario neutralizing liability for someone posing a direct threat would be a diplomat shooting an apparent assassin when the apparent assassin points a gun at him—even though the gun is really a hologram (Frowe 2014: 87). People posing an indirect threat need to meet a lower reasonable belief threshold, but one that is still too demanding to neutralize the liability of most combatants posing indirect threats in war (Frowe, personal communication).

No matter how much research they do prior to deployment and how much evidence they find in favor of their side's just cause, it will still almost always be the case that all combatants on the unjust side contributing to the main strategic thrust are liable to defensive violence for being indirect threats or indirect causes of threats. Since almost all personnel on both sides of the war are in this same epistemically challenged position and engage in the same action of deployment, it is merely a matter of luck (assuming all hew to *in bello* norms) whether one group of personnel assigned to the main strategic thrust of their respective campaigns wind up being unilaterally liable to defensive violence. Yet Frowe's second argument is supposed to link liability to moral responsibility, not mere bad luck. A similar critique of agent-responsibility-derived liability will be developed in section IV of this chapter.

III Contributions to collective action

The previous section raised concerns about attempts to base liability on objectively unjust actions. Some revisionists go beyond objective proceedings to pay attention to the subjective states of actors, which could perhaps lengthen the liability list by including people who are not objectively posing an immediate unjust threat. McPherson argues that combatants on the unjust side of a war are "non-innocent," and so liable to the just side's defensive violence, if they bear "some moral responsibility for wrongdoing through war" (McPherson 2004:

Reductive individualists' theories of liability 35

490). He is not expansive on what he means by moral responsibility, but the concept as he uses it includes the basic physical and mental conditions for moral accountability and would seem to be assessed based on the agent's "knowledge, authority, and viable options" with respect to his ultimate action (McPherson 2004: 497). Service personnel are morally responsible for judging whether wars to which they are deployed are just and so are morally responsible for "wrong-doing through war" if they knew the war was unjust and faced no compulsion to fight.[8]

What does "wrongdoing through war" mean? States, rather than individuals, wage wars. In pre-modern times, when sovereignty was located in the person of a prince, such persons were held accountable (at least in the confessional) for wrongdoing through war. The sins a prince could commit included those that anyone could commit, like murder or theft, but also sins that only sovereigns could commit, like tyranny or launching an unjust war. Yet the modern combat-ant cannot wrong someone by waging war on him in the same way. I suspect McPherson means what Rodin states explicitly, that combatants on the unjust side are morally responsible for wrongdoing in the sense that someone is wrong for contributing to an unjust enterprise. I will turn now to Rodin's argument with my comments also applying to McPherson.

Rodin asserts that personnel on the unjust side are liable to defensive viol-ence because they are responsible for the injustice of the war in the sense that people are responsible for their contribution to a mutual project (2002: 173). Rodin's brief comments leave a question unanswered: exactly how are people responsible for their contribution to a mutual project? Rodin takes into account an agent's power, intentionality, and knowledge with respect to a specific action in addition to his general capacity for moral understanding in order to assess his moral responsibility for an action (2002: 90–97). A consideration of these factors, with their inherent variability, suggests that there is not a uniform type of responsibility associated with contribution to a common project, contrary to Rodin's, and perhaps McPherson's, assumptions. As I will argue at length in Part II, this variety of responsibility types is not based simply on the agent's internal state, but on the nature of the collective action as well.

At the level of physical behavior, some collective actions reduce down to identical component actions in the sense that a group of people raising their hands is reducible to identical component acts of individuals raising their hands. Yet some collective actions, like setting up a campsite, are the result of actors doing different things in loose coordination. There is a further difference between the intentionality and epistemic perspective of members of what Tracy Isaacs calls a "goal-oriented collective," an *ad hoc* group voluntarily assembled by its members for the accomplishment of a particular shared goal—like a group of campers, picnickers, or bank robbers—and an "organization," a highly structured collective with a set purpose and formal roles, often arranged hier-archically (2011: 24). Whereas all campers in a group share, and know, of the collective end of setting up a campsite, and all intend to contribute by volunteer-ing to perform a different component action (nailing tent stakes, unfolding the

36   *Revisionist just war theory*

tent, starting a fire, etc.), organizational actions are centrally coordinated and guided by a corporate intention. A corporate intention may not be natively shared by any one of the organization's members, but instead reflects the interest of the organization as a whole. Organizational members are then expected or compelled to make the corporate intention their own in the course of fulfilling their organizational role responsibilities. Even if guided by the vague, over-arching corporate intention, the organization's compartmentalized and hierarchical structure may keep organization members from knowing the specific collective actions their contributory actions further.

These different types of collective action prompt a number of questions with obvious relevance to responsibility for wrongdoing in war. Does it make sense to charge an individual with responsibility for a collective action, like charging a football player with winning or losing a game? Would the fractional causal responsibility, limited epistemic perspective, and an intention only to perform a contributory action, particularly within an organization, not mitigate responsibility for a collective action? If one claims that combatants on the unjust side are responsible for wrongdoing through war, how grave is this wrongdoing? Is a combatant responsible for the whole war, the operations in which he was involved, or just his contributory actions? Several revisionists argue that personnel can be non-liable to defensive violence if they are participating in a just mission within an unjust war. Yet this argument raises complex questions about how actions should be delimited for the purpose of assigning liability.[9] We need to consider the duration of non-liability associated with a particular mission, the status of personnel engaged in multiple missions at once (e.g., guarding a hospital *and* reporting passing enemy troop movements), the significance of the opportunities putatively non-liable personnel present to their colleagues to engage in unjust missions, the right method for distinguishing sub-missions from the macro mission of a war, and, relatedly, the interplay between combatants' subjective aims and the leadership's aims in distinguishing different missions or causes from one another (Steinhoff 2012: 352). Further, are these aims relevant at the beginning of a war alone or throughout the war? If the combatants' aims make missions just, then many ostensibly unjust aggressive missions can be made just in that the combatants may be fighting in order to prevent a just counter-attack that will threaten the aggressive side's civilian population or that promises unjust peace terms being imposed on the aggressive side (ibid.).[10]

We can eliminate many of the questions about compartmentalized epistemic perspectives and minor causal responsibility (if not all the problems associated with corporate intentions in the form of military orders) for the macro actions of the war and component operations if we focus on combatants' contributing actions. However, the difficulty in focusing on the actions that are most uncontroversially the combatant's own is that they are often morally trivial apart from the larger context of the war effort they further.

If the combatant's contributory actions to the war effort—reading satellite imagery, fueling aircraft, fixing vehicles, doing payroll, reading radar signatures,

Reductive individualists' theories of liability 37

researching insurgent networks, etc.—are not the sort normally making one liable to violence, perhaps the combatant's knowledge that his actions contribute to the unjust war effort or his intention to further the unjust war effort suffice to inculpate him in the morally significant collective action. If knowledge or intention inculpate a service member, then what if a combatant lacks the larger epistemic view or intention? Further, does the intention to participate in a collective action make one responsible for the outcome even if one's contribution makes no difference to the outcome (cf. Fabre 2012: 76–77)? A trivial effort might accrue because the outcome was already determined, as when a bombardier drops an incendiary bomb on a city already engulfed in an inferno or when one is deployed to the front the day the armistice is signed. Does the intention to participate in a collective action inculpate one for the outcome even if one's contribution is ineffectual, such as when a sniper's rifle jams at the moment of truth or when a sonarman's readings are so bad that his submarine spends the duration of the war chasing whales?[11]

Perhaps the combatant is liable simply for enlisting in the military prior to the unjust war, knowing that deployment to an unjust war was possible. We should then ask if there is no difference in responsibility for collective outcomes when one joins an *ad hoc* group expressly assembled to accomplish a particular goal like robbing a bank, and when one joins a group with long-standing priorities and a formal structure like the military. At the point of enlistment, one does not know what wars will be fought in the future, just that one's military is (perhaps) generally disposed to the good purpose of national defense. Should one then be responsible for the sort of wars one reasonably believed one's military would fight or the wars it actually ends up fighting?

So clearly it is not adequate to simply say a combatant is liable to defensive violence because he is responsible for contributing to an unjust war. The preceding questions will be addressed in detail in Part II. Perhaps in acknowledgement that his brief mention of responsibility for contributing to collective activity was insufficient, Rodin explicitly endorses McMahan's agent-responsibility account explaining how contributors are liable for collective action in a later work (2008: 46). It is to that account that we now turn.

IV Agent-responsibility-derived liability

McMahan argues that nearly all combatants on the unjust side of a war can be unilaterally liable to defensive violence. This follows because any person capable of rational agency is morally responsible for unjustified threats accruing as a result of actions he performed that he could have foreseen bore some risk of unjustly threatening others.[12] Therefore, combatants who were capable of moral agency (e.g., mentally competent adults not under the influence of drugs or hypnosis, etc.) at the time of their enlistment or acceptance of conscription can be unilaterally liable to the just side's defensive violence, despite their possible non-culpability for the unjust war and minimal causal contribution to it (2009: 183). They are liable even when not directly posing a threat to combatants on

38 *Revisionist just war theory*

the just side such as when they are training, sleeping, or engaged in some non-violent support role. Thus, McMahan would seem to have a more promising model of liability than those dependent on combatants directly performing unjustified violent actions, discussed above.

I will argue that agent responsibility is merely re-described causal responsibility in all cases relevant to war. By McMahan's own standards, those who are merely causally responsible for unjust threats, like people thrown from windows and hurtling toward pedestrians, are not liable to defensive violence. Thus, agent responsibility fails as a theory of liability capable of undergirding the asymmetry thesis. While I will focus mostly on McMahan's argument, my points also apply to Strawser, Rodin, and, in part, Frowe and McPherson, who use the same account of liability.

i Strict liability

McMahan argues that a person, X, is liable to defensive harm if the person he threatens, Y, has no alternative but to fight X in order to survive a threat born of an action X performed as a responsible agent, foreseeing that his action posed at least a slight risk to others (2005: 394–395).[13] This formulation ostensibly respects a person as a moral agent—and precludes liability in cases when he exercises no agency—and still provides an unjustly threatened person a right to defend himself against many innocent threats and innocent attackers. The unjustly threatened person can even defend himself against a non-culpable (but responsible) unjust threat who is not exercising agency at the time the threat actualizes, such as when a car a person is driving malfunctions and skids out of control (2005: 393–394, 2009: 165). The driver created the causal conditions for the skid to occur when he was in a responsible mental state, when he could have known that driving imposed some risk on others. Re-directing harm toward the casual creator of the conditions for unjust harm is just because the agent voluntarily undertook an action he foresaw could impose unjust harm on others. If that harm eventuates, it is only fair that harm be re-directed toward the agent, the beneficiary of the original action, rather than inflicted on a bystander.

The agent responsibility model solves a problem for reductive individualists who object to the traditional post-Westphalian collective liability argument that marks all able-bodied combatants on both sides of a war as legitimate targets. Lest they be pacifists, reductive individualists need some kind of collective designation of at least strategically significant numbers of personnel on the unjust side in order to facilitate defense of just states. By the lights of the agent responsibility argument, even if personnel on the unjust side are naïve, ignorant, or misled by government propaganda, they can be liable to defensive violence when the risk of being deployed to an unjust war they knowingly embraced comes to fruition.

Agent responsibility is a moral version of strict liability in torts (McMahan 2005: 395). Analysis of the law can give us insights into its moral analog.

Strict liability deems a person liable for damages absent culpability, recklessness, or negligence, such as when a pharmaceutical manufacturer is held liable for product tampering even after the product was out of the manufacturer's direct control. Law may capture popular moral conceptions, but it does not capture such conceptions with strict liability. Strict liability is a blunt instrument of social policy rather than a direct legal application of a moral rule (Coady 2004: 49). It serves a practical political and social function by ensuring self-regulation of dangerous private activities the state can ill-afford to closely monitor. The logic of strict liability is evident when analyzed along rule-consequentialist lines. Two good outcomes accrue if everyone respects the fact that X will be liable for any unjust harm occurring in the causal sequence of events made possible by X's action. (1) X will be forced to act with maximum caution and (2) victims will be compensated. Since a pharmaceutical manufacturer is legally liable for tainted products even if someone completely unrelated to the manufacturer poisons a bottle of pills while it is *en route* to the store, the manufacturer is incentivized to take maximum precautions in the manufacture, shipping, and storage of the drugs—to the benefit of the public. If all producers are extraordinarily, even excessively, careful in producing pharmaceuticals, there will be fewer accidents than if pharmaceutical producers exercised a lesser (and perhaps more reasonable) standard of caution. Strict liability creates a further social benefit by determining ahead of time whom will be blamed if a product is tainted.

While strict liability can achieve morally worthy goals, it does so through an unjust mechanism of punishing people for events for which they are not at fault and that did not flow from their negligence or recklessness. The dubiousness of a principle asserting that one is liable for any event made possible by the physical conditions set through one's deliberate actions is suggested by the principle's inability to survive a universalization test. The scope of liability would be so wide under this universal condition that everyone would be liable, through a distant chain of causality, for nearly every event in the world.

The harshness of strict liability is mitigated by its rare application in law to very risky activities the risk-taker is free to avoid (Feinberg 1991: 56). Yet agent responsibility widens the scope of liability past even strict liability's standard of non-faulty risky activities to include *any* activity foreseeably posing a *slight* risk of unjustly harming others. This would include nearly every action one might perform. Many rightly object to the disproportionate nature of a potentially lethal defense against someone only agent-responsible for an unjustified threat (Lazar 2010: 189; Kaufman 2008: 102; Bazargan 2014; Rodin 2011).[14] Whatever slight type of liability is arguably created by responsibly engaging in a permissible activity with a tiny foreseeable risk of harming others, this degree of liability does not seem sufficient to warrant death. McMahan acknowledges this very point and so also rejects agent responsibility's utility as a general moral point regarding liability (2005: 395). He stresses that these slight types of liability are germane to defensive violence only in forced-choice scenarios where the victim has no alternative to save himself

40 *Revisionist just war theory*

except by resorting to violence (2009: 178; cf. Ferzan 2012: 682). War is a paradigm example.

ii Critique of agent responsibility: responsibility and luck

The intuition behind agent-responsibility-derived liability is that it is unfair for an innocent party to suffer harm when harm results from someone else's non-culpable, but still risky, action. When the harm is indivisible, it is only fair that it be redirected back to the beneficiary or initiator of the action (usually, the risk-taker) rather than imposed on a bystander. It would seem that this argument about fairness would be undercut if both parties are engaged in the same risky behavior when the unjustified harm develops, because then both parties are beneficiaries of the risky action. However, agency-responsibility-reliant reductive individualists argue that symmetry of threat imposition does not change the situation. Liability accrues when agent-responsible risk imposition matures into an actual unjustifiable, unavoidable, indivisible threat, even if both parties imposed risks on one another. I agree with Lazar and Kimberly Kessler Ferzan that "this gives luck too great a role in determining liability" (Lazar 2009: 722; Ferzan 2012: 678).[15] When personnel on both sides of a war "fight in the reasonable belief that their cause is justified, each imposes on the other the risk of being victims of unjustifiable harms" (Lazar 2009: 723). This characterization can be read as consistent with the collective nature of military threats. The issue is less that the individual combatant engages in a risk-imposing action that could mature into an unjustified threat, and more that he risks contributing to a collective activity that would unjustifiably harm others. Each combatant involved in a war is causally responsible for contributing to a collective material threat to his opposite number. In many cases, personnel on both sides are *in bello*-compliant, subjectively justified in believing that they fight for a just cause, and acting in response to orders rather than personal motives. It is just a matter of luck that one side happens to be fighting for an unjust cause.

A broader argument in keeping with McMahan's more recent expression of agent responsibility would start by pointing out that combatants engage in symmetrically risky behavior when they *enlist*. At that point, service members in different states both risk deployment to an unjust war they will reasonably believe is just. At that point, they will both thrust their enemies into forced-choice scenarios. Since service members are equally responsible for the same risk-bearing activity, the only thing distinguishing them is the fact that one group's risk-taking terminates in an objectively unjustified threat. The asymmetrical nature of their actions is added after the point of the agent's conscious control, because, by hypothesis, the enlistee does not reasonably think the war is unjust and therefore cannot consciously act with the intention of enlisting in order to contribute to an unjust war. Thus, we can see that a pat formulation of reductive individualists' views is easily misunderstood if McMahan's unusual (but influential) notion of responsibility is read into the following claim:

Reductive individualists' theories of liability 41

combatants responsible for unjustified threats do not have the same set of permissions and liabilities as combatants responsible for justified threats. The pat formulation makes it sound like combatants A *choose* to perform unjustified actions on the battlefield and combatants B choose to perform justified actions. Rather, on McMahan's view, the actions for which personnel earn liability to defensive violence is mere enlistment or acceptance of conscription. While combatants B may well enlist with the same level of knowledge and same motivation as their adversaries in state A, the actions of A's leaders, in planning and/or launching a war with a certain character, provides the moral content making combatants A's subsequent *in bello*-compliant actions unjustified. The moral asymmetry of a war comes from other agents and circumstances, after the completion of the enlistment action supposedly triggering liability for all service personnel. I contend (and will explain in detail in Chapter 4) that the collective action of war is morally separate from the risk-inducing action of enlistment.

The contention of the model's advocates is that agent responsibility for an unjust threat is sufficiently connected with the agent's moral faculties that we can legitimately speak of his responsibility for that threat and justly ascribe unilateral liability to him on its account. Yet the above argument about luck would appear to completely undercut the concept of agent-responsibility-derived liability in cases where the two relevant parties undertook the same risky action. Agent responsibility liability must have something to do with responsibility, but luck is unrelated to responsibility.[16] We say "he suffered bad luck," not "he suffered a lack of responsibility" because luck just happens—it befalls a person— apart from his conscious efforts and intentions. Without a connection to the agent's moral faculties, agent responsibility is simply causal responsibility. Agent-responsibility-derived liability is an undefended assertion that remote causal agents should be liable to unilateral defensive harm in forced-choice situations.

One might object that this luck-based critique of agent responsibility is too dogmatically Kantian, improperly limiting the scope of morality to the agent's intention. Some argue there is such a thing as moral luck—the proper ascription of moral responsibility to an agent for events that occur outside of his full control. McMahan explicitly invokes this concept, rhetorically asking, "Is it really sufficient for liability that [service personnel on the unjust side] voluntarily choose to harm or kill someone and have bad luck to be objectively mistaken, when a Just Threat [i.e., a soldier on the just side] makes the same choice in indistinguishable conditions, yet has the good luck to be correct, and is therefore not liable?" McMahan then responds affirmatively.

> [W]hen two people have acted in the same way, it can then be a matter of luck that one becomes liable to defensive action while the other does not. What we are liable to is a function of what happens as a result of our action, which is a matter over which we have imperfect control.... [The liable party] acted in the knowledge that bad moral luck was a possibility.
>
> (2009: 176–177)

42 *Revisionist just war theory*

The luck-based critique is a powerful one against agent responsibility, but it seems inadequate to end the discussion here given that agent responsibility advocates seem to embrace the very feature Lazar, Ferzan, and myself find problematic. Also, many thinkers find the general idea of moral luck plausible such that they would not see the luck-based critique as fatal. Appeals to conventional cases where people accept a burden of bad moral luck suggest two routes to generating moral justifications for strict liability: appealing to internally generated forms of the actors' consent and externally imposed regimes justified by rule-consequentialism. I will now show that both of these defenses fail.[17] The luck-based critique of agent responsibility persists—to the detriment of the reductive individualists' asymmetrical thesis.

iii First luck-acknowledging defense of agent responsibility

The generally accepted means of generating moral liability—fault, negligence, recklessness—see liability as stemming from the liable party's violation of a duty.[18] His prior express consent to a rule making someone in his position liable is unnecessary. By contrast, advocates of agent responsibility may be envisioning the agent-responsible person acting as a kind of surety to himself, *extraordinarily* guaranteeing his responsibility for compensating those hurt by his risk-imposing action in the case of bad luck. Both McMahan and Otsuka link liability to agents' knowledge that bad moral luck is a possibility when engaging in a risky activity. We can think of examples where people accept sole responsibility for prospective bad luck by engaging in practices where they know they will bear special costs associated with their risky (bad-luck-tempting) activity. For example, two duelists agree to abide by the outcome of a coin flip to determine who will fire first and who—mimicking a conventional kind of liability—will remain still and not defend himself. The duelists agree to "own" their bad luck by volunteering to treat associated consequences of the randomizing device of the coin flip the same as consequences brought about by faulty, reckless, or negligent actions.

Agent responsibility advocates would need a non-express variant of consent to "own" bad moral luck since they wish agent-responsibility-derived liability to pertain to innocuous activities people would never explicitly connect to unilateral liability to defensive violence. Tacit consent operates like express consent in giving others' permission to treat the consenter in ways that might otherwise wrong her, but conveys this permission without a normal sign of consent. The way to show that tacit consent attaches to a rule present in a practice the agent voluntarily entered is to show that a denial of the rule would be self-defeating to the practice. Hypothetical consent, a third type of consent discussed in the consent literature, can be modeled, for instance, in cases of binary choice where one option is so superior to the other that any rational person could be expected to consent to it.

Regarding tacit consent, a refusal to accept financial liability as a result of bad luck would make chance-based enterprises like gambling impossible, because no one would play with someone unwilling to take a reciprocal risk of losing his stake. Thus, we can say that people entering into games of chance tacitly consent to accepting liability for harms unluckily accruing from causal conditions their action created. Yet tacit consent cannot be modeled for extremely unlikely eventualities possibly connected to certain activities (e.g., a car careening out of control) as opposed to eventualities inherent to the activity (e.g., losing a poker hand).

We can also reject hypothetical consent to agent responsibility liability for permissible, non-chance-based actions like driving. Agents cannot be modeled as hypothetically consenting to an agent responsibility regime invoked in forced-choice scenarios because they would not be advantaged by it. Under the terms of agent-responsibility-derived liability, an unjustly threatened person can permissibly kill a responsible, but non-culpable, unjustified threat. However, he in turn is liable to the same violence if he non-culpably, but responsibly, poses an unjustified threat to someone else. Therefore, there is no *ex ante* advantage to consenting to an arrangement in which one might be permitted to violently defend oneself or might be killed with no recourse to a just defense, when one has no control over the circumstances leading to one's designation as a justified killer or the justly killed. Similarly, a military enlistee cannot be modeled as hypothetically consenting to unilateral agent-responsibility-derived liability to defensive violence if he poses a threat to personnel contributing to the main strategic thrust of the just side. A generic enlistee is just as likely to be on the just as on the unjust side of a war, and so privileged with belligerent rights or stripped of them and assigned unilateral liability to violence on the agent responsibility rule under consideration. One might object that a *particular* enlistee in a particular state might have a better or worse chance of being on the just side given the state's political composition, current relation with other states, and history. This is an empirical question that cannot be considered at length here, but consider any Western liberal democracy with more than, say, four military conflicts in the twentieth century. The track record of even liberal states is not very good, suggesting that an enlistee with a 20-to-30-year career might well be deployed on an unjust operation at least once.

We have ruled out the three kinds of consent that might be used to link moral luck with responsible action: express, tacit, and hypothetical. Thus, it seems that we cannot identify consent-based grounds internal to the agent to defend agent-responsibility-derived liability's reliance on luck.

iv Second luck-acknowledging defense of agent responsibility

Agent responsibility's similarity with strict liability also suggests a charitable reading of it as externally *imposed* on agents. Perhaps the underlying rationale of agent responsibility liability is rule-consequentialist as it is in the case of strict liability. Actions justified along rule-consequentialist lines may not be fair

44 *Revisionist just war theory*

to a given actor and may not lead to the best consequence in a given instance, but lead to the best consequences over time when all relevant actors follow the rule. Victims are compensated and agents engaged in risky behavior are incentivized to exercise maximum caution.

In an effort to exhaustively canvas permissible risk-imposing activities where liability might be justly externally imposed relevant to war, we will consider bilateral risk-imposition and two forms of unilateral risk-imposition where the threatened party generally benefits from the practice (one self-oriented and one other-oriented).[19] Combatants are clearly engaged in bilateral risk imposition, particularly if enlistment or acceptance of conscription is seen as the relevant risk-imposing action. Noncombatants menaced by combatants who are attacking nearby military targets might be described as endangered by the combatants' unilateral, other-oriented risk-imposition. We will see that consent-based waivers and/or other-oriented behavior will eliminate a rule-consequentialist justification of agent responsibility.[20]

The mutuality of permissible, voluntary, risk-imposing activities like contact sports removes the victim compensation element of a possible rule-consequentialist reading of agent responsibility. Participants expressly or tacitly consent to participate in an activity they know bears some personal risk. The practice they wish to engage in could not proceed if they refused to pose a risk to other participants, demanded that other participants not pose a risk to them, or refused to reciprocally bear the same risk that they imposed on others (threatening to hold other players liable for injuries inflicted in the normal course of the game). Fear of liability to lawsuit or lethal defenses consequent to one party feeling threatened would inhibit participation in the risk-imposing action.

Imposing liability on people responsible in some way for harms in cases of unilateral risk imposition creates a kind of mutuality between agent and victim. The promise of liability is a way for the potential victim—who may have no prior or on-going connection with the agent—to threaten the agent with harm *ex post facto*, thus leading agents to exercise extreme caution before acting. Yet the mutuality of contact sports eliminates the need for this *ex post facto* element. Mutual participation in the activity is adequate to encourage all participants to act cautiously in order to avoid hurting other participants.

In cases where the risk imposition is unilateral but coming as part of a practice that generally benefits the potential victim or which the victim sometimes pursues (e.g., a driver endangering a pedestrian), various types of consent usually indemnify the risk imposer. This indemnification may be express, as when a patient requests a surgeon operate on her.[21] Tacit and hypothetical consent covers a broader range of potentially risky activities where there is no formal relationship between the relevant parties. As we saw with internal grounds for moral luck, it is not rational *ex ante* to consent to a rule by which one is permitted to kill responsible, non-culpable innocent threats (e.g., the conscientious driver in an out-of-control car) if one would be liable under the same conditions and one is not able to avoid becoming that sort of threat (e.g., one has to drive). Mutual

Reductive individualists' theories of liability 45

interest in perpetuating the practice and avoiding personal liability if and when one engages in the practice is sufficient to encourage mutual caution and remove the victim compensation element of a rule-consequentialist justification of agent responsibility.

Let us next consider cases where potential victims also generally benefit from the practice but do not participate in it as an agent. Imposing defensive harm on the risk imposers engaged in other-oriented actions (e.g., a pedestrian shooting the driver of an out-of-control ambulance) fails to justly re-distribute harms to those unilaterally enjoying the benefits of the risky activity (e.g., the patient on whose behalf the driver is driving), per the desiderata of agent responsibility advocates. Hypothetical waivers further indemnify risk imposers engaged in generally beneficial, risk-imposing actions, be they other-oriented like ambulance driving or not strictly other-oriented actions like delivery driving, since the withholding of such a waiver should lead to the risk imposer abandoning the risky activity. Ambulance and delivery trucks are harder to control and pose more risk to pedestrians than passenger vehicles. Would drivers be willing to drive them if, according to a law or convention, doing so exposed them to unilateral risk of lethal defense when pedestrians felt threatened? One might answer in the affirmative, because people often take risky jobs if they need the money. Hypothetical consent makes normative claims about what people ought to endorse, not merely empirical assumptions about what they would endorse. For example, we can model people consenting to being warned if they were acting on false information. The modeling is based on a normative picture of people's epistemic duties as well as other duties to self and others. One ought to base one's actions on true information lest one harm oneself or others. Yet many actual people may prefer to believe false information that makes them feel good or allows them to maintain membership in some group. The hypothetical consent model assumes that autonomous people cannot be modeled as consenting to being unilaterally and unjustly stripped of rights. So truck drivers ought not to consent to a rule that would unfairly strip them of a right to defend themselves against lethal violence. (Even empirically, I expect that there would be a different reaction to the prospect of risking injury in an accident in return for pay versus the prospect of being stripped of a right of self-defense in return for pay.) Finally, a fair-play duty suggests one must indemnify risk imposers acting for others' benefits (but not one's own benefit) if one wishes to enjoy the benefits of risk-imposing activities that do not benefit other groups of potentially threatened parties but benefit oneself.[22]

Thus, a rule-consequentialist defense of agent responsibility's reliance on luck fails in cases of bilateral risk imposition and unilateral risk imposition when the victim generally benefits from the action, be it self-interested or other-oriented. A rule-consequentialist defense does succeed in cases of frivolous, self-interested, non-culpable, risk-imposing actions like skydiving (cf. Lazar 2009; Ferzan 2016: 247).[23] Imagine that a cautious, experienced recreational skydiver is blown off-course by a freak wind and suffers a parachute malfunction. He can only break his fall by landing on an insurance agent. The victim can

46 *Revisionist just war theory*

defend himself in cases like this when an unjust threat emerges from a permissible, self-serving action lacking the mutuality of a widely practiced action the victim also enjoys. Here is a case where the agent responsibility advocates' intuitions are well-taken. The agent was non-faulty, non-negligent, and non-reckless, but chose a risky action for his own benefit. Why should anyone else suffer if his risky action matures into an unjust threat? The victim compensatory element of the rule-consequentialist justification remains in force in this case because the insurance agent is in no way benefited by the skydiver's actions. He cannot be modeled as consenting to the activity or to indemnifying the skydiver. The self-regulation element also endures because the extreme caution agent-responsibility-derived liability prompts would likely exceed the ordinary care skydivers assume. Factoring in the threat of defensive violence from below from people who believe they are in danger might prompt skydivers to refrain from jumping altogether or to do so only in the remotest locations.

The difficulty for reductive individualists relying on agent-responsibility-derived liability is that the very circumscribed application of agent responsibility to self-interested, frivolous actions like skydiving is not germane to military enlistment. Military enlistment is the action supposedly rendering all service personnel liable to defensive violence when they are ultimately deployed to an unjust war. Yet clearly, enlistment is neither purely self-interested nor frivolous. Enlistment in the military can entail certain benefits for the enlistee but involves so much sacrifice and hardship for the benefit of others—and a level of hardship incommensurate with the salary and benefits—that it has to be seen in the first order as an other-oriented activity (Rodin 2014: 88). Even if a particular person enlisted for completely self-interested or frivolous reasons, the profession itself is not oriented toward these ends. Broad levels of liability for service personnel cannot therefore be assumed based on enlistees having to adopt a self-interested orientation as part of a professional role.

Perhaps one might object that military service is self-interested in that the individual service member can more ably defend himself against foreign enemies by serving in the military than by remaining a civilian. It is true that there are self-interested defensive attributes to military service, but most service members will serve their time without ever fighting an enemy who actually menaces their homeland. Among those personnel who do face such an enemy, very few of them will spend their entire career focused on that threat as opposed to other military tasks. Most of those who do fight the enemy directly will likely do more than what is necessary and sufficient to defend themselves and whatever personal interests would be threatened by their country's defeat. Finally, so long as the enemy was not bent on genocide or mass enslavement, a safer route for most civilians would be to remain a civilian rather than join the military.

Internal and external defenses of the agent responsibility model of liability's dependence on luck have been overcome in cases plausibly relevant to war. In bilateral cases of risk imposition, I showed how there are no internal, consent-based grounds to model a non-culpable risk imposer's acceptance of his bad luck as incurring liability in the manner of his faulty, negligent, or risky behavior. Concern for others, mutual benefit, and/or various kinds of consent also strip away all liability and prevent the agent from being "assigned" bad luck with a rule-consequentialist rationale. Stripped of liability, the relation of the remote causal agent of an unjust threat to the impending unjustified harm is simply indirect causality—causality that is effectively only of descriptive, rather than moral, interest. Thus, the luck-based critique of agent responsibility's relevance to war remains.

V Conclusion to Part I

Nearly all reductive individualists use one of three models of liability initially articulated by Thomson, Anscombe, and McMahan, with McPherson and Frowe using hybrids of the latter two. We have seen, contra Anscombe, Thomson, Mapel, Fabre, Bomann-Larsen, and others, that it is extremely unlikely that merely physically presenting an unjust threat is sufficient for liability. Some attention must be paid to the internal states of people posing unjust threats to others. Contra McMahan, Strawser, and Rodin, liability does not accrue on agent responsibility grounds in conditions relevant to service members' participation in war. One of Frowe's three grounds of liability falls prey to the same luck-based argument.

None of the reductive individualists' signal revisionary claims can get off the ground without a viable account of liability. I have gone a long way in this chapter toward rejecting the reductive individualists' chosen forms of liability, but have to wait upon developments in later chapters to complete the critique. Frowe's argument about the permissibility of targeting direct threats, regardless of liability, awaits engagement in Chapter 6. Advocates of the objectively unjust proceedings approach may be willing to bite the bullet and accept that the whole list of non-culpable posers of unjust threats are indeed liable to defensive violence, particularly if the alternative is to prohibit self- or other-defense against psychotic attackers. To overcome this concern, I need to explain in the next chapter how this sort of defense is possible without embracing a minimal model of liability focusing on the objective physical behavior of the agent.

Notes

1 Tadros argues that there is no single account of liability (2011: 260). His just war theory is not vulnerable to this chapter's critique. Critiques of elements of his theory occur in later chapters.
2 McPherson partially draws on McMahan's argument about the liability-conferring conditions of combatants' moral responsibility for entering the unjust war and bolsters it with Anscombe's objective argument to render liable even morally innocent combatants who had no way of knowing the war was unjust (2004: 498).
3 Reductive traditionalist Steinhoff adds some nuance to Thomson's theory, writing that all unjust threats lose their claim-rights to life (imposing a duty on others not to attack them) since they have no right to threaten others, but retain liberty-rights to life (meaning they may still defend their lives), if they are not culpable for that threat

48 *Revisionist just war theory*

(2012: 347). Fabre's position on liability is subtly different from Anscombe's and Thomson's in that they see the objectively unjust proceeding as simultaneously making the actor liable to defensive violence and justifying the potential victim's defensive violence. Fabre sees an objectively unjust proceeding as justifying self-defense regardless of the actor's liability. Actors whose threat comes about as a result of their agency are liable whereas those whose threats evolve without their agency, like innocent projectiles, are non-liable. The latter can still be defensively engaged, though they may fight back (Fabre 2012: 59).

4 McMahan here partly rejects his earlier acceptance of this view and concludes that the innocent defenders are often not justified in self-defense in this scenario. See the following note.

5 Frowe takes these thinkers to task for misunderstanding Thomson's conception of rights (Frowe 2014: 47), which, according to Zohar's later, more sympathetic reading, can be violated by states of affair rather than actions, (Zohar 2004: 750). I will show what is problematic with this notion of rights in Chapter 3.

6 As mentioned in the note above, Fabre allows those who threaten innocents without the exercise of personal agency to defend themselves against their potential victim's defensive violence. Therefore, fetuses and defenestrated people could in theory defend themselves. This still leaves a counter-intuitively long list of people who are not permitted to defend themselves.

7 Fabre argues that marginally contributing to an objectively unjust threat can make one liable to defensive violence if one's contribution is of the sort that could be met by defensive harm on its own. For example, a member of a mob unjustly stoning someone is liable to lethal defensive violence (even though his one stone will not kill the victim) because a solitary stone thrower would be liable to some defensive harm, and in this case the stone thrower is part of collective action that poses a lethal threat. By contrast, a voter voting for a warmongering candidate would not be liable to defensive violence when the candidate becomes president and launches an unjust war since voting unto itself is not an action that engenders liability to defensive harm (Fabre 2012: 76). This allowance still will likely not make a strategically sufficient number of combatants liable to harm because of the vast number of personnel who perform actions contributing to violent collective action that do not merit defensive harm unto themselves.

8 McPherson includes an objective Anscombian element to his theory to justify killing completely innocent unjust threats.

9 Frowe acknowledges that the reductive individualist project needs a common, systematic account of how individual actions in collective actions are distinguished from one another (2015: 16).

10 Cf. Tadros (2016). Every combatant could permissibly participate in an unjust war with these kinds of subjective aims, a conclusion Tadros cannot accept without accepting the moral equality of combatants. Bazargan makes a similar argument to Tadros, though focusing on material contributions to just missions within unjust wars. It follows, then, that his position is vulnerable to a similar critique since any material contribution to an unjust aim, say as part of the initial invasion, is potentially also a material part of preventing the degraded enemy military from seeking grossly unjust goals in their counter-offensive (Bazargan 2011: 522).

11 Bazargan focuses on this question (2013).

12 Applying the general principle stated in McMahan (2009: 166).

13 Otsuka, Rodin, Strawser, and Bazargan endorse similar models (Otsuka 1994: 80; Rodin 2002: 86, 88; Strawser 2011; Bazargan, 2014). Otsuka and Rodin discuss the model in interpersonal contexts, though in later work, Rodin (2008) endorses its use for liability for collective action. Bazargan adds a proportionality element so that someone who is n degree (agent) responsible for an unjust threat would be liable to n amount of defensive harm (2014: 122).

Reductive individualists' theories of liability 49

14 Steinhoff argues the driver is not liable because he is not performing an intentional action (2012: 354).

15 Lazar's argument turns on a demonstration of a symmetry of risk imposition between the conscientious driver and the pedestrian in McMahan's famous case. I think his arguments fail, but the larger point about agency-responsibility's fatal reliance on luck in symmetrical cases of risk imposition is sound.

Lazar deploys several arguments for the symmetry between the driver and pedestrian. Lazar argues that someone taking a foolish risk like sleeping next to a highway forfeits his right to self-defense if he finds himself threatened by a truck. Yet the pedestrian is not guilty of such a reckless risk if he is just walking on a sidewalk by a road. This response also undercuts Lazar's argument on the following point. He argues that agent responsibility advocates cannot assert that the pedestrian is merely responding to the driver's initial threat since the pedestrian ceded his right to self-defense by taking on a serious risk.

Three of Lazar's arguments depend on the driver and pedestrian symmetrically imposing risk on each other at the start of their respective actions (2009: 719–721). The driver's beginning to drive and the pedestrian setting out for a stroll while carrying a grenade create the conditions for risk imposition on others. On Lazar's view, there is then no difference between the actors in terms of agent responsibility for an action foreseeably imposing an unjustified threat on another. This is incorrect. Driving is the necessary and sufficient action required for a car to careen out of control toward a pedestrian since, by hypothesis, the driver performs no second action causing the car to lose control. By contrast, the pedestrian has to perform two separate actions, arming and throwing the grenade, in order to impose an imminent threat to the driver. Merely carrying a grenade does not make him liable to defensive violence.

Only theoretical or descriptive distinctions making a difference to defenders' practice count in considering agent-responsibility-derived liability. The theory is one of liability, not desert, which on McMahan's terms, means that harm can be distributed to the agent only if it serves some purpose, like protecting the defender. That the relevant purpose is defense in this scenario means liability has to be linked to the defender's or a third party's knowledge of an imminent threat creating a forced choice. Merely carrying a grenade around outside is not the necessary and sufficient action creating the causal conditions for unjustified threats making a difference to potential defenders' practice. Unlike a pedestrian spying a car speeding toward him, no one can anticipate an imminent threat from a spontaneously malfunctioning grenade, only an imminent threat from someone pulling the pin and rearing back to throw it in one's direction. A fellow pedestrian or a motorist would not know he is in a forced-choice scenario if he merely sees a pedestrian carrying a grenade. A civilian grenade carrier might deserve some punishment for exposing others to unnecessary danger, but cannot be liable to others for defensive violence on account of carrying a grenade. Similarly, a driver is not liable to defensive violence on the agent responsibility account simply for driving, but only for careening out of control.

16 Ferzan argues that a right to life cannot be forfeited by mere bad luck (2012: 675).

17 Some actions or states mentioned in the literature as involving moral luck are not relevant to agent responsibility's potential role in supporting the asymmetry thesis. Moral luck is sometimes invoked in situations in which only one of a malicious, negligent, or reckless pair actually ends up harming someone. Yet the symmetrical triggering condition putatively making combatants asymmetrically liable is not combatants' *bad characters* nor their *culpable intentions* on agent responsibility advocates' view. Rather, the focus is on an objective assessment of the actors' actions.

50 *Revisionist just war theory*

It is true that one actor out of a non-culpable pair is held legally liable if the two were engaged in the same permissible actions and one is the causal factor in the other person's harm, such as when a motorist's car skids on ice and hits another car in traffic. Yet the fact that we sympathize with the liable motorist suggests that *non-fault* tort law does not reflect morality in this instance. I venture that we sympathize with the non-culpable motorist because he has to pay despite having done nothing intentionally wrong. He suffered bad luck. As with strict liability, part of the purpose of non-fault liability is the maintenance of social order. It is neither fair that one motorist has to pay for a twist of fate nor that the second motorist should be stuck with repair bills. Tort law's stipulating liability prevents endless wrangling and conflict over what to do in such a situation. Non-fault causal liability can be justified contractually because no hypothetical contractors we can imagine agreeing *ex ante* to a set of fairly applied rules are unfairly burdened by this arrangement. Every driver in the abstract has an equal chance of being financially liable or financially compensated for a no-fault traffic accident. Things should break even over a person's lifetime. Holding no one liable in such a case is not similarly worthy of *ex ante* consent since the imposition of malicious, reckless, or negligent injury should incur liability and one cannot always tell if the causal agent of his injury was culpable in one of these ways. Designating the causal agent as liable prevents that potential source of uncertainty and conflict.

A rule imposing unilateral lethal defensive liability on the causal agent does not have the same contractual benefit as the analog in torts because one cannot expect to be both the liable party to and benefitee of preventative violence over time, whereas one can expect this mutuality when it comes to *ex post* compensation for car accidents. Given the penalty involved in defensive violence, one would only likely be the liable party once!

Bazargan avers to the law of private necessity's holding people financially liable for damages caused by justified actions to help bolster his case that people can be liable for unjust harms threatened in the course of permissible actions (2017). Bazargan might well appeal to no-fault liability to bolster his case since in no-fault liability, people are also held financially liable for unjust harm resulting from permissible activity. I think sympathy for the party forced to pay damages indicates a gap between legal and moral liability. My sense is that we would not feel sympathy for a hiker who has to compensate a home-owner for damages after he broke into the empty house in an emergency, because he intentionally performed an action that is ordinarily prohibited (2017: 78). By contrast, the no-fault motorist and person held strictly liable performed no action directly leading to harm.

18 Tadros also sees non-standard forms of liability stemming from failures or inabilities to observe one's duties (2011).

19 I focus on the proximate objective end of intentional actions in order to distinguish self-interested from other-oriented actions. I exclude motives and secondary effects of the actions in order to discern whether the actor or other people are objectively benefited by the actions. This permits a firm separation of actions that would otherwise not be so easily distinguishable (cf. McMahan 2005: 399). For example, it draws a clear line between an other-oriented action like a motorist driving his child to the doctor and a self-interested action like a philosopher driving to a conference.

20 The bilateral nature of these actions—evincing some kind of mutual relationship between agent or remote agent and victim—answers McMahan's concern about line drawing. In considering the idea that agents engaged in other-oriented actions like ambulance driving should not be liable for non-culpably imposing unjust threats, he expresses a concern that there is no principled way to distinguish how altruistic an

Reductive individualists' theories of liability 51

action has to be in order to deflect liability (2005: 399). Instead of focusing on the quality of the agent's reasons for acting, I look at the relationship between the unjustly threatened party and the agent to see if there are consensual elements on the part of the victim that forfeit his potential claim for shifting the cost of an unjust threat back to the agent of the threat.

21 A patient may win a torts claim against a negligent surgeon, but not against a surgeon who observed all proper protocols in a case when the operation had complications. Benbaji and Statman make a similar argument (2019: 33).

22 Bazargan makes a similar argument to rule out killing ambulance drivers who non-culpably endanger pedestrians (2014: 131). Unlike me, he permits killing the private citizen in the out-of-control car using a more complex version of the agent responsibility argument. He responds to an objection that *any* level of unilateral liability is unfair by pointing out that the law of private necessity allows compensatory liability in cases of unjust harm posed in the course of justified actions (2017: 77). My view is that the pedestrian would not hypothetically consent to a rule of unilateral liability if he also drives. The pedestrian can also be modeled as hypothetically indemnifying ambulance and delivery drivers. These dynamics trump the private necessity argument. The analogy would be homeowners rejecting a rule requiring desperate hikers to compensate them for damages to their houses caused in an emergency or agreeing to indemnify hikers *in extremis*.

23 I generally agree with Ferzan's point that reasonable choices should not result in liability, but see some exceptions such as the skydiving case (assuming that we can agree that it is reasonable for an experienced skydiver to skydive under certain conditions).

References

Anscombe, G.E.M. (1981) "War and Murder" in *Collected Papers* III, Oxford: Blackwell Press.

Bazargan, S. (2011) "The Permissibility of Aiding and Abetting Unjust Wars," *Journal of Moral Philosophy*, 8: 513–529.

Bazargan, S. (2013) "Complicitous Liability in War," *Philosophical Studies*, 165: 177–195.

Bazargan, S. (2014) "Killing Minimally Responsible Threats," *Ethics*, 125: 114–136.

Bazargan, S. (2017) "Defensive Liability without Culpability," in Coons, C. and Weber, M. (eds), *The Ethics of Self-Defense*, Oxford: Oxford University Press.

Benbaji, Y. (2009) "The War Convention and the Moral Division of Labour," *The Philosophical Quarterly*, 59(237): 593–617.

Benbaji, Y. and Statman, D. (2019) *War by Agreement*, Oxford: Oxford University Press.

Bomann-Larsen, L. (2004) "Licence to Kill? The Question of Just vs. Unjust Combatants," *Journal of Military Ethics*, 3(2): 142–160.

Coady, A. (2004) "Terrorism and Innocence," *Journal of Ethics*, 8: 37–58.

Fabre, C. (2009) "Guns, Food, and Liability to Attack in War," *Ethics*, 120: 36–63.

Fabre, C. (2012) *Cosmopolitan War*, Oxford: Oxford University Press.

Fabre, C. (2014) "Cosmopolitanism and Wars of Self-Defence," in Fabre, C. and Lazar, S. (eds), *The Morality of Defensive War*, Oxford: Oxford University Press.

Feinberg, J. (1991) "Collective Responsibility," in May, L. and Hoffman, S. (eds), *Collective Responsibility*, Lanham, MD: Rowman & Littlefield.

Ferzan, K. (2012) "Culpable Aggression: The Basis for Moral Liability to Defensive Killing," *Ohio State Journal of Criminal Law*, 9: 669–697.

Ferzan, K. (2016) "Forfeiture and Self-Defense," in Coons, C. and Weber, M. (eds), *The Ethics of Self-Defense*, Oxford: Oxford University Press.

Frowe, H. (2014) *Defensive Killing*, Oxford: Oxford University Press.

52 *Revisionist just war theory*

Isaacs, T. (2011) *Moral Responsibility in Collective Contexts*, Oxford: Oxford University Press.

Kaufman, W. (2008) "Torture and the 'Distributive Justice' Theory of Self-Defense," *Ethics and International Affairs*, 22(1): 93–115.

Lazar, S. (2009) "Responsibility, Risk, and Killing in Self-Defense," *Ethics*, 119(4): 699–728.

Lazar, S. (2010) "The Responsibility Dilemma for Killing in War: A Review Essay," *Philosophy and Public Affairs*, 38(2): 180–212.

Lazar, S. (2012) "Necessity in Self-Defense and War," *Philosophy and Public Affairs*, 40(1): 3–44.

Mapel, D. (2004) "Innocent Attackers and Rights of Self Defense," *Ethics and International* Affairs, 18(1): 81–86.

McMahan, J. (1994) "Self-Defense and the Problem of the Innocent Attacker," *Ethics*, 104(2): 252–290.

McMahan, J. (2005) "The Basis of Moral Liability to Defensive Killing," *Philosophical Issues*, 15: 386–405.

McMahan, J. (2009) *Killing in War*, Oxford: Clarendon Press.

McPherson, L. (2004) "Innocence and Responsibility in War," *Canadian Journal of Philosophy*, 34(4): 485–506.

Norman, R. (1995) *Ethics, Killing and War*, Cambridge: Cambridge University.

Otsuka, M. (1994) "Killing the Innocent in Self-Defense," *Philosophy & Public Affairs*, 23(1): 74–94.

Øverland, G. (2006) "Killing Soldiers," *Ethics and International Affairs*, 20: 455–475.

Rodin, D. (2002) *War and Self-Defense*, Oxford: Oxford University Press.

Rodin, D. (2008) "The Moral Inequality of Soldiers: Why *jus in bello* Asymmetry is Half Right," in Rodin, D. and Shue, H. (eds), *Just and Unjust Warriors*, Oxford: Oxford University Press.

Rodin, D. (2011) "Justifying Harm," *Ethics*, 122(1): 74–110.

Rodin, D. (2014) "The Myth of National Defense," in Fabre, C. and Lazar, S. (eds), *The Morality of Defensive War*, Oxford: Oxford University Press.

Shue, H. (2008) "Do We Need a 'Morality of War'?" in Rodin, D. and Shue, H. (eds), *Just and Unjust Warriors*, Oxford: Oxford University Press.

Shue, H. (2014)"The Myth of National Self-Defence," in Fabre, C. and Lazar, S. (eds), *The Morality of Defensive War*, Oxford: Oxford University Press.

Statman, D. (2014) "Fabre's Crusade for Justice: Why We should not Join," *Law and Philosophy*, 33: 337–360.

Steinhoff, U. (2012) "Rights, Liability, and the Moral Equality of Combatants," *Journal of Ethics*, 16: 339–366.

Strawser, B. (2011) Walking the Tightrope of Just War, *Analysis Reviews*, 71(3): 533–544.

Tadros, V. (2011) *The Ends of Harm*, Oxford: Oxford University Press.

Tadros, V. (2016) "Unjust Wars Worth Fighting For," *Journal of Practical Ethics*, 4(1): 52–78.

Thomson, J.J. (1991) "Self-Defense," *Philosophy & Public Affairs*, 20(4): 283–310.

Walzer, M. (2006) "Response to Jeff McMahan," *Philosophia*, 34(6): 43–45.

Zohar, N. (1993) "Collective War and Individualistic Ethics," *Political Theory*, 21(4): 602–622.

Zohar, N. (2004) "Innocence and Complex Threats: Upholding the War Ethic and the Condemnation of Terrorism," *Ethics*, 114: 734–751.

Part II

The foundations of the moral equality of combatants

The main goal of Part II is to articulate how the moral equality of combatants is conceptually possible. To accomplish this goal, I need to show how a sane, adult combatant can make a material contribution to the main strategic thrust of an unjust war without thereby performing an unjustified action. I also need to show how combatants on opposite sides of a war performing the same behavior (e.g., firing a rifle) are responsible for normatively identical actions, distinct from their downstream effects. This two-step argument will create the conceptual space to argue in Part III that two opposing combatants, performing the same actions, can both be justified, even though one is contributing to an unjust war.

Revisionists allow that combatants may be justified in contributing to just missions within unjust wars. I will address the tougher challenge for traditionalists by focusing on combatants' meaningful contributions to thoroughly unjust wars rather than on atypical examples of combatants' contributions to just missions in unjust wars, just phases of wars that started out as unjust, or wars that are unjust but justified. (As examples of the first type of atypical mission, soldiers might be sent to guard a hospital from looters in the midst of an unjust invasion. Regarding the second, an unjust war might unleash sectarian conflict that invading troops are then tasked with suppressing. Regarding the third, troops might unjustly invade a coastal state in order to occupy defensive positions against a seaborne invasion from an aggressive adversary. While the invasion of the coastal state is unjust it might lead to the best overall outcome given the destruction promised by an unopposed invasion attack from the adversary.)

The plan of the argument is as follows. In Chapter 4, I will argue that military action is a special sort of collective action called an *irreducible corporate action*. It does not reduce down for the purpose of moral analysis and critique to individual component actions retaining the moral character of the collective action. The component actions then are not necessarily unjustified by virtue of being meaningfully connected to the unjust collective action or ends. By contrast, other types of collective actions called *goal-oriented collective* actions are aggregates of their component actions. An unjust collective action of the latter sort is an aggregation of individual unjustified actions.

There would seem to be no need to pursue a question of liability for actions that are not unjustified as they presumably do not terminate in unjust effects that need

54 *The foundations of the moral equality of combatants*

to be blocked or punished. The peculiar nature of organizational action means that the collective action of the organization can be unjust without its members' contributory actions necessarily being unjustified. Yet they *can* be unjustified if the members know about the specific unjust ends they are advancing and intend their actions to advance those ends because they are motivated to see their fruition. These actions are unjustified since there are strong objective moral reasons connected to the agent not to knowingly and intentionally advance unjust ends.

Culpability is the liability standard that encompasses an agent's knowledge, intentions and motives, so a defense of a culpability standard in Chapter 3 is necessary to fill out the argument in Chapter 4. The standard inculpates actors differently in organizations and goal-oriented collectives. The interplay of the structure of these collective actions and the requirements of culpability can mean that the member of a goal-oriented collective can be culpable for group actions of which he is ignorant. This is relevant to irregular militant groups and to conventional military units engaged in conspiracies to commit war crimes.

I also need to pursue a rehabilitation of the culpability standard to finish the critique of the objectively unjust proceeding and unjust threat approaches advanced in the last chapter. I need to show how a culpability standard of liability will not prevent innocent people from defending themselves against psychotic or other non-culpable attackers. Again, on most other points, the minimal forms of liability favored by the reductive individualists have been found wanting.

Beyond criticizing the conclusions of revisionism, I also mean this book to defend the traditional exceptionalist and collectivist approach to just war theorizing. Part II presses this methodological point against all reductive *and* individualist approaches to just war theory, including those of reductive traditionalists (e.g., Steinhoff 2007, 2008, 2012; Benbaji 2007, 2008, 2009, 2011; Lazar 2017),[1] individualist traditionalists (e.g., Miller 2017; Handfield and Emerton 2009), and the one prominent reductive individualist who does not endorse a single standard of liability, Victor Tadros.

Most actions in war are irreducibly corporate actions, so a reductivist approach basing prescriptions for contributors to collective actions on insights gained from analysis of individual actions performed *out* of collective contexts may be systematically flawed. Descriptive individualism is a problem for just war theory because it denies that actions in particular group settings should be analyzed differently to the actions of individuals outside of groups, and relatedly, denies the existence of irreducibly corporate actions.[2] Descriptive individualism can lead to evaluative individualism, which might deny unique norms for military personnel. Even prescriptions by traditionalists that are normatively correct—such as those affording most conventional combatants in inter-state war equal belligerent privileges—can be right for the wrong reasons. Wrong conclusions may then follow these methods in other areas. Finally, arguments clarifying the scope of combatants' responsibility in war in Part II will support the traditional separation between combatants' and policymakers' responsibilities for *jus in bello* and *jus ad bellum*, respectively.

3 The culpability standard of liability

I Introduction

Actions for which an actor might be judged culpable are actions that the actor can physically control and intentionally perform; these are also actions whose immediate consequences he can foresee and that provide his motivation. One can also be held culpable for actions one did not specifically intend but that one performed in a condition of recklessness or negligence. In these cases, the standard criteria of culpability apply to the initiation of the benighting condition such as intoxication, rather than the problematic action performed in the condition. Since culpability encompasses aspects of action that are in an actor's control, an actor can usually avoid culpable behavior if he wishes. Others can therefore blame or praise actors for these actions, demand correction of bad behavior, and offer instruction to this end.

Most philosophers, McMahan included, feel that culpability is the most satisfying standard for liability because the innocent party is justly permitted to defend himself and the attacker is ideally prevented from completing a rights violation (McMahan 1994: 263). There is often a rough symmetry between the harm the attacker inflicted or planned to inflict and the harm he suffers in proportionate defense. If the defense is successful, the two parties are largely returned to a *status quo ante* where neither is infringing on or violating the other's rights. Further, a culpability standard provides ample opportunity for people to avoid being stripped of a right to self-defense (a feature of liability) and suffering defensive harm. By definition, culpable actions are within agents' control. The culpable attacker could have avoided liability by choosing to refrain from his unjust action.[3]

As we saw in the last chapter, some philosophers want alternatives to the familiar and intuitive culpability standard of liability because of puzzles the standard seems to raise in unusual cases of self-defense. A culpability standard indicates a non-culpable attacker or non-culpable threat must be non-liable, despite being causally responsible for an unjust threat that would otherwise suggest that the innocent defender has a right to defend herself. Bizarrely, a woman defending herself from a knife-wielding mental patient would seem to make *herself* liable to defensive violence by violently engaging her non-culpable

56 *The foundations of the moral equality of combatants*

attacker. A person's liability is not the only situation making violence permissible, but in cases where the non-culpable attacker does not waive his defensive rights and where killing him is not the lesser evil, it seems that an innocent person simply has to suffer an attack from a non-culpable attacker. The same goes for someone materially threatened by someone falling or slipping out of control. Many feel that it is highly counter-intuitive to say that an innocent person cannot violently defend or preserve herself in such scenarios. For the sake of limiting the scope of the argument in what follows, I will restrict myself to the tri-fold grounds of justified killing admitted by many revisionists: liability, waiver, and lesser evil. I do not claim these are the only grounds for justified killing.

A full defense of culpability's applicability to all variants of non-culpable attackers or threats would require a book. I do not need an exhaustive defense since it is the intuitive form of liability that some only abandon because of the challenges posed by unusual cases. I will sketch out brief responses to cases involving major types of non-culpable threats: non-responsible threats, mistaken threats, and those who pose a threat without the exercise of personal agency. In most cases, consistent with common intuitions, the victim may use defensive violence against the non-culpable attacker or threat despite that party's non-culpability. This is due to a hypothetical waiver ascribable to the party. Meeting the intuition removes the necessity to resort to less satisfying minimal modes of liability discussed in Part I.

i Mistaken and psychotic attackers

A culpable attacker breaches his duty not to unjustly threaten innocent people with imminent violence by knowingly attacking an innocent person. The culpable attacker knows what he is doing is wrong and is able to refrain from the attack. Uncontroversially, the victim may engage in proportionate defensive violence if necessary to ward off the attack and prevent the attacker from immediately re-engaging in the attack.

The mistaken attacker and psychotic attacker non-culpably engage in behavior that is materially threatening to an innocent person. The mistaken attacker and psychotic attacker are behaving violently because of subjectively justified reactions to situations in which they are unknowingly suffering diminished capacities. The mistaken attacker does not understand the true ramifications of his actions; the psychotic attacker may face this difficulty as well as an inability to control his actions. Since they are not culpable for initiating the actions posing an unjust threat, it is wrong to treat their relation to their threatening action the same way as the relation between the culpable attacker and his action. I will refer to the following thought experiment of a mistaken attack as a reference point to defend this assertion. I will stipulate certain commonalities between the psychotic attacker and mistaken attacker in the paragraphs to follow before filling in the argument regarding the psychotic attacker later.

The culpability standard of liability 57

Mistaken attacker: battlefield

The mistaken attacker lives in a city devastated by civil war. His neighborhood is controlled by a brutal militia dedicated to exterminating the ethnic group of which the mistaken attacker is a member. The mistaken attacker traverses streets filled with discarded military equipment. A man approaches him down an alley wearing the militia's distinctive coat. Realizing that he has been spotted, the mistaken attacker jumps behind a turret-mounted machine gun on an abandoned jeep and starts firing at the militia man. Yet the man is not a militia member; he merely put on the discarded coat to keep warm. He is trapped in the alley, but sees a grenade launcher on the ground.

The mistaken attacker has not violated his duty by knowingly attacking an innocent person so is not liable to defensive violence for this action according to a culpability standard of liability. An agent's intentional state gives subjective meaning and organization to the behaviors he materially advances. A culpability standard takes this internal view into account along with an objective description of the situation (broader than the agent's epistemic view) in assessing liability. Taking the internal viewpoint into account, we can see that the culpable attacker's subjective understanding of the action he initiated matches the effects he is actually having in the world in the midst of his action. New information about the effects of his initial action on his intended victim would not alter his behavior since he *wants* to attack this innocent person. By contrast, new, accurate information about the effects their actions were having would cause both the mistaken attacker and psychotic attacker to try to halt their efforts if they were able because their initial subjective understanding of their action does not match reality (assuming that the mistaken attacker and the psychotic attacker, in moments of clarity, are dutiful people). Mid-action, we can refer to the culpable attacker's originating intention to make sense of his action, assess liability with a culpability standard, and identify a permissible reaction for the victim since the culpable attacker's intention is still sufficient to guide the action he wants to complete. We cannot do the same with the mistaken attacker or psychotic attacker. We need to consider, for instance, the mistaken attacker's relationship to the physical behaviors he materially advances in the middle of what a bystander might describe as a single action begun with the mistaken attacker's depression of the trigger and ending with the alley man's death. In a sense, we need to consider the mistaken attacker as a witness to the action he is perpetuating since a full and accurate description of the action he materially advances is alien to him. The mistaken attacker does not know he is attacking an innocent person. The subjective understanding that motivated the mistaken attacker's action is false so cannot play a part in determining the mistaken attacker's liability *now*. The mistaken attacker already met his duty not to knowingly attack an innocent person. Yet the mistaken attacker is not, as he thought, an innocent person pre-emptively attacking a vicious murderer. By

58 *The foundations of the moral equality of combatants*

contrast, the culpable attacker's malicious originating (and guiding) intention has given shape to an action ceding his defensive rights and making him liable to the victim's proportionate defense or a bystander's proportionate defensive assistance.

We need to reconsider the mistaken attacker's relation to the action he is materially advancing. The mistaken attacker's reasonable heuristic—any adult man wearing a militia coat is a militia member—failed to yield the correct decision this time. We sometimes engage in hypothetical exercises in exigent circumstances when considering how to interact with people who are ignorant, ill, mistaken, or incapacitated, by asking how this person would want to be treated if he suffered no diminishment. In this case, we can ask how would, or how must, the mistaken attacker act if he suddenly became aware of his mistake? Imagine that the first rounds the mistaken attacker fires at the alley man miss and then the man cries out in the mistaken attacker's own tribal language, making him realize that he is shooting at an innocent person. Obviously, the mistaken attacker's duty not to threaten innocent people means that he must immediately stop firing. The moral nature of his action would change if he persisted in shooting.

What if the gun jams and the mistaken attacker cannot stop firing? Perhaps he is also stuck in the turret so the victim cannot disable the machine gun with his grenade launcher without killing the mistaken attacker. The mistaken attacker must attempt to halt the action he is materially advancing. He is therefore dutybound to attempt to disable the gun or to ask for help to that end from bystanders if he realizes his action threatens an innocent person, but he cannot arrest the action himself. He is also duty-bound to accept help to stop the action even if he did not ask, but help was offered and he was unable to self-arrest the action.

Asking for help or accepting help includes waiving whatever rights would normally deter others from interacting with the agent in the way that is now necessary to halt the action and that is proportionate to the threat posed by the action. Similarly, a choking victim, gesturing for someone to help her, waives the right that normally entitles her to forcibly fend off others manhandling her. Giving someone permission means waiving the rights that ordinarily prevent the person from acting in the arena covered by the permission.

The mistaken attacker's duty to halt the action unjustly threatening others extends to his requesting proportionate *violent* interference with his actions, if that is the only way to arrest the actions. Since the mistaken attacker's actions pose an imminent threat to an innocent person's life, the mistaken attacker cannot demand that his life be preserved in this case instead of his victim's.[4] While the mistaken attacker and the victim are both non-culpable, they are not in the situation of shipwreck survivors who are both threatened by the same menace and retain an equal right to a life-saving resource like a lifeboat or an equal claim to being saved by a third party. Scholars employing a minimal standard of liability ascribe the inequality between the mistaken attacker and his victim wholly or in part to the fact that one party is causally responsible for, or causally involved with, an unjust threat posed against the other. Even the non-culpable threat presses the victim into a forced choice. This causal responsibility does not necessarily make a difference for culpability-based liability. Rather, there is a

The culpability standard of liability 59

morally relevant difference between the parties in this case because the mistaken attacker's negative duty not to unjustly threaten others (broader than the related duty not to attack innocent people) means he is responsible for attempting to halt the action he non-culpably initiated.[5] He may still be able to ask for help in arresting the action in a case where he understands the ramifications of his action but is unable to halt it himself. In any case, he can omit a defensive action that would halt the victim's or third party's arresting of the action. In such a case, he must ask for help, omit defensive actions, and waive defensive rights thereby giving others the permission to intervene.

The situation is clear if the mistaken attacker realizes the victim's innocence, is unable to self-arrest the action, and cries out to the victim or a bystander: "I'm sorry! I don't want to kill you! Please stop me!" Yet it needs to be explained how a waiver can be ascribed to someone who does not explicitly grant it, given that waivers are typically given by explicit, unambiguous signs with clear, mutually understood meanings to cede a right the waiving party would otherwise retain.

ii Hypothetical waivers

We act on *hypothetical* waivers when getting express waivers is impossible and it is reasonable to think most people in the patient's situation would grant a waiver in order to protect their rights or interests. For example, one might perform a life-saving operation on an incapacitated person or jump into a stranger's rolling car to apply the emergency brake. One's positive duty to render assistance to others is insufficient to justify the action without an express or hypothetical waiver in these cases, because unlike giving money to charity, the agent's good deed requires her to materially infringe on someone's rights. The person to whom the hypothetical waiver was ascribed might actually be aggrieved, but most would argue that the Good Samaritan was right to intervene and performed an action that anyone similarly able, and similarly situated, should perform.

There are also situations in which the coupling of a person's negative right and positive duty indicate that one has a *duty to waive* a negative right in order to behave correctly with others. Others may act on the duty-holder's hypothetical waiver in some such cases. For example, consider *Tsunami*.

Tsunami

Sara survives a tsunami by climbing a tree. Most of the surrounding structures are covered with water. After half a day in the tree, she decides that no rescuers will likely come before sundown. She swims to a nearby marina past capsized boats toward a still-sea-worthy yacht. The high sides of the yacht make it impossible to board. The yacht's owner, Maria, is safe ten stories above in her well-stocked apartment watching Sara's plight. Maria can remotely lower a ladder on her yacht to the waterline.

60   *The foundations of the moral equality of combatants*

Ordinarily, Maria has a right to refuse anyone access to her yacht, but she must waive that right now as an expression of her positive duty to assist others, given the extremity of Sara's need, the slight cost to Maria, and the unique nature of Maria's ability to render aid. Maria's general positive duty to offer assistance to those in need does not compel her to directly rescue Sara with bodily actions, as the duty would in a case where an able-bodied adult sees a toddler drowning in a nearby wading pool. In *Tsunami*, Maria's duty to assist means that Maria must waive part of the package of rights associated with private property ownership because she is too far away to directly rescue Sara and Sara needs entry onto the yacht in order to survive. Maria's full package of rights to private property is not forfeited. Another boat-owner cannot come and tow her yacht away; Sara cannot take the yacht's brass fixtures home with her. One might object that a duty to waive seems oxymoronic because waivers need to be freely given. Duties compel us to voluntarily perform morally prescribed acts or refrain from prohibited acts. So indeed, the right thing for Maria to do is to choose to waive her right to refuse Sara entry to her yacht. Refusal would make her liable to proportionate measures to force her to lower the ladder (Tadros 2011: 265).

Unable to communicate with the yacht owner, Sara may pull a latch she finds on the yacht's exterior to manually lower the ladder. Her rights to board the yacht and stay there until help arrives or the water recedes are the reciprocal aspect of Maria's duty to waive her rights to refuse access. Sara's entry is not necessarily consequent to Maria's liability and forfeiture of her relevant rights. Maria has not, as far as Sara knows, forfeited any rights through a breach of duty. Sara is acting on a hypothetical waiver, assuming the yacht owner would waive her right to refuse entry because she has a duty to permit Sara's entry. Were the two able to communicate by a diver's phone on the side of the yacht and Maria explicitly refused her entry, Sara could board knowing she was justified through Maria's ceding of her right to refuse entry.

While the status of positive duties is somewhat controversial, there should be even less doubt that one must waive one's right(s) if doing so is necessary to meet a negative duty that cannot be met without such a waiver. This dynamic will help us address the non-culpable attacker cases.

The mistaken attacker retains his two defensive rights—the right against being violently confronted and the right to defend himself—through the initiation of his action endangering the victim. He retains these rights because he did not culpably engage in the action. His non-culpability means he is not liable to defensive violence. As already argued, he would be violating his duty by persisting in the action after becoming aware of the victim's innocence in a moment when he is able to self-arrest the action. He would be liable under such a scenario.

If he becomes aware of the true nature of his action but is unable to self-arrest, there is no commission or omission he can perform to *directly* arrest his action. The only way he can aid the victim is to omit a defensive action that would prevent the victim from defending himself or a bystander from intervening to defend the victim. The mistaken attacker's duty to avoid unjustly

The culpability standard of liability 61

threatening others means that he must omit this defensive action and waive the defensive rights that would morally inhibit the victim or a bystander from violently halting him with force proportionate to the threat he poses. Again, all would be clear if the mistaken attacker shouted at the victim "Do what you must to stop me! I don't want to kill you!" Without any way to communicate with the mistaken attacker, the victim in the alley may act on a hypothetical waiver. He may defend himself without wronging the mistaken attacker because the mistaken attacker has a duty to waive his defensive rights.

What if the mistaken attacker remains ignorant? With people whose faculties are compromised, we model the duties they would have if their faculties were intact. Generally, others can act in a way preventing one party from wrongly infringing on another's rights by forcing the first party to occupy a space or posture he would have adopted voluntarily if self-limiting his actions in accord with his duties. Paradigmatically—with a non-ignorant actor—one can force a culpable attacker to desist from his unjust violent actions (to be clear, the culpable attacker cedes his defensive rights rather than waives them). This permission to intercede extends even to interceding against non-malicious ignorant actors in an exigent circumstance where verbally warning them might not make them halt fast enough. Imagine a nurse grabbing the arm of a surgeon who is about to amputate the wrong limb. These are cases where dutiful actors should welcome an intercession preventing them from causing harm. The interceding party is acting in a way the ignorant actor would presumably want her to act because the intercession forces the ignorant actor to occupy the space or posture she would voluntarily occupy in keeping with her duties. So the ignorant mistaken attacker can be forced to occupy the physical space or posture vis-à-vis the victim he would voluntarily occupy if he had the knowledge to perform his duty to waive his defensive rights.[6] The victim's self-defense is not justified through the mistaken attacker's liability because he has not culpably initiated the attack or culpably persisted in it as the victim began to defensively respond.

Note, there is a moral difference between forcing someone to physically desist from materially infringing on others' rights in response to a duty breach versus a hypothetical waiver. In *Tsunami*, Sara can board the yacht without communicating with Maria, reasoning that she is permitted to do so because the yacht owner has a duty to waive the rights that would otherwise entitle the owner to refuse a stranger's boarding. Sara is not in the same situation she would be if facing a villain whom she defensively forces to occupy the space or position he would voluntarily occupy if he was meeting his duties. Unlike a confrontation with someone attacking her or trying to steal her property, Sara does not have reason to believe that Maria is breaching her duty to waive her rights relative to the use of the yacht. Sara's actions are consistent with the belief that the yacht owner really would waive her relevant rights and gladly welcome a tsunami victim aboard. Whereas the victim defends against an apparently culpable attacker with the understanding that he has already breached his duty and so has to be compelled to reassume the position he should have voluntarily occupied, the victim can reasonably assume that she is engaged in a cooperative

62 *The foundations of the moral equality of combatants*

venture with the person to whom a hypothetical waiver is ascribed. The deeper moral and practical differences between forfeiture and the waiver approach will be discussed in sub-section iii, below.

The psychotic attacker may be in a similar situation as the mistaken attacker, though his epistemic problem has a different etiology. At least during the violent episode, the psychotic attacker lacks accurate knowledge of the situation and lacks the ability to control his inordinate emotions. He acts with agency in that he is trying to hurt (or defend himself against) the particular victim, but he lacks many of the markers of culpability for the attack because his psychosis leads him to think that the victim is actually a vicious enemy whom he feels an irresistible urge to confront. We will assume he did not refuse to take anti-psychotic medication in a prior moment when he was able to make responsible decisions.

In this case, we can model what the psychotic attacker would be duty-bound to waive were he to have a moment of clarity and become aware of his victim's innocence mid-attack. The psychotic attacker may also be like the mistaken attacker in the variant in which he is aware his victim is innocent but is unable to halt the attack. People with severe mental illness sometimes report that a "part of them" watches their actions during a psychotic episode as though from a third party's perspective. Perhaps the psychotic attacker cannot stop his violent actions even if, on some level, he perceives them to be wrong. As with the mistaken attacker, we can model what rights the psychotic attacker would be duty-bound to waive if he could not stop himself from attacking an innocent person and permit the victim to act accordingly. This argument meets Fabre and Frowe's concern that a culpability standard would seem to force someone to submit to a psychotic attacker's attack. Rather, the victim may defend herself without wronging the attacker despite the attacker's non-liability.

iii Significance of the waiver approach

Other scholars solve the non-culpable attacker problem by arguing that the non-culpable attacker is liable to being violently confronted,[7] meaning he is not wronged by the victim's proportionate and necessary defensive response. Others argue that the non-culpable attacker is permissibly targetable, but nonetheless wronged (Frowe 2009: 268). There is a split among these scholars on the question of whether the non-culpable attacker retains a right of self-defense.[8] A third group argue that killing the non-culpable attacker is wrong but the victim can be excused.[9] In most of these cases, the mistaken attacker does not enjoy a right to self-defense (though he might be excused as well).[10] These somewhat messy formulations are the result of conceiving the two parties in an adversarial forced-choice situation native to the culpable attacker scenario. The victim's defensive rights are privileged as they would be in a culpable attacker case but then the novel element of the attacker's non-culpability is also factored into the equation.

The noncompossibility of both non-culpable threat and defender succeeding in their defensive actions poses no conceptual problem to granting both

The culpability standard of liability 63

defenders and non-culpable attackers permission to engage in defensive violence, according to Jonathon Quong (2009: 520). He is correct to point to sports and games as examples of this juxtaposition of noncompossibility with adversarial permissions. Both boxers can contend with one another, but only one can win. Yet this arrangement may strike some as dissatisfying when it comes to the forced-choice approach to non-culpable attacker scenarios since that approach purports to distribute justice, and in matters of justice, unlike sports, it is usually not just as well that either one of an adversarial pair "loses."

The forced-choice approach the deontologist scholars use, which takes into account the victim's defensive rights and the attacker's non-culpability, does not capture all the relevant moral phenomena despite the complexity of the above-mentioned formulae. The forced-choice approach is indicated when we just look to the external effects of the parties' bodies. Yet it is limited compared to an approach taking into account the internal states with which a culpability standard is partly concerned. The non-culpable attacker has nothing against the victim *really* and the victim should have nothing against the attacker if understanding that he is non-culpable. We can imagine an actual non-culpable attacker being horrified to learn that he was menacing an innocent person and overcome with guilt if his attack was successful. The defender would probably feel terrible if forced to kill the mistaken attacker or psychotic attacker.

The waiver approach extends the mistaken attacker's responsibility to the temporal middle of the action he materially advances, at which point we re-assess the implications of his duty not to threaten the victim. We then conclude that his duty entails waiving all the rights that need to be waived to permit the victim's non-wrongful proportionate defense. This treatment of the problem seems to more accurately capture the moral complexity of the action and, interestingly, yields a theoretically tidier outcome. The non-culpable attacker has a duty to waive both his right against being violently confronted, which some scholars grant, and his right to self-defense, which far fewer grant. The victim is justified in defending himself, rather than merely excused, because the attacker can be modeled as waiving his defensive rights and this waiver permits the victim to do something he has strong moral reasons to do. The waiving party is not wronged by the victim's necessary and proportionate violence.

Excused parties may not be aided by third parties. Some see this as a reason why deeming the victim merely excused is implausible, while others question why a third party should not assist a mental patient who is about to be killed by a sane defender or assist two non-culpable attackers being fought by a single victim (Alexander 1987: 1188). The waiver approach dissolves this debate since a duty to waive a right also means refusing third-party intervention to defend that right. An exception would be a third-party intervention that saved both parties.

Thus, I have articulated a way in which a non-culpable attacker can be permissibly killed by a victim without the attacker being deemed liable. The desire to explain why the victim should be able to defend himself, recall, led some to abandon a culpability standard and to seek out minimal standards of

64 *The foundations of the moral equality of combatants*

liability. There may be a practical difference in the violent defense permissibly elected by the victim if the attacker is understood to be vulnerable to defensive force on grounds of liability versus hypothetical waiver. The victim should certainly use minimally effective defensive force against an attacker to whom a waiver of defensive rights is ascribed since he is acting on the waiving party's behalf, doing what the waiving party should endorse if he was able.[11] Further, the victim should flee instead of confront the non-culpable attacker—if this is possible—because the attacker is non-culpable. This deference to the attacker may make a practical difference when compared to what is advocated for culpable attackers since some thinkers argue victims may be freer in their use of force against culpable attackers.

Even if the same level of force is used against attackers for different reasons, there is a moral difference between defensively killing the mistaken attacker or psychotic attacker on grounds of liability versus on the grounds of their hypothetical waiver. The approach ascribing a waiver to the agent assumes a non-adversarial moral relationship between the parties, despite the apparent adversarial relation of their physical actions. We can model a dutiful person waiving his two defensive rights when he has no other way of arresting an action unjustly threatening another that he causally advances. The agent is thus ascribed a kind of dignity by the victim in that the victim acts with the understanding that the dutiful agent would have waived the two rights inviting the defensive action if he had full knowledge of the situation. By contrast, liability is understood as a condition that is forced on the agent regardless of his subjective state, as a kind of consequence to the outward effects of his action (e.g., posing an unjust threat to another). Liability based solely on the outward effects of an agent's action disrespects the agent's autonomy in the sense that his treatment is inattentive to his own decisions, but only pays attention to the position of his body in space (see Nagel 1972; Rodin 2002: 88–89). The culpable attacker, of course, has no grounds to complain about this disrespect since the defensive response is commensurate with an action he freely chose. While a liable party might not be culpable, liability is the solution to the forced-choice problematic conceptualizing two parties as being in an antagonistic or competitive zero-sum relationship native to the culpable attacker case (see Kaufman 2008: 105).[12] This antagonistic dynamic is present in the explanation made by some of why liability is the appropriate justification for the targeting of the non-culpable attacker: unilateral absorption of harm is forced on the non-culpable liable party because he is the one who materially forced the devilish choice on the victim.

II Innocent projectile

Finally, we will discuss the most fantastical of the oft-discussed thought experiments: the innocent projectile. The innocent projectile is someone who poses an unjust threat to others without exercising agency, like someone about to land on a pedestrian after being thrown out of a window. Assume the innocent projectile did nothing to merit his defenestration and the pedestrian is on crutches and

The culpability standard of liability 65

cannot get out of the way quickly. Here, it is important to distinguish three different scenarios.[13] In the first scenario, the innocent projectile is falling down a ventilation shaft and cannot avoid landing on a pedestrian below him. He has no room to maneuver in the air in order to avoid the pedestrian. He will survive if he lands on the pedestrian but the pedestrian will die. In the second scenario, the innocent projectile is in a Pareto-inferior position of being doomed whether he hits the pedestrian or hits the sidewalk. The third scenario is similar to the first, but now the innocent projectile has enough room to twist away from the person beneath him and fatally hit the ground instead.

Recall, the mistaken/psychotic attacker would be duty-bound to try to halt his action if he realized he was performing a materially unjust action or to ask for help in arresting his action if he was not able to self-arrest. Asking for help would involve waiving his defensive rights to proportionate harm if outside intervention involved his being harmed. Others can act on what would be a hypothetical waiver in the event that the mistaken attacker/psychotic attacker was ignorant about the material injustice of his action with the understanding that the mistaken attacker/psychotic attacker would be duty-bound to give the waiver if he was knowledgeable.

Yet the innocent projectile is not performing an intentional action like the mistaken attacker/psychotic attacker. So the preceding argument obligating an agent to waive his defensive rights upon realizing that his intentional action is unjustified is inapplicable. The innocent projectile is not performing an action for which he is then primarily responsible for halting. The innocent projectile knows he is falling and knows his falling endangers an innocent person, but can do nothing to arrest his fall. The mistaken attacker/psychotic attacker merely has to change his intention to halt his action but innocent projectile 1 is a non-agent with respect to the pedestrian because his intentional state has no bearing on what his body does regarding the pedestrian. Since the innocent projectile lacks a duty to halt his action (because he is not performing an intentional action), he lacks a duty to waive the defensive rights it would be necessary to waive to give others permission to violently halt a non-liable person whose death is not the lesser of two evils. Therefore, others, including the pedestrian, cannot ascribe a hypothetical waiver unto him. The pedestrian does not have permission to shoot him on grounds of a waiver.[14]

Innocent projectile 1 of course cannot be killed on grounds of culpability-based liability either. Further, neither the pedestrian nor a third party can kill innocent projectile 1 with the argument that doing so is the lesser evil.[15] The death of either innocent projectile or pedestrian in this context is an equally bad result because both are non-culpable. Innocent projectile 1 and the pedestrian also cannot be modeled as partners in a hypothetical contract where they agree *ex ante* that someone in the pedestrian's place can permissibly kill someone in innocent projectile 1's situation because neither one of the hypothetical contractors would benefit from the rule compared to the morally sound *status quo* in which the pedestrian is prohibited from self-defense. One might just as likely be the unlucky person defenestrated by some villain as the unlucky pedestrian

66 *The foundations of the moral equality of combatants*

beneath the relevant window. Hence there are no rational grounds for permitting a rule granting the pedestrian permission to shoot. Having canvassed the reasons for permissible rights infringement entertained by most revisionists, we can conclude that the pedestrian may not shoot the innocent projectile. Therefore, the innocent projectile could defensively shoot the pedestrian if he sees the pedestrian aiming at him.[16]

However, the pedestrian could defend himself with a shield even if anticipating the innocent projectile might be killed by the impact. The armed innocent projectile may not shoot the pedestrian to prevent him from picking up the shield. One may shield oneself, foreseeing that it might lead to another's death, as one can duck a missile, foreseeing it might lead to another's death.[17] Generally, one does not have to sacrifice himself to save another innocent person.[18] A contract in which someone in the pedestrian's situation takes an ordinarily permissible, passive defensive action and someone in innocent projectile 1's situation waives a right of self-defense can be agreed to by hypothetical contracting parties because the arrangement grants both contracting parties a better-than-50% chance of survival compared to the just *status quo* in which the pedestrian has to defer to the non-culpable, non-waiving innocent projectile.

Let me explain further. A hypothetical contract permitting one party to intentionally kill a non-culpable threat in self-defense in exchange for the threatening party's waiver of defensive rights offers no extra benefit to the contracting parties compared to the just *status quo* in which the pedestrian must defer to the innocent projectile's non-culpability and non-waiving status. Yet a contract permitting shielding or ducking has two advantages over one permitting direct and intentional killing of a non-culpable person (or the just *status quo* in which the pedestrian may not shoot). First, a passive defense like shielding is ordinarily permissible and so does not require contracting parties to agree to a *prima facie* immoral action like intentionally killing a non-culpable, non-right-waiving person. Second, the defensive action exposing the other party to risk gives that party a better chance of survival than the defensive action that intentionally kills the threatening party or the just *status quo* in which the pedestrian must omit defensive action. The threatening party might survive the passive defensive action like shielding, but not the defensive reaction in the first hypothetical contract since the defensive action in that contract necessitates the threatening party's explosive death.[19] Though the *status quo* is not open to hypothetical contract—it is the alternative to a special contractual arrangement—we can compare the odds of the two parties' survival there with contractual arrangements to see if any morally sound arrangements are practically preferable. The odds are similarly bad for the pedestrian according to the just *status quo*. He will die and the innocent projectile will live. The hypothetical contracting parties have an equal chance of being the innocent projectile or the pedestrian in either contract; the worse-off party (the pedestrian) in the first contract (and in the just *status quo*) has a 0% chance of survival but the worse-off party in the second contract (the innocent projectile) has a greater-than-0% chance of survival.

The culpability standard of liability   67

This shielding contract also must involve innocent projectile 1's waiver of his right to self-defense since a retention of that right—which innocent projectile 1 could act on if he was armed and could shoot the pedestrian to prevent him from picking up the shield—would be no more advantageous than the first contract for contracting parties. This follows if we assume there is an equal chance of either party succeeding in his defensive efforts. *Ex ante*, without hypothetical contracting parties knowing their marksmanship abilities or the likelihood that their bodies would be unable to withstand a collision with a shield, there are no grounds to assume that there would not be an equal chance.

Innocent projectile 2 is in the Pareto-inferior position of being doomed no matter what he does. It follows that innocent projectile 2 has a duty to waive his right against being violently confronted and his right to self-defense. The pedestrian can act on these hypothetical waivers (in the event the innocent projectile does not shout his permission) and blast innocent projectile 2 apart with a shotgun if he chooses.[20] The justifying argument for this position turns on innocent projectile 2's positive rather than negative duties. Innocent projectile 2 does not have the duty not to unjustly threaten others while falling because he is not able to halt his descent or to maneuver in the air in order to avoid the pedestrian. Innocent projectile 2 lacks the capacity—and not just the opportunity—to act on the duty not to unjustly threaten others from the moment he becomes a material threat to the pedestrian. Innocent projectile 2 has the duty to refrain from actions he is still able to do as he falls, like divulge others' secrets, but he is not a dutyholder with respect to actions he has no capacity to execute.

I rejected the idea in Chapter 2 that unilateral defensive violence is justified against non-agents whose bodies pose a material threat to others because (the advocate asserts) the non-agent's body is having a material effect normally associated with a duty breach. I also reject the idea that the non-agent can be forced to absorb the level of harm he would have the duty to absorb if he was able to intentionally act. If he is armed, the only area of efficacy he has is with respect to his acting or not acting on his right to self-defense. Innocent projectile 2's negative duty not to unjustly threaten others does not demand his refraining from defensive action against the pedestrian because the threat innocent projectile 2's body poses to the pedestrian does not issue from his direct intentional action, indirect intentional, or intentional omission. The threat to the pedestrian could issue from innocent projectile 2's indirect intentional action if he fell because of his negligence, recklessness, or fault. Innocent projectile 2 would be intentionally omitting an action that would otherwise halt the danger posed to the pedestrian if he refrained from engaging in a mid-air maneuver that would have allowed him to avoid the pedestrian. Since innocent projectile 2 lacks agency in all these spheres—lacks the capacity to intentionally threaten others unjustly—he lacks a negative duty to avoid unjustly threatening the pedestrian.[21]

Innocent projectile 2's duty to waive his defensive rights stems from his positive duty to aid others in distress. Innocent projectile 2's predicament obviously makes it impossible to take active steps to act on his positive duty to protect the pedestrian. The only way for innocent projectile 2 to act on his positive duty, if

68 *The foundations of the moral equality of combatants*

both he and the pedestrian are armed, is to refrain from defending himself and allowing the pedestrian to shoot him. It may be more common to think of negative duties demanding omission of actions. Yet the relevant negative duty is not present, as just discussed, and *Tsunami* provided an example of where a positive duty to render assistance prompts a waiver of negative rights.

Ordinarily, one does not have to sacrifice oneself in order to save another because one's claim-right to life competes against, and usually supersedes, one's positive duties. Yet in this case, innocent projectile 2 cannot insist on his claim-right to life since there is nothing the pedestrian can do or refrain from doing to save him. Like an adult seeing a toddler drowning in a wading pool, innocent projectile 2 must act on his positive duty to render assistance to another because doing so comes at virtually no cost to him and no one else can preserve the pedestrian's life. Again, unfortunately, he is doomed. The cost for him associated with waiving a right to self-defense would be losing an extra few seconds of life. Innocent projectile 2 must waive his defensive rights because the only way to save the pedestrian is to permit the pedestrian to blow him apart.[22] The pedestrian can act on a hypothetical waiver in the event innocent projectile 2 does not or cannot shout his consent.

In the third scenario, the innocent projectile has room to twist in the air in order to avoid killing the pedestrian, though doing so would lead to the innocent projectile's death. He is non-culpably posing an unjust threat to the pedestrian, but, unlike the innocent projectiles in the other variations, he has some potential for agency. He must act to spare the pedestrian.[23] Having the power to act on the negative duty is the necessary precondition for his having the duty in situations where the duty is relevant. He may not use an innocent bystander like the pedestrian to save himself from the villain's murderous action any more than someone unjustly attacked by a gunman could use an innocent bystander as a human shield. Assuming he is able to twist away, falling on someone to cushion his impact or holding her body as a shield is an opportunistic killing, where one uses another to advantage oneself in a way that would not be possible in the victim's absence. Opportunistic killings are widely seen as presumptively worse than eliminative killings, where the killer is not left better off by the killing had the victim not been present. They are seen as morally worse because the killer is using the victim as a means to his benefit. While he was wronged by the villain, the innocent projectile cannot redirect the harm from that unjust action to an innocent bystander.[24] The innocent projectile is liable to defensive violence for culpably omitting a saving action that he is able to perform. While his inaction is less grievous than the culpable attacker's action—otherwise suggesting in a proportionality calculation that the pedestrian should absorb a greater degree of risk than if facing a culpable attacker—his liability tips the balance in favor of the pedestrian when the pedestrian cannot mitigate the innocent projectile's risk without lethal risk to himself. The pedestrian is permitted proportionate methods to stop innocent projectile 3. The pedestrian may shoot, spear, or hold a shield up to him and the (armed) innocent projectile may not shoot back.

The culpability standard of liability 69

One might object that innocent projectile 3 is not liable despite the danger his body poses to the pedestrian because of the difference between his omission of a saving action and a culpable attacker's commission of a threatening action. Innocent projectile 3 is not choosing to use the pedestrian for his purposes in the premeditated, malicious manner of a culpable attacker nor did he choose to initiate the sequence of events terminating in his body posing a threat to the pedestrian. Yet his omission of a saving action he is able to perform does not have the same exculpatory force it normally would when contrasted with commission of a threatening action. This follows because he does not need to commit any action—does not need to alter the causal structure of local events—to obtain a self-beneficial result that poses an unjust threat to another. To cite a similar example involving a lower-grade menace, there is a moral difference between ogling a naked person through a peephole and ogling a naked person when a locker room door swings opens. Yet the difference erodes as the seconds pass and the accidental voyeur chooses not to turn away. In these cases, an omission should be seen as morally closer to commission of a wrong action, because the agent is deciding to benefit himself at the expense of another and electing to accomplish that action through inaction—*because* action is unnecessary. That the omission regards a "crime of opportunity" rather than a premeditated one mitigates, but does not remove the culpability. The accidental voyeur and the peeping Tom's mental state is almost the same five seconds into the event.

Thus, while innocent projectile 3 is not exercising agency, he *has* agency with respect to the pedestrian's life. Innocent projectile 3 does something wrong by omitting a saving action he is able to perform. Innocent projectile 3 is not merely hoping to survive as in the first scenario, because he also choosing to sacrifice the pedestrian for that end. This choice to use the pedestrian also distinguishes this case from one where he might permissibly compete with another to get a scarce resource (e.g., the last seat on a lifeboat) with the knowledge that it will spell another's doom.

The mistaken attacker's victim in the alley could also choose to omit self-defense in order to save the mistaken attacker. One might wonder if his election of defensive actions makes him liable like innocent projectile 3, but he has the latitude to act on the mistaken attacker's hypothetical waiver. The pedestrian in the innocent projectile case could refrain from shooting innocent projectile 3 and offer his body as a cushion. His omitting this saving action does not make him liable—as innocent projectile 3's omission of a saving action does—because, unlike the mistaken attacker, there are no duty-based grounds to model the pedestrian's waiving his defensive rights to innocent projectile 3.

III Conclusion

With the exception of the first variant of the innocent projectile case, we have seen that a culpability standard can still yield intuitive responses in non-culpable attacker and threat cases if common intuition permits targeting the non-culpable attacker or threat. I do not take these kinds of thought

70 *The foundations of the moral equality of combatants*

experiments to be the end-all and be-all of moral argumentation because of the indeterminacy of intuitive responses, even among scholars who share a common cultural and educational background. My point here is to meet critics' concerns that a culpability standard of liability encounters grave problems when it comes to non-culpable attacker and threat cases.

Part I argued that the reductive individuals' minimal standards of liability are flawed and so cannot support the asymmetry thesis. In this chapter, I suggested we return to the more familiar culpability standard of liability and addressed how such a standard can still yield intuitive answers to the thought experiments that are often used to criticize the culpability standard and defend minimal standards of liability. I added to the critique of the objectively unjust proceedings and unjust threat models of liability discussed in Chapter 2 by showing how innocents can in most circumstances defend themselves against non-culpable unjust threats despite the threatening parties' non-liability. I have thus overcome a strong argument those models' advocates have in favor of otherwise-counter-intuitive minimal models of liability: that a culpability standard of liability would seem to prohibit self- or other-defense against non-culpable unjust threats.

I do not imagine this chapter to have exhaustively defended the culpability standard. I wished to do enough to meet the above concern and to make use of the standard plausible as a reference for discussions of collective actions in Chapter 4. There, we will see that culpability, but not more minimal forms of liability, makes a difference for the justification of contributory actions to unjust collective actions. Given the peculiar type of collective action that is military action, only culpable contributions to unjust collective military actions are unjustified. Yet due to the structure of military actions, most combatants are blocked from having the necessary elements of culpability present in their contributory actions. The irreducibility of military actions to their component actions will be invoked to explain how one's meaningful contributions to the main strategic thrust of an unjust war are not necessarily unjustified and, more broadly, to argue against the use of individualist *and* reductivist approaches in just war theory.

Notes

1 Lazar has expressed some sympathy to collectivist approaches to just war theory (2017: 4).
2 For other critiques of descriptive individualism, see Kutz (2005) and Walzer (2006).
3 Other just war theorists endorsing at least a minimal culpability standard for liability include Lazar (2012, 2015); Pattison (2011); and Zohar (1993). Tadros might be included as well since he considers culpability as one possible factor leading to liability (2016).
4 I agree with Wallerstein on this point (2005: 1030).
5 Causal responsibility for an unjust threat does not help distinguish attacker from victim because the victim's presence also causally contributes to the forced choice (Grabczynska and Ferzan 2009: 249; Lazar 2009: 721).
6 I take it that a person is not actually doing her duty if being physically moved or shouted at so that she halts her action in surprise. One has been prevented from

The culpability standard of liability 71

materially infringing on a right but has not freely chosen to refrain from an action out of respect for a right.

7 See Chapter 2. Also, Benbaji (2007: 571), Quong (2009: 520), Fabre (2012: 59) (in the case of the psychotic attacker, interpreting her terming the psychotic attacker's lack of a right to self-defense as liability).

8 Frowe, Benbaji, Quong, and Steinhoff permit self-defense. Fabre does not extend this privilege to the psychotic attacker (2012: 59); Wallerstein (2005: 1031), Anscombe (1981), and Thomson do not permit any non-culpable threats or attackers to defend.

9 Ferzan (2005: 734); Alexander (1987: 1187); McMahan (1994: 286; though as Chapter 2 showed, McMahan's position evolves); Rodin (2002: 98).

10 Ferzan seems to do no more than excuse the non-culpable attacker's self-defense (Grabczynska and Ferzan 2009: 249; see Frowe's discussion, 2009: 267). Alexander's consequentialist approach might permit self-defense in some instances. McMahan clarifies in his later work that the non-culpable attacker is not justified in self-defense.

11 Though Kasachkoff deems the innocent attacker liable because he is causally responsible, she argues his non-culpability suggests using less force than would be permitted with a culpable attacker (Kasachkoff 1998: 529).

12 Consequentialist approaches adopt a third party's perspective, inquiring which innocent party's death is the lesser evil instead of conceiving innocent attacker cases as zero-sum or antagonistic distributive justice problems.

13 The necessity of such a distinction can be seen in Øverland's explanation for why the innocent attacker should shoulder the burden of harm.

> [If the innocent attacker] has innocently initiated or sustained a causal sequence the effect of which is to put someone else in harm's way, then … he has a duty as a matter of fairness to shoulder his share of the cost.
>
> (2009: 215)

As we will see, the innocent projectile has *sustained* a causal sequence in the third, but not the first scenario, and this action is relevant to liability.

14 Several authors agree that the innocent projectile cannot be killed for different reasons (Rodin 2002: 86; Otsuka 1994: 75; McMahan 2005: 401; Ferzan 2005: 734; Wasserman 1987: 366).

15 Cf. Frowe (2014: 67–71), Tadros (2011: 254–255), Kamm (2001: 47–48), Wallerstein (2005: 1027). These theorists seem to conceive of claim-rights in a stronger manner than I do, such that Frowe, for one, holds that a person may use lethal violence to defend against all direct threats, no matter the threatening party's liability. I think the rights of the defender and the threatening party must both be taken into account. Hypothetical consent can be used to model what moral rules these unhappy pairs are rationally committed to endorsing *ex ante* in order to balance their rights.

16 My critique of Frowe's argument on this point is in Chapter 2.

17 The pedestrian would also be permitted to "passively" spear the innocent projectile if this entailed huddling under a pole in the anticipation that the innocent projectile would be skewered and halted before colliding with the pedestrian. I conceive of this type of spearing as a type of shielding even though it might seem closer to an offensive action like shooting. If the only shield available was a small upturned table the pedestrian quickly lifted and slid under, the innocent projectile might be speared by a table leg. In this case, the permissible use of the shield also happened to spear the innocent projectile. If we shrink the table and extend the leg, we get a shielding implement more and more like a spear. Frowe has a similar idea (2014: 64).

18 Zohar and Frowe make the same connection with deflecting a falling body and ducking though appeal to intuition for justification (Zohar 1993: 609; Frowe 2014: 64–65). On ducking, see Boorse and Sorensen (1988) and Alexander (2005: 621).

72 *The foundations of the moral equality of combatants*

19 The pedestrian with a shield is not using the innocent projectile in order to survive—the innocent projectile's survival after hitting the shield would in no way detract from the pedestrian's survival. Quong uses a similar logic to assess the permissibility of killing someone who is innocently blocking one's path to safety (2009).

20 Øverland and Arthur Applbaum make a similar argument regarding the Jim and Indians thought experiment (Øverland 2005: 693; Applbaum 2000: 162).

21 See my argument to this effect in Chapter 2 in the section on Frowe.

22 One might have a preference that one's remains be handled in a certain manner, say, for religious reasons, but this interest does not trump the duty to defer to the pedestrian's right to life.

23 Frowe has a similar view, but does not think the falling man incurs liability if he refuses to twist away when the ensuing impact will kill him (2014: 79). Frowe, Tadros, and Kamm think the falling man must accept injury, but not death, in order to save the person he will otherwise crush (Frowe 2014: 70; Tadros 2011: 254; Kamm 2000: 48). I think one is not permitted to re-direct one's bad luck toward another so the amount of the harm should not matter so long as it is proportionate to the harm threatened.

24 I agree with Wallerstein (2005: 1030), Tadros (2011: 272), and Zohar (1993: 609). Øverland argues that the non-culpable aggressor generally may not transfer risk to an innocent (2009: 214).

References

Alexander, L. (1987) "Justification and Innocent Aggressors," *Wayne Law Review*, 33: 1177–1189.

Alexander, L. (2005) "Lesser Evils: A Closer Look at The Paradigmatic Justification," *Law and Philosophy*, 24: 611–643.

Anscombe, G.E.M. (1981) "War and Murder" in *Collected Papers* III, Oxford: Blackwell Press.

Applbaum, A. (2000) *Ethics for Adversaries*, Princeton, NJ: Princeton University Press.

Benbaji, Y. (2007) "The Responsibility of Soldiers and The Ethics of Killing in War," *The Philosophical Quarterly*, 57(229): 558–572.

Benbaji, Y. (2008) "A Defense of the Traditional War Convention," *Ethics*, 118: 464–495.

Benbaji, Y. (2009) "The War Convention and the Moral Division of Labour," *The Philosophical Quarterly*, 59(237): 593–617.

Benbaji, Y. (2011) "The Moral Power of Soldiers to Undertake the Duty of Obedience," *Ethics*, 122: 43–73.

Boorse, C. and Sorensen, R. (1988) "Ducking Harm," *Journal of Philosophy*, 85(3): 115–134.

Fabre, C. (2012) *Cosmopolitan War*, Oxford: Oxford University Press.

Ferzan, K.K. (2005) "Justifying Self-Defense," *Law & Philosophy*, 24: 711–749.

Frowe, H. (2009) "A Practical Account of Self-Defence," *Law and Philosophy*, 29(3): 245–270.

Frowe, H. (2014) *Defensive Killing*, Oxford: Oxford University Press.

Grabczynska, A. and Ferzan, K.K. (2009) "Justifying 'Killing in Self-Defence,'" *Journal of Criminal Law and Criminology*, 99(1): 235–254.

Handfield, T. and Emerton, P. (2009) "Order and Affray: Defensive Privileges in Warfare," *Philosophy and Public Affairs*, 37(4): 382–414.

Kamm, F. (2001) *Morality, Mortality, Volume II*, Oxford: Oxford University Press.

Kasachkoff, T. (1998) "Killing in Self Defense: An Unquestionable or Problematic Defense?" *Law and Philosophy*, 17(5–6): 509–531.

The culpability standard of liability 73

Kaufman, W. (2008) "Torture and the 'Distributive Justice' Theory of Self-Defense," *Ethics and International Affairs*, 22(1): 93–115.

Kutz, C. (2005) "The Difference Uniforms Make," *Philosophy and Public Affairs*, 33(2): 148–180.

Lazar, S. (2009) "Responsibility, Risk, and Killing in Self-Defense," *Ethics*, 119(4): 699–728.

Lazar, S. (2012) "Necessity in Self-Defense and War," *Philosophy and Public Affairs*, 40(1): 3–44.

Lazar, S. (2015) *Sparing Civilians*, Oxford: Oxford University Press.

Lazar, S. (2017) "Just War Theory: Revisionists vs. Traditionalists," *Annual Review of Political Science*, 20: 37–54.

McMahan, J. (1994) "Self-Defense and the Problem of the Innocent Attacker," *Ethics*, 104(2): 252–290.

Miller, S. (2017) *Shoot to Kill*, Oxford: Oxford University Press.

Nagel, T. (1972) "War and Massacre," *Philosophy and Public Affairs*, 1(2): 123–144.

Øverland, G. (2005) "Contractual Killing," *Ethics*, 115(4): 692–720.

Øverland, G. (2009) "Forced Assistance," *Law and Philosophy*, 28(2): 203–232.

Pattison, J. (2011) "When is Right to Fight? Just War Theory and the Individual-Centric approach," *Ethical Theory and Moral Practice*, 16(1): 35–54.

Quong, J. (2009) "Killing in Self-Defense," *Ethics*, 119(3): 507–537.

Rodin, D. (2002) *War and Self-Defense*, Oxford: Oxford University Press.

Steinhoff, U. (2007) *On the Ethics of War and Terrorism*, Oxford: Oxford University Press.

Steinhoff, U. (2008) "Debate: Jeff McMahan on the Moral Inequality of Combatants," *Journal of Political Philosophy*, 16(2): 220–226.

Steinhoff, U. (2012) "Rights, Liability, and the Moral Equality of Combatants," *Journal of Ethics*, 16: 339–366.

Tadros, V. (2011) *The Ends of Harm*, Oxford: Oxford University Press.

Tadros, V. (2016) "Causation, Culpability, and Liability," in Coons, C. and Weber, M. (eds), *The Ethics of Self-Defense*, Oxford: Oxford University Press.

Wallerstein, S. (2005) "Justifying Self-Defense: A Theory of Forced Consequences, *Virginia Law Review*, 91(4): 999–1035.

Walzer, M. (2006) "Response to Jeff McMahan," *Philosophia*, 34(6): 43–45.

Zohar, N. (1993) "Collective War and Individualistic Ethics," *Political Theory*, 21(4): 602–622.

4 Responsibility, justification, and liability in war

I Introduction

A visitor to a battlefield might see personnel in different uniforms performing largely identical actions: operating weapon systems, driving vehicles, tending to the wounded, etc. If asked why they are doing these things, any combatant might reply "because those were my orders," or, more expansively, "to the win the war." The revisionists provide a philosophical argument as to why what appear to be identical actions are morally asymmetrical. This chapter will attempt to explain how *in bello*-compliant actions on opposite sides of a war can be morally symmetrical—in other words, how the moral equality of combatants is even possible. Part III (Chapters 5–7) will argue that conventional combatants or privileged irregular combatants on opposing sides of a war *are* morally equal under certain conditions.

Much philosophical work has to be done to defend the idea that combatants on opposing sides of the war are performing morally identical actions. The argument will proceed in two steps. First, I will argue that contributions to the main strategic thrust of an unjust operation or war are not necessarily unjustified. Assuming that combatants' actions pursuant to just ends are justified, opposing combatants' actions are then not necessarily asymmetrical on account of supporting opposing collective actions and outcomes. The second step of the argument provides a positive account of how combatants on the opposite side of the war can be performing identical actions, distinct from the morally unequal ends they enable. Again, later chapters will show how both actors can be justified in performing their identical actions.

The implication of this argument for the reductive individualists' asymmetry thesis is as follows. I argued in Part I that extant reductive individualist accounts of liability fail to support the asymmetry thesis. Step one of this chapter's argument entails that the asymmetry thesis *cannot* be defended. In order to defend the thesis, a revisionist philosopher needs to be able to show *a priori* that a strategic number of combatants are performing unjustified actions in contributing to an unjust operation or war, thereby incurring unilateral liability to defensive violence. The revisionist does not refute the moral equality of combatants doctrine if the broad asymmetry between liabilities of combatants on the just and

Responsibility, justification, and liability in war 75

unjust sides is a contingent, empirical matter. Many combatants' non-kinetic contributing actions would only plausibly be unjustified by virtue of a moral connection with the distant ends the actions promote since the contributing actions would not be deemed unjustified unto themselves out of a collective context. Contingent, subjective factors about the actor like a bad will or knowledge of the distant unjust ends will not suffice as a sufficiently broad connection the theorist can cite to refute the moral equality of combatants doctrine. As we saw in Part I, reductive individualists address these challenges by looking to external factors about the action or nearly ubiquitous internal factors about the actors (like the basic conditions of responsibility) in order to have a sufficiently broad base to claim *a priori* that all—or all but exceptional—combatants advancing the main strategic thrust of the unjust war are performing unjustified, potentially liability-earning actions. This chapter will argue that broad-based grounds to deem unjustified all or most contributing actions to the main strategic thrust of an unjust war are not available because of the normative structure of military action.

It is not necessarily the case that most adult, sane combatants on the unjust side of a war are performing unjustified, liability-incurring actions by virtue of contributing to the main strategic thrust of (even) a thoroughly unjust war. Military actions performed by conventional combatants and privileged irregular combatants in war are "irreducibly corporate actions," a type of action distinct from individual actions and from other collective actions. With irreducibly corporate actions, it is possible for a group's action to be unjust without it being the case that most or all the group members contributing to the main strategic thrust of the collective action perform unjustified actions. A theorist lacks grounds to claim that all actions contributing to an unjust end, even those performed under conditions of responsibility, are unjustified.

In service of the second step of this chapter's argument, the contributor to an unjust collective action may only be responsible, and potentially liable, for her normatively distinct contribution rather than for the collective action the contribution furthers. If contributory actions to irreducibly corporate actions are normatively distinct from the collective actions and associated outcomes, it is possible for two riflemen, two pilots, two mechanics, etc., on opposite sides of the war to be performing morally identical actions.

This two-step argument about the grounds for the moral equality of combatants also supports the traditional moral division between *jus ad bellum* and *jus in bello*. The two-step argument explains how typical combatants can be held responsible for their contributory actions, but not for the operations or wars these actions advance. Thus, it makes sense that for centuries, scholars have assigned the responsibilities of *jus in bello* to ordinary combatants, but not held them responsible for judging if the war as a whole is just.

Finally, this chapter aims to advance a point about method in just war theory. We should eschew reductivist *and* individualist approaches to just war theorizing, be they in service of revisionist or traditionalist ends. Reductivism is problematic because if military actions are irreducibly corporate, the moral character

76 *The foundations of the moral equality of combatants*

of the collective action is not necessarily present in the contributing actions. We ought, then, not to expect insights derived from analysis of contextless individual actions (e.g., self-defense scenarios) to apply to war when they are scaled up and aggregated.[1] Descriptive individualism is a problem because it denies that actions in particular group settings should be analyzed any differently than the actions of individuals outside of groups and, relatedly, denies the existence of irreducibly corporate actions.[2] Descriptive individualism can lead to evaluative individualism, which might deny unique norms for military personnel. Individualist approaches are not even congenial to the revisionist project. The chapter will show how the two plausible individual standards of liability for collective action—culpability and participatory intention—also fail to support the asymmetry thesis.

II Argument outline

Generally, there are strong, objective moral reasons against advancing an unjust end. These reasons are independent of the agent's perspective. Others should warn the agent, refrain from helping her, and, perhaps, take proportionate means to stop her. Yet sometimes there are only weak moral reasons to desist from advancing unjust ends, reasons that can easily be overridden by other concerns. Reasons against an action may be weakened because of the existence of intervening agents between the initial contributing agent and the ultimate causal outcome, the indeterminacy of outcomes following the initial causal contribution, a corporate rather than individual intention driving the action, and the advancement of multiple good outcomes alongside the bad ones. Contributory actions may be considered normatively distinct from the collective actions they causally advance under these circumstances. As distinct actions, different sets of reasons for committing or omitting the contributory actions, and for committing or omitting the collective actions, may obtain.

Organizations—formally constituted groups with stable roles and rotating personnel (e.g., companies, the military, religious orders, and government departments)—are typically characterized by these four features separating contributory from collective actions and ends. It follows that irreducibly corporate actions, the characteristic collective actions of organizations, lack the normative architecture to consistently render organization members' contributory actions unjustified when those collective actions are unjust. Different sets of reasons for commission/omission may apply to the collective agent responsible for the irreducibly corporate action and to individual contributors responsible for their contributory actions. Contributors might lack strong moral reasons against contributing to unjust irreducibly corporate actions or might have strong moral reasons for contributing. For examples, recall some of the thought experiments used in this book's Introduction. Imagine that the waitress serving breakfast to police who later engage in an unjustified shooting clairvoyantly knew about this one-off event. She still would not necessarily be unjustified in serving them breakfast. The causal connection between their eating the food she brought and

Responsibility, justification, and liability in war 77

their shooting an innocent person is attenuated. The shooting depends on the officers' agency and is not specifically connected to or influenced by eating the breakfast she served. They could have gotten breakfast anywhere else if she had refused to serve them and would have gone to work even if they had skipped breakfast. No one would blame her for being partly responsible for the shooting. Similarly, the computer chip designer might well have had strong reasons to proceed with her work even if she clairvoyantly knew that her chips would later be incorporated into chemical munitions, among hundreds of other beneficial products, because of the intervening agents and the balance of good outcomes related to bad outcomes.[3]

This normative separation between contributory and collective action is absent in goal-oriented collective actions, which, again, are the characteristic actions of *ad hoc* groups voluntarily entered into in order to accomplish a particular goal. The collective actions of a goal-oriented collective really are the typical contributor's own actions because the contributor joins the group with the same motivation of someone using a tool: to accomplish a particular end. Others join the group with the same motivation. Their combined labor produces the multiplying effect normally produced by a tool. This motivation guides both the contributor's joining of the group and his actions in it. He intends his contribution to the group to advance the group's/his end and his knowledge (or belief) that his contribution contributes to that end leads him to continue his efforts (he might quit the group if it was no longer devoted to his motivating aim). If there are strong moral reasons associated with the group's collective ends, these reasons apply to the contributor's individual action.

Justification and liability are related but distinct. The former concerns moral reasons for acting or refraining from action and the latter concerns the normative mechanism by which a person cedes certain rights through his actions, often through unjustified actions. Uncontroversially, most combatants are not culpable for the unjust war (in the sense their political leaders are culpable). Yet the reductive individualists' standards of liability, far less demanding than culpability, can mean that *in bello*-compliant, subjectively justified personnel on the unjust side are unilaterally liable to the defensive violence of the just side. Minimal types of liability usually find the necessary material to deem nearly any causally linked combatant liable to some degree for participation in an unjust war or operation. Yet denying the action-theoretic differences between different types of collective actions makes reductive individualism overly inclusive when it comes to identifying liable parties. Reductive individualists deem many combatants liable for the wrong action. I do not mean wrong in the sense that they deem a military logistician liable to proportionate defensive violence for the action "waging unjust war" rather than "shipping freight," but that the logistician's shipment of freight is considered an unjustified action because it is interpreted, effectively, as a "shipment of freight pursuant to an unjust war" rather than a shipment of freight *simpliciter*. Attention to action theory indicates that the maximum a typical conventional combatant contributing to an irreducibly corporate action can be liable for is his contributory action, which is normatively

78 *The foundations of the moral equality of combatants*

distinct from the collective action it causally advances. Paying attention to action-theoretic differences between irreducibly corporate and goal-oriented actions indicates that a contribution to an unjust irreducibly corporate action is not necessarily unjustified, but the same physical behavior contributing to an unjust goal-oriented collective action usually will be unjustified.

In all cases of unjustified action, we might ask if the agent of the unjustified action is liable to defensive violence or some sort of sanction. People can sometimes be non-liable for unjustified actions, depending on the standard of liability. For example, on a culpability standard, an adult with dementia should be non-liable to punishment when he takes a bicycle from a neighbor's porch (thinking it his own), even though the action is objectively unjustified. Action-theoretic distinctions precede questions of liability since such distinctions delineate the actions for which an agent *can* be liable. A standard of liability then determines the actual extent of his liability.

Since a goal-oriented collective action is an aggregate of its members' identical motives and intentions to contribute to an end they all have in sight and that they joined the group to realize, a theorist is in the position to say the typical group member will be unjustified in contributing to an unjust collective end. Due to the normative architecture connecting the member with the collective action, a culpability standard indicates that the contributor to an unjust goal-oriented collective action is culpable *for the collective action*, not merely his contribution, even if *ignorant* of the specific end his actions advance. For example, a militia member who joined the group to facilitate its genocidal agenda against group A might be liable to defensive killing (if necessary and proportionate) by representatives of A even though all he did was fix the military's vehicles and even if he was ignorant of the particular murderous operations his colleagues were performing on the day of A's counter-offensive. He might be liable to the same punishment as the front-line killers in a war crimes tribunal.

By contrast, a theorist is not in the position to say that all or most of the contributions to an unjust irreducibly corporate action are unjustified due to the structure of such actions. This is to say, the contributory actions are not *necessarily* unjustified by virtue of contributing to unjust ends. The contributor would not then be liable for anything on account of his own action by the lights of a minimal standard of liability focusing on the actor's causality. (One would only apply those standards in the case of unjustified actions.) Yet a culpability standard of liability can make a difference to the question of justification. Contributory actions are not necessarily unjustified by virtue of causal connections. A culpability standard looks at a not-necessarily-unjustified action that *is* causally connected with an unjust end, and, unlike minimal accounts of liability, considers a combatant's knowledge, intentions, and motives with respect to the unjust end in order to determine the justification of the action.

A given enlistee might join the military with a similar motivation to someone joining a goal-oriented collective: in order to contribute to a specific group project he would have pursued on his own if able. He is an atypical organization member since the typical member is blocked by the organization's structure

Responsibility, justification, and liability in war   79

from knowing the specific outcome of his work product—and therefore from having an intentional state with respect to it. Moreover, usually, the intention to perform his contributory action comes from the organization rather than himself. Yet one can in effect commandeer the structure of an organization and use it as a tool to accomplish an end he desires. Such a combatant would be culpable for an unjust war or subsidiary unjust action (e.g., an airstrike on a hospital) if he knows about and specifically intends to further the unjust elements of the war or operation. As with a member of a goal-oriented collective, his contribution is unjustified. It is not that the strong moral reasons counseling against the group action also apply to his contribution, as with goal-oriented collective action. Rather, there are strong agent-relative and agent-neutral moral reasons against knowingly and intentionally contributing to an unjust end. This is to say, the perhaps otherwise-banal contributory action is re-capitalized (even in the actor's own mind) as a morally rich action, say, from a logistician's "shipping freight" to "shipping freight pursuant to destroying a hospital" or "shipping freight pursuant to an unjust war."

These reasons are agent-relative in the sense that this particular actor should not avail himself of the opportunity to act unjustly, if he knows joining the military at this time will afford him that opportunity. Just as an alcoholic should avoid bars, a bigot against nationality X has strong agent-relative moral reasons not to enlist in the military on the eve of an unjust war against country X. The reasons are agent-neutral in the sense that anyone has strong moral reasons to avoid knowingly and intentionally committing unjust actions. These reasons are more related to the agent than to the effects of the action. For example, the clairvoyant computer chip designer might be justified in making her computer chips if she knew the good effects of making them outweighed the bad effects of them being put into chemical weapons. Yet the balance of reasons changes if we include the negative effects on her character if she builds computer chips with the intention that they will be incorporated into chemical weapons.

The culpable agent acting in this way in an organization is performing a different action to his non-culpable peers who perform the same physical behavior in the same context. The latter typically are ignorant of the specific ends advanced by their efforts and, therefore, are necessarily motivationally aloof from those ends. Yet the culpable actor's knowledge and intentionality change the nature of the action he performs. It is as though the culpable actor was specially briefed on the specific outcome of his work product and just this once, given complete freedom, absent orders from the chain of command, to elect to participate or not. In contrast with this dynamic among culpable organizational actors, nothing about the action changes if we consider a particular organizational actor who contingently has the material connections with the unjust outcome or the knowledge that his action has some risk of terminating in an unjust harm, as the reductive individualists' minimal standards of liability call for. Nothing changes here since per theory—in contrast to contingent knowledge of the target and intentionality—nearly all adult combatants already have those elements characterizing their actions.

80 *The foundations of the moral equality of combatants*

The different features of irreducibly corporate, goal-oriented, and individual actions indicate different horizons of liability for a contributing member— different answers to the question, for what action is he potentially liable? Assuming a culpability standard of liability, a close causal connection to the life-threatening action is less important for liability to defensive violence in goal-oriented collective action than in individual action. We are also less likely to find the requisite levels of knowledge and intentionality in actors for liability for irreducibly corporate actions than for superficially similar individual actions or contributions to goal-oriented collective actions. The contributor to an unjust irreducibly corporate action is potentially liable for a much greater harm than if he committed a physically identical unjustified individual action but is also less likely than an individual actor engaging in identical physical behavior to be liable for *any* unjustified action.

III Argument

i Goal-oriented collective action

Three actors can be responsible for unequally grave actions even if an observer would describe their physical behaviors as identical. This disparity can obtain if one action is an individual action, conceived, carried out, and concluded by a single actor (e.g., a mugger stabbing his victim), a second action contributes to a goal-oriented collective action (e.g., a militia member stabbing a civilian in a pogrom), and a third action contributes to an irreducibly corporate action (e.g., a soldier stabbing an enemy combatant). The actors may be responsible for actions of different gravity because irreducibly corporate actions, unlike goal-oriented collective actions, cannot be scaled down to individual contributory actions that are simple miniature moral versions of the corporate actions. These collective actions' different structures create different normative relationships between contributory and collective actions, typically making contributions to unjust goal-oriented collective actions unjustified, but not doing the same for contributions to irreducibly corporate actions. Individual actions, outside a group context, have a third type of normative structure. These three different actions have different horizons of liability—different demarcations of the action for which an actor can potentially be held liable—which makes a difference for assessments of culpability. These action types are ideal; some goal-oriented collectives may take on some of the hierarchy and formality of organizations over time.

Irreducible actions can best be explained by first examining a reducible collective action. Scaling down to microcosmic individual actions with the same moral character of the macro actions is possible in a goal-oriented collective action. Such actions are often performed by *ad hoc* groups expressly created by their members in order to perform a specific collective action; new members may join because they share the same interests in the collective action as the original members. The distinctive aspect of the collective action relevant to our

Responsibility, justification, and liability in war 81

conversation arises due to the subjective states of the contributors, whereas the distinctive aspect of an irreducibly corporate action initially comes from its organizational context.

The assassination of Julius Caesar is an example of a goal-oriented collective action. The collective action of a group of senators stabbing Caesar can be scaled down for the purpose of moral consideration to a single contributing action of one senator stabbing Caesar (Fain 1972: 79; see also Narveson 2002: 182). This scaling down can be done on both the physical and normative levels. The aggregation of the physical actions visible to witnesses in the senate sufficiently accounts for the collective action of assassination. There is no pre-existing institution accounting for the assassins' training, no vast support staff behind the scenes making the assassination possible, and no figure coordinating the actions prospectively or in real time in the manner of an orchestra conductor. Instead, coordination of physical actions transpires more or less spontaneously and "horizontally" between conspirators as each is independently guided by a shared motive of killing Caesar (see Bratman, 2006).

Due to the normative structure of a goal-oriented collective action, the strong moral reasons (we will assume) counseling against the assassination of Caesar also apply to one senator participating in the assassination. They apply to him since he joins the cabal in order to assassinate Caesar, knows his contributions will result in the assassination, and intends to assassinate Caesar. The group's actions are his actions. Had he the prowess, he could have and would have acted alone. The moral reasons for the group not to assassinate Caesar (or, more generally, why assassination is wrong) are the reasons why a senator ought not to assassinate Caesar.

One is not always liable for performing an unjustified action. First, we need to determine which liability standard to use and then assess whether the actor fulfills the elements of responsibility the standard deems relevant. A culpability standard of liability looks for the actor's power to plan, commit, and complete an action, awareness of his action and its likely outcome, personal intention to commit the action, and motive to bring about the associated end. Such a standard finds sufficient material to analyze in the person of each senator to deem him culpable for the assassination. We come to the same conclusion of culpability for assassination whether we analyze a senator acting in concert with others or a senator assassinating Caesar on his own. Each Roman senator voluntarily performs a physical action in concert with others' identical performances—an individual action sufficient on its own to kill Caesar—fully aware that stabbing can lead to death, intending to stab him, and hoping he dies as a result.

A culpability standard can inculpate actors for graver outcomes when they act in groups than when they perform the same physical behaviors outside of a group. It is not the case that each senator would be culpable for assassination only in the event that each contributory action was a lethal blow. Due to the structure of the collective action, each senator is culpable for murder even if one of the senator's sword thrusts by itself was insufficient to kill Caesar. Had he acted alone, he

82   *The foundations of the moral equality of combatants*

would be culpable for assault or attempted assassination, but he is culpable for assassination even if his sword thrust lightly wounded the dictator since he knowingly and intentionally joined a group that intended to kill Caesar and that did kill Caesar (Isaacs 2011: 127). The same holds true if he stabbed Caesar after he was mortally wounded (Kutz 2010: 157). The structure of a goal-oriented collective action makes him the "inclusive author"[4] of all the group's actions so the relevant action for which we assess the liability of the weak-wristed assailant is "assassination" not "scratching with a knife." The assassin contributing to an overdetermined action engages in "assassination," not "mutilation of a corpse."

While the case is intuitively clearer when the constituent physical behaviors are identical, culpability is equally shared even when members contribute diverse physical behaviors to the collective end. Their knowledge, intention, and motive are all directed toward the common end and they perhaps chose to adopt a physical behavior inefficacious to the end (e.g., pushing him or smuggling the swords into the senate) only because it complemented the behaviors of their colleagues (Sadler 2006: 139; Bratman 2006). Their participation empowered their colleagues to land mortal wounds. Thus, by participating in a goal-oriented collective action, one can be culpable for grave collective actions despite the fact that one's personal contribution was relatively insignificant unto itself.

Goal-oriented collective members can also be culpable for specific actions they did not know would occur if those actions are consistent with the characteristic ends of the group (Kutz 2010: 156). One's membership in the group empowers others to do things they could not do alone. One may have trained one's peers, offered advice or encouragement, worked collaboratively with them, and given peers the confidence that someone "has their back." A's presence in the group creates opportunities for B to perform actions that B could not have accomplished were she busy doing A's portion of the task. So A can be culpable for B's action X even if A is not aware of what B is doing. A joined the group, motivated to see X-like actions performed, intends her contributory actions to advance X-like actions, empowers B to perform X through her presence in the group, and knows that B, like herself, is engaged in X-like actions.

In a martial context, unprivileged irregular militant groups, including many militias and insurgent groups, are goal-oriented collectives, and their members are inclusive authors of everything their groups do. These sub-state armed groups lack belligerent privileges if they fail to wear uniforms and to adhere to the laws of war.[5] These groups typically have a well-publicized, singular cause and use tactics that are also well-known because their theatrical and shocking violence is itself used as an advertisement for the group. People typically join the group because they want to achieve the end through the publicized tactics. Unlike organizations, these groups also usually have relatively flat hierarchies and rely on informal networks of pre-existing friendships or family or tribe relations that are conducive to members knowing about and intentionally orienting themselves toward specific operations. So the member of such an irregular group can be considered culpable, say, for a particular terrorist bombing, even if he did not know about that particular operation.

Responsibility, justification, and liability in war 83

ii On the use of realistic examples in just war theory

I want to introduce a realistic picture of a modern military action as an example of an irreducibly corporate action and a reference for the arguments to follow. The use of unrealistic thought experiments unrelated to war is one of the aspects of revisionist just war theory that is most jarring to scholars who were introduced to the subject in the context of studying theology, political science, international relations, or applied ethics.[6] Reductive individualists use examples of people falling down wells or being brained by meteorites in order to isolate variables and to bracket any prejudices readers might have regarding real historical cases (see Frowe 2014: 5).[7] Given their evaluative individualism, there is no need to use realistic examples of collective action. Given their reductivism, they feel there is no concern that insights garnered from cases of civilian self-defense will not apply to military action in war.

While fantastical thought experiments are fine to exemplify subtle distinctions, I think it is important for just war theorists to also attend to realistic military examples. Doing so will take one in a different direction than revisionism. Modern military action is irreducibly corporate, there is an action-theoretic difference between irreducibly corporate action and individual and other collective actions, and this action-theoretic distinction makes a difference for the moral connection between collective and contributory actions. I suspect that many reductive individualists are reductive individualists instead of traditionalists because they began their reflection about war using thought experiments familiar from the self-defense literature rather than with analysis of actual military behavior. Reductive individualists might say this kind of study is unnecessary because current practice is not normative for scholars—revisionary conclusions may instead call for reforms to military doctrine. Yet this response begs the question against the view that an accurate description could yield different normative conclusions.

The critic who wishes to dismiss empirical matters' relevance to just war theory should exercise some care about the empirical assumptions present in her avowedly purely theoretical work (Fishback 2016: 281). Standard self-defense thought experiments make certain empirical assumptions about the functionality of guns, knives, and clubs, as well as assumptions about human beings' physical abilities and vulnerabilities. One might object that the typical thought experiment only requires the most general definition of a gun or a knife. This is fair, but I wonder how many empirical details can be waved away as contingent—deemed inessential to a general definition of a thing—if we wish to invoke some more complicated instrument or event like an airstrike in a thought experiment.[8] There has to be a limit where the critic cannot wave away empirical facts as mere contingencies and still be invoking an actual practice or instrument for the purpose of tailoring a theory. I include the richly detailed picture of an airstrike below in the interest of finding that point where empirical details matter to the phenomena being invoked in thought experiments (see Walzer 2015: postscript).

84 *The foundations of the moral equality of combatants*

The following scenario is long—which is rather the point—including many early steps in the causal sequence of events leading to the airstrike. This is appropriate if we wish to include intentionality in assessments of the pilot's responsibility, as we do in cases of psychotic, hypnotized, or coerced aggressors. While not all the actions described below are necessary to drop a munition from a jet, not all bombing runs are combat actions in war. The reason this release of a munition is an "airstrike on an enemy target" rather than a training mission or contractor's demonstration is rooted in the prior political decision to go to war. I therefore include the political decision at the start of the causal chain of discrete acts that in sum constitute the airstrike.

Airstrike

A carrier-based FA-18 drops a munition on an enemy target. One month before the Director of National Intelligence (DNI) delivered the president his morning intelligence briefing, written by senior analysts, coordinated among intelligence agencies, and based on the cumulative work-product of numerous intelligence collectors. The report contained troubling information about military preparations in an adversary country. Afterwards, the Joint Chiefs of Staff ordered a crisis plan group to work with the Combatant Commander of the Unified Combatant Command (UCC) with jurisdiction over the relevant portion of the globe to generate contingency plans for military actions against the country in question. A few days later, this plan was presented to the president, who ordered its implementation. The order was related to the UCC, which determined the necessary mix of forces to implement the plan, began to marshal its forces, and routed a request for additional needed units through the Joint Forces Command. The Command in turn relayed "warning orders" to the relevant units around the world.

The rear admiral in command of a particular carrier strike group relayed orders to the captains of the various ships required for the mission. The carrier's captain called the Tactical Action Officer who called the Officer on the Deck who ordered the helmsman to set a particular course and speed. The helmsman relayed the latter command to the engine room, where a team of engineers set to supplying the requisite power.

At command headquarters, intelligence analysts consulted satellite imagery and other intelligence sources to update their existing contingency targeting packages to determine militarily-relevant targets. Targeteers determined which of the available targets' destruction would contribute to the strategy determined by the command and civilian leadership. This "strike package" was relayed to the carrier. At this point, perhaps 24 hours before the first sortie, the carrier's commanding officer, the carrier Air Wing Commander, and other senior leaders met to determine which assets would be used in the attack. The relevant aircrews consulted with intelligence officers to select the aimpoints on the targets and the munitions to be used in the attacks.

Responsibility, justification, and liability in war 85

> The FA-18s to be used in the mission were maintained by a group of sailors on board the carrier. The planes were brought to the deck, fueled, and inspected by another group of sailors, armed by a third group, and launched from the deck catapult by a fourth group. The launch was scheduled and overseen by the "air boss" in the carrier's tower. The aircraft were under the air boss's authority until they reached a five-mile perimeter, when they switched radio contact to the strike warfare officer on board the carrier. They then checked in with an air warfare officer on a nearby destroyer who monitored their flight until they reached a range when they became the responsibility of a circling E-2 Hawkeye. Once over the target, the FA-18 aircrew made the final decision to release or not release the weapon based on their assessment of the target's viability (e.g., its match with the analysts' depiction of it, the proximity of civilians nearby, etc.).

iii Irreducibly corporate action

Irreducibly corporate actions do not scale down to the individual contributory level retaining the physical and moral character of the macro action (Runciman 2003: 41; Cooper 1991: 45; Fain 1972: 81; Isaacs 2011: chapter 2). They are not the mere aggregate of morally identical actions. In irreducibly corporate actions, very different contributory actions performed by actors with varying levels of knowledge about the wider enterprise are combined by means of a corporate intention to form a collective action. The corporate intention plays the same functional role a personal intention does in an individual person's action. The corporate intention itself may be irreducible even to the intentions of the actors involved in the group's executive decision-making sub-group as it is a synthesis of the members' individual inputs and the sub-group's pre-existing decision-making procedure. As a result, the collective action is more than the sum of its parts.

Bearing in mind a comparison with the scaling down of assassination by a group to assassination by an individual, the strong moral reasons against an organization performing a collective action do not necessarily apply to the individual contributory actions advancing that collective action. The structure of organizations often means that contributory actions are normatively distinct from the collective actions they causally advance. A different set of reasons for the action's commission or omission may then exist. Four structural aspects of organizations lead to this separation. First, the collective action is spurred by a separate intention to the contributory action, a corporate intention. Second, the corporate intention and the organizational procedures expressing this intention arrange the efforts of intervening agents in a way that can alter the initial contributor's work product. Third, due to these interventions, there is a genuine indeterminacy of the contributory action with respect to future effects. Fourth, and relatedly, the contributory action may causally advance good and bad actions and outcomes, frustrating attempts to justify the

86 *The foundations of the moral equality of combatants*

initial action based on a causal connection with one of the outcomes. I will discuss each aspect in turn.

Corporate intentions. Some scholars distinguish an agent's intention from her motive, where the former is the mental order for an action originating in the actor sufficient to spur, guide, and complete the action, and the latter is the reason she has for undertaking the action. The distinction between the terms is helpful in order to distinguish the permissibility of certain actions from the goodness or badness of the motives animating the agent.

Next, it is important to clarify the difference between individual and corporate intentions. The agent's intention organizes his body's movements into a coherent action reflective of his plans. The intention makes the action his own and makes it into an event for which he can be held accountable. Since we think using language, the actor's subjective intention guiding his action can also objectively describe the action with the substitution of third- for first-person pronouns. This fact reflects the actor's responsibility for the action; he can fully envision the action (as both he and others would describe it) in anticipation, just as an outsider will actually see it in fruition (Davidson 1980). Others can hold the actor accountable for an intentional action since he planned the action with the same morally weighty description (say, "stealing" rather than "borrowing") they ascribe to the action. His intention also creates the grounds for him to defend himself against a misinterpretation of the action. "I was just borrowing it!"

There is considerable debate in the collective responsibility literature about whether groups can have intentions that are irreducible to the intentions of their members. Individualist philosophers claim that group intentions are really just the aggregate of individuals' intentions within a group. This dynamic can be seen in one type of action executed by goal-oriented collectives. Group members each have the same intention when the collective action is the aggregate of largely identical individual actions, like the assassination of Julius Caesar. We can say the group "intended" to kill Caesar because each group member intended to kill Caesar.

One cannot describe the scenario in the same manner in a second kind of goal-oriented collective action, composed of different contributing actions, like setting up a campsite (one person collecting firewood, one person preparing food, two setting up the tent, etc.) since each actor must intend her proximate action (e.g., collecting wood) that contributes to the collective action. Each actor cannot, strictly speaking, intend to set up the campsite, since this is an action accomplished by a group in this context. Yet each camper intends to perform her contributory action with an eye to the collective action of setting up the campsite and the collective end of enjoying a campsite. We can therefore speak of a collective motive to accomplish that end, reducible equally to each participant. Like the collective intention in the first kind of goal-oriented collective action (e.g., the assassination of Caesar), the collective motive in the second kind of action is the aggregate of the individual motives of the group members. Each intends her proximate action because she wants to enjoy a campsite.

Responsibility, justification, and liability in war 87

Collectivist philosophers argue that organizations can have corporate intentions (e.g., French 1987: 143; Pettit 2003: 182; Isaacs 2011: 68). Corporate intentions are irreducible to the intentions of the group's members for two reasons. First, individuals cannot intend complex collective actions because intentions are mental events to initiate discrete actions and individuals cannot perform collective actions. General Patton cannot intend to wage the Second World War. Second, something functionally similar to an individual's intention is created through the organization's unique protocols, irreducible to any one organization member's intention. These protocols are what Seumas Miller calls "joint mechanisms" or Peter French calls "corporate internal decision structures" (Miller 2001: 174–176),[9] sets of interlocking behaviors such as decision-making procedures or protocols for transmitting orders used to coordinate actions and bring about certain types of outcomes within organizations. Joint mechanisms reproduce aspects of humans' rational faculties, making it possible for groups to do things paradigmatically done by individuals like evaluate options, decide, and implement plans. Joint mechanisms allow for variations based on the participants' varying desires and inputs. For example, a joint mechanism within a planning cell in the military might indicate that proposals for action should be discussed and voted on by the attending officers; the varying desires of the officers will affect the outcome of the vote (Miller 2001: 174–176; French 1987: 148). It follows that the mechanism's output (a subordinates' carrying out orders, the outcome of a vote, etc.) can be contrary to some of the participants' preferences. Particularly since executives participating in joint mechanisms may feel they have to embody a professional persona when using their joint mechanism-provided power to vote or issue or transfer an order, the resultant corporate intention may not reflect the personal intention of *any* of the participants (Isaacs 2011: 30).

Corporate intentions are functionally identical to human intentions in the sense that they have the same relation to corporate actions as individual intentions do to individual actions (Isaacs 2011: 30, 37; Pettit 2003: 179, 182–183). They lead the collective to act. They can be very broad, shared with all organizations of their type (e.g., winning wars, for militaries) or be for specific subsidiary actions (e.g., "increase acquisition of FA-18s by 20% in 2019"). They are corporate in the sense that they are irreducible to the intentions of any one group member. The joint mechanism transforms the particular inputs of executives to create something that cannot be divided into its component inputs. Using this term of art does not commit us to talking about corporate emotions or superentity minds (cf. Miller 2001: 165). Objections to the idea of corporate intentions will be addressed below.

We are at a point where we can briefly digress and assert a point about the agents behind military action. Organizations are the agents performing irreducibly corporate actions and organizational members are the agents performing contributory actions (Isaacs 2011: 118–119; Erskine 2003: 21; Harbour 2003: 71–73; Copp 2006: 206–208; Narveson 2002: 184). For the purposes of identifying the collective agent performing the irreducibly corporate action "unjust

88 *The foundations of the moral equality of combatants*

war" we need to consider the corporate intention driving all the combatants' lawful actions. (We will assume that when militaries engage in lawful actions, it is a result of their proper functioning. While unlawful action may be a result of corporate intentions, they are more likely the result of personnel deviating from their training and orders; more below.) The broadest relevant corporate intention is "win the war." While the political leadership and citizenry want to win the war, the military is the agent that can both intend this action in the literal sense of spurring action with the functional equivalent of a mental event (in the form of joint mechanisms) and that has this intention embedded in its structure. States are collective agents that can intend to win wars but are not constitutively defined by the intention in the way militaries are so defined. Just the same, "the military" is always a politically and socially embedded entity. In the American context, the military is an organization that is led by the civilian president, bound by Congress's laws and beholden to its funding, and constrained by rulings by the Supreme Court. So the collective agent waging wars that are irreducible to the contributory actions of combatants is the military rather than the state, but "the military" is conditioned by indirect influence from the wider society.

So the military wages war. Smaller groups perform subsidiary collective actions that are irreducible to the contributory actions of their members. The carrier strike group (the carrier, its support ships, and stateside support systems) carries out airstrikes. Considering subsidiary collective actions, the maintenance crew fixes the airframes; the deck crew maneuvers and launches the aircraft; the engine room team provides the carrier's steam power. Individual combatants perform contributory actions to these collective actions. For example, one member of the maintenance crew services the FA-18s' avionics pods. While he is not individually responsible for the state of the aircraft as a whole, he can be held accountable for the job he does on the pods.

When people are wronged by a collective action, the organizational group at the lowest level with operational oversight of the relevant action is the responsible agent. Possible punishments can be directed at that group. A series of technical aviation mishaps might lead to collective punishment and remediation of the maintenance crew. For example, they might all lose their holiday liberty and be forced to undergo re-training. They work as a team and so have to be re-trained as a team. Yet the engine room crew would not be punished since they had no visibility or control over the matter. The entire carrier crew might be punished and re-trained following a series of botched airstrikes. There may be glaring exceptions where some incompetent or malicious team member is singularly responsible for the mishaps, but mishaps accruing from organizational action often are the result of a host of reasons besides contributing actions including deficient policies and control systems, deficient funding or staffing, poor leadership, etc.

So, there are separate agents spurring an irreducibly corporate action such as a war and an individual contributory action in the war. These collective and individual agents have corporate and individual intentions, respectively. The

Responsibility, justification, and liability in war 89

military's corporate intention to win the war is irreducible to a combatant's individual intention, say, to fire his rifle. Intentions are what spur and organize physical behavior into normatively distinct actions. The separation between individual and corporate intentions, then, suggests drawing a normative separation between individual and irreducibly corporate actions. The intention-based distinction by itself does not show that separate moral reasons necessarily apply to the two actions. Yet as there may be different sets of reasons for omission or commission for any two distinct actions, we have grounds related to the structure of irreducibly corporate actions to think that there could be entirely separate moral reasons applying to an individual contributory action and a causally related irreducibly corporate action.

Intervening agents. Collective actions in organizations are typically initiated by high-ranking personnel who order their subordinates to act. The order may subsequently be instantiated in physical action at a quite low level in the organizational hierarchy. Importantly, the intervening agents who take up the work product after that initial physical action may be superior in rank to the first actor. They may have the power to change the work product as they see fit or may be directed via joint mechanism to contribute to the evolving project in a particular way. Actions are shaped from physical behaviors by the agent's intention. So subsequent actors, acting outside the first actor's authority, can re-cast the action with their intervening intentions, sometimes in a manner completely opposed to the first. The lack of authority the first (physical) actor has over her colleagues suggests looking at subsequent contributory actions in the causal stream as normatively distinct.

Indeterminacy of outcome. Action X may happen to causally contribute to unjust action Y or unjust outcome Z, but the nature and context of X may make it effectively indeterminate with respect to outcome. This is obviously not the place for an extended discussion of determinism. By effectively indeterminate, I mean there are many potential outcomes potentially flowing from X and that there is little or nothing in X's nature to predispose X's termination in Y or Z. It then follows that there is no set of reasons for X's commission or omission connected with a particular outcome. This is the case, even viewed retrospectively, when the entire causal train leading up to Y or Z is considered. Put another way, it would be irrational, or would have been irrational, to desist from X due to a concern that it could lead to Y or Z.

For example, consider the unjust shooting of an innocent person. First, consider different actions that could have led directly or indirectly to the victim's being shot:

a   pointing a gun at an innocent person and squeezing the trigger
b   firing a gun into the air on a city street
c   leaving a loaded gun on a park bench

There are strong moral reasons to refrain from a–c because of the strong likelihood that an innocent person will be injured. Despite the increasing

90 *The foundations of the moral equality of combatants*

indeterminacy of the three actions, a through c, there is still a strong causal potential for even c leading to an unjust outcome. Now consider d–f in the causal train of an unjust shooting:

d   selling a gun
e   making a gun
f   making steel

These latter three examples suggest that unlike *corporate intentions* and *intervening agents*, *indeterminacy* is scalar. Actions d and e are far more indeterminate than a–c with respect to the unjust shooting; it is less likely that d or e will terminate in an unjust outcome compared to a–c. Yet clearly, both d and e are fraught actions requiring careful execution and numerous safeguards. Whereas there are always strong reasons against doing a–c, there may be strong reasons in some contexts for not doing d or e at all.

Making steel, while causally necessary to make, sell, and fire a gun, is the kind of extremely indeterminate action for which the case of normative distinctiveness can be made most strongly. Steel can be used for millions of purposes. The steel mill worker would have no way of knowing how a given ingot he works will be used. It would be irrational for him to put down his tools out of fear that the steel would be used to make a gun and that the same gun would be used in a murder.

In *Airstrike*, we can trace a series of actions terminating in the killing of human beings with similarly increasing levels of indeterminacy as we go farther back in time: from the aircraft's dropping of the munition on the target, to the FA-18 taking off from the carrier, to the aircrew performing maintenance on the aircraft, to the intelligence cell researching targets, to the engine room staff supplying power to the engines, to the helmsman steering the carrier, to all the support functions in the carrier's home port. Consider the helmsman's action. He is ordered to turn the wheel a certain number of degrees to change the heading of the carrier when the carrier is 1,000 miles away from the target. This action creates the possibility of innumerable actions by the 5,000 sailors aboard the carrier, some of them unplanned at the time when the order to re-direct the carrier is given. (For example, one officer told me that on his first deployment, his destroyer was headed from Virginia to support operations in Iraq but then was re-directed on the way to do humanitarian assistance in Haiti, evacuate an embassy in South America, and then do a freedom-of-navigation operation in the Gulf of Sidra after Col. Qadaffi threatened to turn it into a lake of fire.) The helmsman's maneuvering the carrier is causally necessary for everything else the carrier and its crew will do but is not inherently linked to any particular unjust action. In certain contexts, it would not be reasonable to think that a particular unjust action will occur as a result. The helmsman could not (or it would be irrational to) refuse to steer the carrier because of it leading to a particular unjust airstrike several weeks hence. Again, *indeterminacy* is a scalar category. The helmsman would be in a less indeterminate situation if his country was

Responsibility, justification, and liability in war   91

engaged in a genocidal war such that the helmsman could reasonably think that his action would facilitate airstrikes in that war.

While the helmsman's situation can change depending on context, farther back in the causal chain are actions approaching the context-independent indeterminacy of steel making. Consider the logisticians who develop lists of goods needed for different kinds of carrier operations years before the carrier actually leaves port. Their actions are of the sort that may never be utilized in any further actions, and if utilized could be employed for vastly different purposes. The set of reasons for working on a logistics spreadsheet years ahead of a particular carrier's deployment are different from the reasons pertaining to fighting a particular war or bombing a particular target. The logistics work might be justified even though the downstream actions are not.

Multiple effects. A certain set of reasons for commission or omission of an action exist at the moment of its performance given that the future is unknown to the actor and, let us say, genuinely undetermined. It is still challenging to determine if an action is objectively justified if we retrospectively view the entire chain of outcomes causally issuing from a given action, because of the plurality of positive and negative outcomes the action makes possible. The actions in the causal train of *Airstrike*—the enlistment of the personnel involved, the activities conducted by the personnel while the carrier is in port, the support activities once the carrier is underway, and the strike operations launched from the carrier—can all facilitate just, unjust, or mixed operations within a war that is itself, on the whole, just or unjust. A given action may lead serially to phases of the war that are just or unjust. For example, consider one ordinary support activity in a war: maintaining a small boat in the aircraft carrier's hold.

Engine repair

A mechanic fixes the boat's engine. The boat is used to ferry a squad of special operations troops ashore. In the next few weeks, the squad destroys a mosque that is an inspirational national symbol, kills five militia members who were *en route* to a massacre, and frees a chai boy who was kept as a sex slave by a local warlord. One of the special operators rapes a local woman.

On the revisionists' view, support actions leading to killing of combatants in unjust wars or unjust operations are typically unjustified due to that material connection even if they are not the sort of action that would be unjustified out of a collective action context. Was the mechanic's action objectively justified or not, given its plethora of downstream effects? The answer seems to change depending on which outcome is linked to the engine repair. Many scholars argue that assessments of *jus ad bellum* have to be made throughout a conflict, not just at its start or in summary fashion. A just war may become unjust, say, as the proportional assessment of goods and evils associated with continued fighting

92 *The foundations of the moral equality of combatants*

changes. So if we consider the possible justification of the mechanic's action insofar as it supports an initially just war, we might see the balance of reasons making the action justified or unjustified depending on whether the downstream effects at a particular moment made the war proportionally justified.

The trend among revisionists is to not to look at the justice of a war as a whole, but that of certain operations within the war. I criticized revisionists for their lack of clarity in distinguishing subsidiary collective actions for this purpose earlier. We can now see the importance of clearly distinguishing different actions. Each downstream outcome of the engine repair brings a different set of reasons for omission or commission. The repair might be justified if we consider its role in forestalling a massacre, but unjustified if we consider its role in facilitating a rape. Does assessing the "deep morality of war" require a net assessment of all the outcomes? Scholars disagree about the commensurability of different kinds of goods and evils, a conversation I cannot enter into here. On its face, though, it would seem particularly challenging to weigh all the good and evil outcomes made possible by the mechanic's repair in order to assess if the action was justified overall, given the heterogeneity of the outcomes. Each day may bring a different mix of reasons for and against the repair. Absent a net assessment, there is no non-arbitrary reason to halt our analysis on a particular day following the repair to see if the outcome occurring then generates strong reasons for or against fixing the engine. This quandary suggests looking at the engine repair as a normatively distinct action and considering reasons for and against performing the action apart from its possible downstream effects.

While indeterminacy is scalar, the other three categories just discussed are not, and so would be in play even in cases with low degrees of indeterminacy. These factors serve to make contributory actions to irreducibly corporate actions normatively distinct from the collective actions they causally advance. The set of reasons for the commission or omission of the contributory action may be separate from that set of reasons applying to the collective agent's performance of the irreducibly corporate action. An irreducibly corporate action may then be unjust without it necessarily being the case that its contributory actions are unjustified.

We are now in a position to see how the moral equality of combatants is conceptually possible. State A's war against B is unjust. Mechanic A and mechanic B serve on opposite sides of the war. Each mechanic's actions are normatively distinct from the collective actions they help advance. The mechanics fix engines and the militaries of which they are a part wage war. There are two important conclusions to be drawn from this normative separation between contributory and collective actions. The first conclusion is that A's action is not necessarily unjustified by virtue of his participation in an unjust war and B's action is not necessarily justified by virtue of his participation in a just war. The two mechanics' actions are not morally asymmetrical on account of their downstream effects. Now just because a theorist lacks the grounds to claim moral asymmetry does not mean she can claim moral symmetry. For the actions to be morally symmetrical, the bounds of the action for which the

Responsibility, justification, and liability in war 93

agents are responsible—and potentially liable—must be the same and both actions have to be equally justified or unjustified. An argument regarding the bounds of actions was developed in this section. This is the second conclusion to be drawn from the normative separation between contributory and collective actions. Each mechanic performs the same action: "repairing engines," rather than, say, "contributing to a just/unjust airstrike" or "contributing to a just/unjust war." Part III will articulate how both mechanics' actions can be objectively justified.

iv Culpability for not-necessarily-unjustified action

The conclusions of the previous section assume a typical organizational member in a typical organization. The mechanic's contributory action in *Engine repair* is not *necessarily* unjustified on account of being causally linked to an unjust collective action or end. However, it could still be unjustified. There are strong moral reasons not to knowingly and intentionally contribute to an unjust collective action or outcome. The culpability standard has to refer the mechanic's contributory action to the collective action in order to discern if his material involvement with an unjust outcome makes him liable for an unjustified action given unique subjective factors. His contributory action gets its moral weight in reference to the collective action, dependent on his contingent knowledge of and intentional state with respect to the collective action.

Imagine that the mechanic is friends with some of the special operators and so knows about their unjust mission to destroy the mosque. He is bigoted against Muslims and so intends his contribution to further this unjust aim because he is motivated to see its fruition. He is doing everything in his power to facilitate the specific attack. His knowledge and motive recast the authorship of his contributory action as his own rather than the organization's (Kutz 2010: 73). He would bomb the mosque unilaterally if he could. He instrumentalizes the organization like a participant in a goal-oriented collective, harnessing others' power to accomplish his goal. (This culpability might be of practical relevance in a war crimes trial, if it could be proven through his contemporary statements that he knew he was facilitating destruction of a holy site.) He does not get credit for the good downstream actions his repairs enabled because he did not know about them or have any intentional relation with them. Provided these markers of liability, we can fairly re-describe his intention as not simply "to fix the engine" but "to do [anything] to facilitate the destruction of the mosque." So characterized, it is clear that he has strong moral reasons to desist aiding in the destruction of a holy site.[10] Section IV of this chapter will consider how widely a theorist can ascribe this kind of culpability for downstream effects to modern combatants.

v Objections

McMahan aptly characterizes the individualist aspect of reductive individualism when he says a sentence like "the team won the game" is not a reference to

94 *The foundations of the moral equality of combatants*

irreducible collective action performed by a collective, but an abbreviation for thousands of sentences describing individual actions like "the quarterback threw the ball at 3:01:00," "the receiver caught the ball at 3:01:04," etc. (2015).

In Part I, I criticized reductive individualism internally, arguing reductive individualists' approaches failed to meet their own aims or had dubious implications. Part II develops an external critique of individualist and reductivist approaches to just war theory. I am arguing some scholars are wrong because of an argument they do not accept or have not considered. Why should any individualist philosopher, revisionist or traditionalist, accept that there are irreducibly corporate actions? No concrete, substantive account of a phenomenon is logically binding in the way that some formal accounts of phenomena strive to be binding. One can refuse a concrete, substantive account of something provided a plausible alternative. One man's "trash" is another's "treasure," and so on.

In describing phenomena as irreducibly corporate actions, or some alternative, one must strive for descriptive adequacy, pointing out how one's favored account addresses nuances of the phenomena with fewer gaps, difficulties, or problematic implications than alternatives. So to individualists' objection that they do not see why they have to accept collectivist descriptions of collective action, I grant there is no logical trap that will spring shut if they reject a collectivist account.[11] Ultimately, my claim is that the collectivist description of military action is an account that is more faithful to people's experience.

Also, there are weaknesses with the individualist account of action that should make us leery of *its* adequacy as an approach to just war theory. First, generally, when we seek to describe a complex phenomenon, innocent of any particular action theory, it seems to make sense to start with a top-down description that tries to capture the complex experience of an observer before analyzing components of the action. By contrast, individualists start with simple actions superficially dissimilar to the complex action, which individualists *assume* compose the complex action. Further, individualists who are also reductivists assume that any moral insights generated from an analysis of the simple actions will apply to collective actions (see Fishback 2016: 286). Most relevant to our conversation, reductive individualists stipulate without argument that superficially dissimilar peace-time civilian individual actions are morally indistinct from the individual component actions of military collective actions (see, e.g., McMahan 2009: 156; Frowe 2014: 5).

Second, individualists' denial of collectivist accounts of collective action works both ways. There is no logically binding reason for a collectivist to accept an individualist account of collective action. With respect to the reductive individualists in particular, I am not familiar with any reductive individualist accounts defending the individualist approach to examining action.[12] Some seem to opt for the individualist approach based on the perceived weakness of collectivist approaches or for lack of a compelling reason to accept even strong collectivist accounts.[13]

Third, adding up all the individual, contributory actions of a collective action does not seem to fully describe the action, contrary to McMahan's assertion

Responsibility, justification, and liability in war   95

about the football game, above.[14] The theorist cannot assume that the military's corporate intention, say, to seize a valley from the enemy, reduces to the intentions of combatants to do the same for reasons already discussed.[15] Individualists would say that all the combatants nonetheless chose to act on certain reasons, reasons that might include "I have to do X because it's my job," and so they become responsible for those actions (Flores and Johnson 1983: 542). This analysis seems to miss two elements necessary to fully describe the collective action: the origin of these reasons the personnel adopt as their own and the social background motivating them to accept these reasons.

Individualists take the animating principles of collective action to come from the collective members since the collective itself is not an animated being. I agree in the case of goal-oriented collectives like the Roman cabal or a group of rioters; the members create and drive the group. We have a sufficient picture of what is animating the collective action if we add up all the sentences describing the individual actions of one of these groups. There is no pre-existing or even contemporaneous executive command structure shaping and directing the members. In the case of military action, however, the individualist approach does not account for the fact that the military organization is oriented toward certain ends, and collective decision-making and communication structures like planning cells and chains of command are embedded in the military before anyone is recruited. The organization persists even with a complete turnover of staff. Further, a popular political and social theory has inculcated recruits with values that lead them to privilege military role-based reasons over their personal intuitions (Crawford 2007: 190). That which drives service personnel to act on certain reasons is not accounted for when we add up all the sentences of the form "SGT Smith did X after he chose to see his orders as action-guiding." The institutional structure producing the orders and the complex social practice leading personnel to feel it is compulsory to take those orders as action-guiding are not accounted for with an individualist account.

Fourth, in tandem with the reductivist aspect of their approach, reductive individualists' individualism leads to a host of morally disturbing conclusions. (Individualists are not always reductivists, but their two approaches are allied. Descriptive individualism usually leads to evaluative individualism, and, like evaluative individualism, reductivism denies any special moral status to collectives.) Service members should sometimes or always refuse to deploy to wars they think are unjust. Captured members of the unjust side should in principle be denied POW privileges and exposed to prosecution (Rodin 2002: 64). Service members on the unjust side should turn their guns on their comrades to prevent them from furthering the unjust cause (Fabre 2012: 79). Noncombatants can in principle be targeted,[16] including attacks strictly meant to terrorize civilians into withdrawing material support for the military (Frowe 2014: 199–202). Moreover, professionals of all sorts need to constantly make *ad hoc* moral decisions on the job without steady deference to their professional norms (e.g., a lawyer's code of confidentiality, a doctor's oath to do no harm, etc.).

96 *The foundations of the moral equality of combatants*

IV Culpability for collective actions

The collective action called the assassination of Julius Caesar is normatively reducible to its component actions in two respects. First, the strong moral reasons applying to the collective agent regarding the collective action apply to the individual agents' contributory actions. Second, given that each senator's contributory action is unjustified, a theorist finds ample material in each senator's action to deem him culpable for the assassination. Given the structure of the collective action, conspirators are culpable for the assassination even if they were not directly involved in the violence, or if their violent actions were inefficacious to the end of killing Caesar. Focusing now on the second aspect of irreducibility, this section will exemplify the dynamics of organizational action in military action and show how those dynamics deny a theorist grounds to deem strategically significant numbers of combatants culpable for the unjust collective actions and ends they materially advance. This argument blocks another potential basis for the asymmetry thesis since, as we saw above with the knowledgeable mechanic, culpability for collective action makes not-necessarily-unjustified contributory actions in organizations unjustified. Culpability can be demonstrated in specific situations where combatants atypically know and intend to bring about specific subsidiary outcomes. An individual liability standard is therefore useful to distribute responsibility for contributions to unjust subsidiary collective actions in war, like massacres.

Further, while the previous section's discussion of irreducibly corporate actions provided reasons to eschew *individualist* approaches to just war theory writ large, this section will offer more reasons to eschew *reductivist* approaches to just war theory. It makes sense to apply the same moral rules to agents in different contexts only if those agents have the same capacities for moral action. This section will show how combatants' agential, epistemic, and intentional states are so different from the imagined civilians in philosophical thought experiments that it would be folly to place normative demands on the former based on prescriptions derived from considerations of the latter. Finally, this section will provide the material necessary to defend combatants' traditional responsibility for answering to the demands of *jus in bello* rather than *jus ad bellum*.

i Criteria for culpability for collective military actions

The point to be made in this section about culpability for collective action is a related but different point to one arguing that most combatants are non-culpable for unjust killing or the threat of killing.[17] Most combatants are not directly committing the sort of violent actions that in civilian contexts might make them liable to defensive violence. Even if they are, they do not have sufficient knowledge about their immediate target to judge necessity or proportionality. These points challenge revisionists regarding whether it is

Responsibility, justification, and liability in war   97

appropriate to model combatants' duties by reference to civilian self-defense thought experiments. These points also question if the deep morality of warfare requires reductivist approaches given that resultant norms do not seem to be action-guiding for combatants in the fog of war.[18] Since contributory actions in war are unjustified if the actor culpably contributes to an unjust end, the concern in this portion of the chapter is instead to consider whether theorists can defend the asymmetry thesis by claiming that a strategically significant number of combatants are culpably contributing to unjust ends (Dill and Shue 2013: 8).

A combatant causally contributing to a collective action would need to know and be motivated by the specific collective action his contributory action furthers (e.g., bombing the XYZ munitions plant) rather than the general sort of action it furthers (e.g., airstrikes) if he is to be culpably connected to that action. His knowledge and motive have to be specific with respect to collective actions/ends, because "airstrike," *simpliciter*, is not a specific enough action for the participant to know if he is furthering a just or unjust action/outcome (Crawford 2007: 189; Harbour 2003: 71). Therefore, the epistemic material is not present for him to effectively instrumentalize the organization like a goal-oriented collective. So, we cannot make moral judgments about the participants' contributory action simply on the grounds that he knows he is aiding the group in conducting its characteristic activity, unless that activity is inherently immoral.[19]

Some theorists look to participatory intention—the intention to be part of a particular group—to deem even marginally contributing and ignorant group members liable for group actions (Kutz 2010; Bazargan 2013). Participatory intention works for this purpose in the case of goal-oriented collectives because typical members know the group's *raison d'être* and join the group because they want to do something to bring about those ends. They empower their peers through their mere presence. Yet participatory intention to be part of an organization that, without the agent's knowledge, is performing unjust actions is not inculpating if the agent reasonably thinks the organization is oriented toward good ends. As already explained, organizations can accomplish many different ends using the member's work product and the structure of the group typically blocks members from knowing about those ends. It is unfair to deem someone responsible for something that happened out of her control and beyond her knowledge in a group she was permitted to join.[20]

Bazargan, the one prominent non-reductivist revisionist, uses participatory intention to support the asymmetry thesis, charging combatants on the unjust side as complicitous in the unjust ends they advance because they intend to be members of the military. This argument works to deem members of a goal-oriented collective like an unprivileged irregular militant group culpable for everything their group does, but not the members of conventional militaries—except militaries infamous for systematic war crimes, mutinies, and brigandage.

98 *The foundations of the moral equality of combatants*

ii Combatants' causal contributions toward, and knowledge of, military action

A war is an irreducibly corporate action composed of irreducibly corporate actions. (The irreducibility refers to contributory individual actions with the same moral character of the collective actions rather than to subsidiary collective actions.[21]) The corporate actions are almost all complex actions performed by teams of people acting in coordination within a hierarchical and compartmentalized organization. Many of the relevant actors make minor causal contributions and are prevented by the structure of the organization from knowing the details of the larger collective action they help advance. The actors always act in the absence of personal intentions for that action and usually without a personal motive to advance it. This section will show how the organizational structure of the military typically blocks two potential markers of liability—power over, and knowledge of, morally significant collective actions—from being present in contributory actions. This feature frustrates attempts to deem participating combatants culpable for unjust wars via these inculpating vectors. Sub-section iii will address issues related to intention and motive.

Regarding culpable knowledge, a combatant might know that:

- he is targeting an unlawful target like a hospital
- it is unnecessary or (narrowly) disproportionate to kill the combatant he is targeting[22]
- it is disproportionate to engage in a particular harm-causing action given the objectives of the current phase of the war (and the good done by the action)
- the war has entered an unjust phase and the agent's contributory good-making action is either insufficient to balance the phase's negative aspects or indirectly contributes to the bad-making features of the phase
- the war as a whole is unjust

A preliminary point complicating the task for one trying to determine combatants' liability for unjust, life-threatening collective actions should be clear from *Airstrike*. Contrary to what many civilians assume, most combatants in war are not involved in kinetic operations and so do not make themselves liable to defensive violence (in the usual way) by violently threatening innocents.[23] For example, the percentage of US service members at the "pointy end of the spear"—tasked with the kinetic operations that civilians think of when they think about warfighting—is as small the metaphor suggests. The percentage commonly invoked by officers and trade publications is 10%. Direct commission of an unjust violent action does not always make one liable for the action. However, direct commission of such an action helps a theorist reach a conclusion about liability since a sane, adult actor directly committing a violent action usually has the freedom to refrain from the action, knows what she is doing,

Responsibility, justification, and liability in war   99

and—since intentions are necessary to guide specific actions—usually intends the action.

Most combatants are not choosing to *contribute* to specific violent actions either. Due to the hierarchical and compartmentalized nature of modern military action, as well as the need for speedy, efficient, and classified actions, very few support actors know details about the target their efforts will ultimately help destroy. For example, consider the aircraft carrier helmsman: his epistemic position is especially limited compared to others in the airstrike's causal chain (Zupan 2008: 218). He has been ordered to turn the steering wheel a certain number of degrees and knows that executing this command will cause the carrier to change course. He will typically not be told in that moment where the carrier is going or for what purpose. The helmsman may know his country is at war, or the carrier's crew (and even its captain) may not be informed of the purpose of its maneuvers until hours before the first attacks. In the case of war, the helmsman can reasonably assume that strike aircraft will bomb enemy targets. Yet typically, he will know nothing about the targets to be bombed, the munitions to be used, the amount of collateral damage forecast, nor the utility of the targets' destruction. Since he is only fractionally and indirectly causally involved in airstrikes and has no knowledge of any particular airstrike, unlike the culpable mechanic in *Engine repair*, he cannot intend his actions to support a particular airstrike, much less an unjust one.

The issue here is not whether the combatant *knows* his actions support a war (as opposed to training or other non-kinetic operation) since this knowledge would not distinguish most combatants on just and unjust sides. Whether or not the combatant *believes* the war is unjust is relevant. Much has been written since the middle ages about whether combatants can be expected to judge for themselves whether a prospective war meets the *ad bellum* criteria. In general, I do not think we have grounds to make bold non-empirical claims on this point. Like civilians, combatants sometimes have access to non-ambiguous information about the justice of the war and sometimes they do not. They will have less access to information if they are already stationed at a foreign base, on a sea tour, or engaged in operations. We do have grounds to make claims about combatants' knowledge of specific collective actions within war, which is of more interest to many revisionists anyway (see below). We also have grounds to make broad claims about the intentions and motives of most conventional combatants even if they believe the war or operation they are advancing is unjust (sub-section iii).

Let us consider kinetic actors with these qualifications in mind. The FA-18 pilot directly commits an act of violence. She is in a more epistemically privileged position than the helmsman in that she has been briefed about the target type (e.g., bridge, barracks, etc.). She has more liberty of action in the cockpit than the helmsman on the bridge. She knows she is causing destruction to a particular target type and intends to cause that destruction. Still, the pilot's situation is disanalogous to that of an individual actor in a self-defense scenario or one of the Roman senators in terms of agency. These actors' actions usually fully

100   *The foundations of the moral equality of combatants*

originate with the actors. By contrast, the airstrike originates much farther back in a causal chain of actions in an organization, the last of which is the pilot's releasing of the weapon. Intuitively, it seems unfair to deem the pilot liable for the airstrike—because she engaged in a kinetic action—to the exclusion of the thousands of other people in the causal chain. The pilot would not be in the position to release the weapon without the analysis, decisions, orders, and actions of all the others. True, she decided to pull the trigger, but exploring her culpability on this point requires a discussion of intentionality to determine the relevance of her reason for pulling the trigger (see sub-section iii).

The pilot's epistemic position with regards to her target is also very different to that of an individual in a self-defense scenario or one of the Roman senators. The pilot knows general information about the target, but usually nothing about whom is killed, much less details concerning their activities at the moment of the airstrike. She cannot direct her actions toward specific lawful but unjust outcomes such as unnecessary or (narrowly) disproportionate killings of combatants or destruction of materiel or personnel that is (widely) disproportionate given the objectives of the current phase of the war.[24] Also, this knowledge is not generated like the analogous information about the target for a civilian in a fight or Roman senator in that it is not generated by the pilot's own epistemic faculties. Rather, it is wholly dependent on the information received from the targeteers, which is dependent on the information they get from the analysts, which is dependent in part on the quality of the analysts' training and the available surveillance technology. To say that the pilot acts on information provided by others does not automatically exonerate her if that information is faulty. Her enlistment decision and her trust in her colleagues must be assessed, but the corporate structure eliminates the grounds for deeming her culpable for subsequent bad effects due to faulty reasoning in the way we might deem an individual actor culpable who wrongly judges that someone is liable to defensive violence.

Perhaps one might object that airstrikes are non-representatively complex examples to use in critique of revisionism. The combat scenario that might seem the best candidate for scaling down to an individual action performed by an actor with the same markers of power, knowledge, and intention as an individual violent attacker in a civilian context or a member of a group-oriented collective would be one where one combatant shoots another. At first glance, this sort of infantry combat case would be the most like the one involving the cabal of Roman senators; the group of soldiers/senators is engaged in a collective action composed of nearly identical component actions. We might expect this to be the sort to reflect the injustice of an unjust war on an individual level.

Yet first, there is a relevancy problem if scholars are conceiving of rifleman versus rifleman as the paradigm case in war or the only case in which the injustice of a war can be ascribed to the individual service member. Only around 10% of wartime casualties in twentieth- and twenty-first-century conventional warfare are from bullets—the rest from the effects of high explosive and shrapnel. Most of this explosive is delivered via airborne platforms or indirect fire, meaning that the shooters usually do not see the people they injure or kill. Even

Responsibility, justification, and liability in war 101

regarding shootings, before the recent wide distribution of telescopic sights in some countries' militaries, presumably few of these bullet wounds were fired at a range where the shooter could clearly see his target, in a sense, as a man (as opposed to a muzzle flash in the darkness or a shadowy movement at the tree-line). So even among the roughly 10% of combatants engaged in kinetic operations, a very small percentage of *them* see their human targets individually and therefore could potentially have knowledge about their targets that would indicate killing them was unnecessary or (narrowly) disproportionate, or that destroying materiel or a larger group of combatants was (widely) disproportionate given the objectives of the current phase of the war.

Second, combatants who shoot an enemy at a range where they can at least briefly see him can often deflect much of the responsibility that normally stems from directly causing harm because of the mechanistic, horizontally coordinated movements enabling one combatant to fire his weapon at the enemy. An infantryman firing his rifle rarely shoots in the individualist manner of a solitary hunter firing a rifle, both in terms of physical behavior and intention. Infantry squads usually are trained to engage targets en masse—everyone starts firing if one man starts firing—and to coordinate fires with one another during extended engagements, with some operators tasked with distracting or pinning down the enemy while others maneuver for a direct shot. The coordination of unit-mates extends to the intentional level as each intends to do something because he knows his unit-mates intends to perform some coordinating behavior, each squad member developing sub-plans for his own behavior in order to mesh with what he assumes are the others' sub-plans.[25] So it is as misleading to think of the combatant who shot an enemy to be solely or even mostly responsible for wounding him as it is to consider the pilot solely or mostly responsible for the airstrike. The shooter directly, causally responsible for wounding an enemy combatant might reasonably deflect responsibility for the shot to his squad because the shooter just happened to be in position to fire directly at the enemy after a series of coordinated movements that could have put any other squad member in the same place (cf. Fabre 2012: 79).

Third, focusing on the 90% of causalities from blast waves or shrapnel further reveals how the collective structure of the relevant actions strip participants of potential markers of liability relevant to culpability. The vast majority of combatants maimed or killed by mortar, mines, artillery, bombs, and missiles are unseen by the attacker, not specifically aimed at (as opposed to a general area or building), and attacked by a team operating in concert in a highly rehearsed, mechanistic manner. The import of this last clause should be made clear. The lethal effects of indirect, ballistic projectiles like artillery, mortars, or ground-to-ground rockets are typically achieved through mass or blast yield rather than accuracy, against largely unseen enemies. Therefore, they require teams acting in concert, either irrespective of enemy actions (e.g., preplanned barrages prior to a ground assault) or in response to categorical states of affair ("is the enemy still firing?"), rather than ones admitting of proportional judgments. More accurate satellite-guided munitions are programmed before they are

102   *The foundations of the moral equality of combatants*

even loaded into firing tubes; they are then aimed at locations, not personnel. The mechanistic and indirect nature of these actions suggest that it would only be in extremely atypical scenarios where kinetic actors would have specific knowledge about their targets sufficient for a theorist to say that the actor was culpably choosing to tie his contributory action to a particular unlawful, or lawful but unjust, end.

Finally, one might argue that engaging in violent behavior when one is unsure about target details is culpably negligent. Negligence is socially determined, based on an assessment of what constitutes adequate care in a given context. It would be negligent for a private citizen to sleep with an unlocked assault rifle next to his bed but not for a soldier in a forward operating base. The standard for negligence in soldiering has to be determined in reference to all those affected by their actions, including enemy combatants and noncombatants. The contractualist scheme of *jus in bello* developed in Chapter 6 will permit kinetic action coupled with a level of uncertainty maximizing efficacy for the agent and minimizing risk to the target combatants and collaterally threatened noncombatants. Hewing to *jus in bello* without 100% certainty is usually not negligent.

In sum, most military actions are structured in such a way to inhibit reduction to component actions that are morally controversial unto themselves or that provide the actor with a direct epistemic perspective on the proximate or ultimate collective ends he is advancing. Even if technological changes made military actions less segmented or gave operators a better epistemic vantage point,[26] the corporate intention that leads combatants to act under orders would make their actions importantly different to actors in self-defense scenarios or the assassination plot. Even the individual rifleman who actually shoots an enemy is still performing a corporate action inasmuch as he is part of a coordinated team, acting under orders rather than by native personal volition. His intentional state with respect to the proximate or ultimate collective ends he advances is not conducive to culpability. We will address this subject now.

iii Corporate intentions in military action

As we saw above, military actions almost never involve individual intentions sufficient to guide the actions to completion. The military's corporate intention driving the collective action of fighting the war and subsidiary collective actions like airstrikes does not scale down to an identical personal intention on the part of contributors because individuals do not win wars, conduct airstrikes, fire howitzers, and so on. Instead, the average combatant performs—and so has intentions to perform—a subordinate part of violent collective actions (e.g., loading a missile, reading a radar screen, entering coordinates into a computer, etc.).

One might suspect this person-sized intention offers grounds for liability. Individual intentions offer grounds for liability for collective action in the case of goal-oriented collectives. In goal-oriented collectives, the actor forms the

Responsibility, justification, and liability in war   103

intention to perform a contributory act as a conscious contribution to a collective action he joined the collective to see come about. However, in the case of military action and other irreducibly corporate actions, the combatant's intention to perform a contributory action is not a self-generated intention but a "person-sized" segment of the group's corporate intention impressed by others for actions contributing to still other agents' broader ends. Since lawful military actions are definitionally those passed down the chain of command, pursuant to military ends, this description of combatants' personal intentions supervenes over any given moment when a combatant might also subjectively share the ultimate end of defeating the enemy or of acquitting her proximate task. She is making her commanding officer's interpretation and application of the corporate intention of winning the war her own insofar as she is acting as a professional (Isaacs 2011: 29). Thus, the corporate intention of fighting the war does not scale down to a participating combatant's individual intention because she does not and cannot intend her contributing action as a professional absent the larger chain of command compelling her to adopt the intention.

These claims require further explanation. The president of a country in *Airstrike*, above, orders the military to overthrow an enemy regime. What is characteristic about a hierarchical organization is that the superior who determines the end to be pursued usually does not materially contribute to its fulfillment. Instead, the president sets the collective end of overthrowing the enemy regime and this dictates the collective action to that end, fighting the war against the enemy regime. By contrast, in an egalitarian group like a group of hikers or bank robbers, all participants natively share the same end and join the group in order to reach the end.

Given this broad corporate end of winning a particular war set by the president, subsidiary corporate intentions to accomplish subsidiary collective actions, like neutralizing the country's air defenses, are determined through joint mechanisms in planning cells, wherein a staff of general officers and their advisers determine the war plans. Certain officers' ideas may win out over others' through a more or less formal deliberation process. The joint mechanism transforms the votes of the minority bloc into an outcome contrary to the minority members' preferences, while in a sense keeping it their own. These decisions are then imposed and communicated throughout the organization according to a particular procedure, at which point group members are institutionally obliged to act according to these directives. They are required to act as if the corporate intention was their own. The chain of command itself is a joint mechanism in that it is a set procedure for communicating information and coordinating action that can yield different outcomes along its tributaries than the higher echelon officers might have desired and would have intended had they been the lower-echelon personnel receiving the orders.

For example, in *Airstrike*, the Crisis Plan Group's (CPG) master plan called for destroying the air defenses of the enemy state. Lower in the chain of command, the Chief of the Air Group (CAG) on the carrier may interpret that fairly broad order to entail the destruction of a radar station one of the admirals

104 *The foundations of the moral equality of combatants*

in the CPG would not have thought necessary to destroy. We can imagine a conversation taking place after the fact in which the admiral asks why the radar station was destroyed, with the CAG replying "I was following *your* orders, sir." The admiral could demur, but destroying the station may have been a reasonable entailment of the CPG's order given the information and resources the CAG had at his disposal. The joint mechanism of the chain of command permits the lower-ranking commander on the scene to adapt and apply orders as necessary. The CAG is fulfilling his professional role and carrying out the military's corporate intention of fighting the war. We can expect a tactical action diverging from the first order-giver's original intent to a greater extent the farther down the chain of command the order travels.

Let us focus further on this example to explain how a corporate intention is spread throughout an organization. Such attention will eventually help us to distribute responsibility among contributors to complex collective actions within war. It will be helpful to refer to a distinction Seumas Miller makes between type-a and type-c intentions. Type-a intentions are for the actor's own actions; type-c intentions are for someone other than the intending agent to do something, as when a teacher tells a student to complete an assignment. In this case, the teacher has a type-c intention that the student completes the assignment.

The rear admiral in charge of the carrier strike group relays the CPG's strategy to the captains of the ships in the group. The captain of the carrier confers with the CAG who derives a type-a intention from these orders to tell his squadron commanders to destroy the enemy air defenses, fulfilling the president's type-c intention that he do so. To be clear, the CAG needs a type-a intention in order to do anything, in this case, give an order. One of the squadron commanders, a lieutenant commander, is left to tease out the derivative end of assigning one of her pilots to destroy a particular target that is an application and specification of the broader end of destroying the enemy's air defenses. She derives a type-a intention she needs to make her own from the CAG's type-c intention to order her squadron pilots to pursue their assigned targets. One of the pilots derives a type-a intention to release a weapon at a pre-assigned location in response to his commander's type-c intention. Each officer (type a) intends to act on the orders he or she was given, reflective of his or her superior's type-c intention. Each officer descending in the chain of command has a more tightly focused end for his or her type-a intention compared to his or her superior.

Not only are the agents' intentions the vicarious vestige of their superiors' intentions, the vector of transmission of these intentions and ends is "pushed" rather than "pulled"; it is characterized by compulsion rather than voluntary choice. This vector is a key reason the collective action and its potential injustice is irreducible. This vector means that the theorist has no grounds for assuming combatants would have intentions for their contributory actions absent the institutional framework of the chain of command. The lower-echelon officer pursues a particular end and makes a particular intention his own, not necessarily from personal affirmation in the way that the Roman assassins all personally have "killing Caesar" as their end, but, characteristically, because he was so ordered.

Responsibility, justification, and liability in war   105

This point about the compulsory vector is not an empirical claim that combatants are often acting under orders. A combatant's orders might coincide with personal intentions to do the same thing, but obeying orders, internalizing these vicarious intentions and ends, is the precondition for his professional actions. Military actions are constituted by military professionals contributing to collective actions in coordinated series under orders. War re-enactors dressed and equipped like service personnel cannot perform military actions, because they lack an authentic political corporate intention channeled through the chain of command (Pitkin 1966: 50; Copp 2006: 206). The institutional frame explains why one person's type-c intention is taken on by another and turned into a type-a intention. Each link in the chain of command segments the corporate intention and assigns it in the form of a type-c intention to a subordinate.

In the military, the only point when a person's self-originating individual ends (e.g., like those of the senators who each individually want to kill Caesar) are put into a joint mechanism where they are melded with those of others is when a civilian, animated, perhaps, by the end of joining the military, or the vaguer end to serve his country, takes an induction oath and becomes a service member. Once the civilian becomes a service member, his intentions for professional action are assigned through the chain of command. The enlistee's end of national service, or even to fight in a particular war, is transformed into his intentions to fire this weapon, fuel this vehicle, analyze this satellite image, etc., in the context of a particular exercise or campaign, regardless of his personal preference to perform that action.

From the perspective of each service member, then, there is a pre-existing corporate intention each person has to adopt in an appropriately segmented parcel (Arnold 2006: 288–289). This, as opposed to a collective "intention" that is the aggregate of participants' native, identical, individual intentions, as in the Roman cabal. Again, a given service member might or might not personally have winning the war as an end, but cannot *intend* to win the war, because fighting and winning wars are actions done by militaries or states. Individuals can intend individual actions while in uniform; a *service member* is professionally obliged to intend to contribute to the war effort in the specific way dictated to him by his chain of command.

This combination of individual and corporate intention does not causally over-determine contributory actions. While the committed helmsman on the aircraft carrier bridge may naturally intend to contribute actions to the war effort he personally supports, the helmsman only intends to turn the wheel *as a military action*—as a fulfillment of his lieutenant's order—when the helmsman internalizes the appropriate segment of the corporate intention to win the war, communicated by the lieutenant, into his individual intentions (cf. Miller 2001: 168–169). A civilian could not intend this military action, because she is not implicated in the chain of command—not professionally obliged to internalize military superiors' type-c intentions as type-a intentions—even if the civilian sneaked onto the carrier and formed and acted on the intention of turning the ship's wheel.

106 *The foundations of the moral equality of combatants*

iv Corporate motives in military action

One might object that if a person cannot, strictly speaking, intend to perform a collective action like an airstrike or unjust war, surely one can intend to do something like fuel an airplane *in order to contribute* to a war. One can enlist hoping to do *something* to aid the war. These aims should count for some level of liability for collective action. Indeed, group members can intend to *participate* in a group and/or, once in a group, can intend to *contribute* to a particular group action. They will intend to contribute to a particular group action when they are motivated by the end the group action accomplishes. In a military context, it is possible that an individual combatant would be motivated by the end of the collective action his contributory action advances. He can want to contribute to the announced strategic end of the military's actions such as defending the homeland, liberating a country, destroying a terrorist group, etc.

A person who joins the military expressly in order to contribute to a particular unjust war is culpable for the phases of the war following his induction and subsidiary collective actions (including those he unwittingly advances) under the title of his reasonable subjective understanding of the war. The reasonableness of the subjective understanding of the war is based on the actor's knowledge of the constitutive aspects of the war. In other words, the combatant does not have to think of a war as unjust in order to be culpable for participating in an unjust war, but has to know the constitutive features of the war (e.g., widespread massacres of civilians) that make it objectively unjust. If he thinks killing noncombatants is just, he is culpable just like he would be for knowingly performing an individual unjust action for which he had an irrational justification. Epistemic expectations should be modest here since the relevant standard is individual culpability, rather than a more minimal standard of liability indexed to objective states of affair. The question would be "should any rational enlistee (of the enlistee's age) understand that the announced aims of the war are unjust?" It strikes me that genocidal aims or aims of natural resource acquisition have this flagrant nature, but some cases of territorial dispute would not. The enlistee non-culpably ignorant of the true nature of the war is not inculpated. We might see this in a state with pervasive propaganda or even in a state with a free but polarized and partisan press.

The enlistee who joins the military expressly to prosecute the objectively unjust ends of a war, like slaughtering a hated ethnic group or seizing natural resources for the glory of his own state, is culpable for the war and for specific subsidiary unjust actions he unknowingly furthers, such as specific massacres, even if his causal contributions are marginal and even if he is ignorant of the specific massacres (cf. May 2006: 317). Regarding that marginal contribution, by enlisting, the malicious enlistee has done everything he can or (more likely) everything the military judged he was capable of doing to further prosecute an unjust end. The degree of his causal involvement is less important compared to individual action since he intentionally sought to combine his efforts with those of others to magnify the unjust effect and then left it to his leadership to

Responsibility, justification, and liability in war 107

determine his specialization and location in the battlespace. Thus, for example, a file clerk supporting the German war effort in the Second World War because he passionately supports Hitler's vision of an ethnically pure Europe is culpable for the frontline soldiers' battlefield actions and the concentration camps along with other military contributors who are similarly disposed. His otherwise-banal actions pick up the taint of the collective actions they help enable. They are unjustified.

We will now consider if a theorist has grounds to deem a strategic number of personnel culpable for unjust collective action by dint of an inculpating motive in this manner. Motivation would appear to be a compelling candidate for involvement with liability. It is much more likely than intention to reduce down to identical individual-sized segments original to the contributing actors, since individuals can coherently want to contribute even a small effort to help bring about some broad state of affairs (e.g., end global warming), whereas they cannot intend the collective action bringing about that collective end.

To be confident that all causal participants in a collective action are motivated by the end of the action, we would want some steady connection between motivation and causal involvement discernible from the theoretical vantage point. Observers can usually only initially guess at motives, whereas an observer can usually assume that a sane agent's intention matches an objective description of the action. For example, a church parishioner putting cash in a collection plate presumably intends to give alms. However, she might be motivated by concern for the poor, a desire to bolster her reputation, and so on. Motives are usually connected with the anticipated outcomes of actions, but it will be hard to find a way to theoretically link collective outcomes with contributors' motives since motivations can be expected to vary among contributors. Also, a single contributor might have multiple motives for participating in a collective action.

Distinguishing professional from personal motives will help link outcomes with motives. A professional motive directs one to act according to the received standards of her professional role. By contrast, a personal motive originates in, and reflects, an agent's character or personality; the resulting action is something the agent chooses to do because she wants to achieve the end associated with the motive. This is a comparative rather than a precise definition. Personal motives are more closely linked to culpability than other motives because they do not "explain away" the action from the actor's perspective. The actor asks not to have her character judged when she says, "I'm just doing my job."

A person might sincerely want to perform her professional role well. I mean to emphasize with the distinction between motives the fact that a profession has certain institutional standards that the diligent professional then accepts as action-guiding motives. For example, even if a misanthrope, a diligent doctor wants to care for her patients because that is what doctors must do; a diligent teacher wants to ensure each of her students learns, because that is what teachers must do.

Professional motives linked to good professions can guide the professional to perform actions that are permissible or obligatory for her even when

108 *The foundations of the moral equality of combatants*

non-professionals should or could omit the actions. External observers cannot ascribe a bad motive to the professional based on his contribution toward a bad end because of the plausibility that he is acting on a professional motive. Consider the following scenario.

Minefield

A farmer lives in a country where a sectarian militia is engaged in a genocidal campaign against a minority sect. The farmer comes across an injured stranger in a minefield. The farmer enters the minefield and delivers first aid to the man.

Someone risking his life to save a stranger must have strong motives. An observer could reasonably assume that the farmer either:

a   supports the genocidal campaign and so hopes the man he helps is a militant
b   wants to aid the oppressed group and so hopes the man he helps is a member of the sect
c   or feels that no human being should suffer and so would not feel regret regardless of the patient's identity

Now consider *Minefield 2*, the same scenario as *Minefield*, but involving a doctor instead of a farmer as the rescuer. An observer could reasonably assume that the doctor has motives a through c but also motive d, a professional motive. She might be non-partisan with respect to the conflict as well as a misanthrope, but her professional motive still directs her to do a technically sound job, healing all wounds, and impartially treating all patients the doctor comes across, because this is what doctors do.

A layperson does not have training or an institutional frame compelling or disposing her to pursue a particular end. So a layperson is more likely motivated by the ends she brings about when she acts in a private capacity. A farmer motivated by a or b would only aid one of two injured people if one was clearly identified as a militant and one as a minority sect member. By contrast, the identity of the patient would not affect the doctor's motivation to aid him if the doctor was behaving as doctors should. Thus, an observer cannot assume the doctor was motivated to save a militant or sect member *per se* even if the wounded man was clearly identified as one or the other.

Combatants are often in the doctor's position in *Minefield 2*. They enter dangerous environments unsure if their actions will contribute to objectively good ends. If the FA-18 pilot who releases the weapon in *Airstrike* is acting on a professional motive, she is not motivated to destroy this particular target even though she engages in an intentional action to destroy it. If asked what she was trying to do, she would say "I'm trying to destroy this target," but if asked why, she would probably say "those were my orders." Her terse response implies a

Responsibility, justification, and liability in war 109

rejection of a layperson's assumption that actors must be motivated by the ends they bring about. Rather, a professional motive is aloof of the particular end assigned to the professional. Assuming she acts on a professional motive, we cannot then assume the bad outcome motivated her to act.

Professionals cannot necessarily shirk responsibility, and perhaps culpability, for their actions and ends. The Nazi file clerk is culpable for unjust killings because he knowingly contributes to them motivated by Hitler's racist vision. Yet we cannot *assume* potential culpability via an inculpating motive to bring about a bad end if the doctor or pilot does something in her professional purview indirectly contributing to this end. Actions performed in the professional arena can have the same neutral motive despite leading to good or bad outcomes: being a professional, doing one's job.

Yet we also cannot assume a layperson performing a generically permissible action with a bad result (e.g., the farmer aiding an unidentified militant) performed the action due to a bad motive—he may want to help all suffering people—so how does a possible professional motive help us? While we are not in a position to make a general claim about the ubiquity of good or bad motives in laypeople, the corporate intention and motive in military action provides grounds to assume the ubiquity of a professional motive for service personnel when we assess competent military action.

First, a professional motive among a unit's members (as opposed to a motive to accomplish their particular end) would be sufficient by itself to competently execute military action. Second, it is unreasonable to assume the ubiquity of any one personal motive in a particular operation since we observe a wide range of motives among service personnel for military service. Third, we cannot infer the ubiquity of a self-centered motive like earning a salary since these motives could be met without performing one's assigned role in a competent manner. These three reasons all apply to competent medical practice. The fourth reason distinguishes the medical and military professions. Medical practice usually does not unfold in perilous environments like minefields so we do not have the grounds to assume a powerful professional motive overriding inconstant personal motives in medicine. It can be assumed that only a professional motive would be adequate to compel proper military behavior in the face of horrible conditions that would be expected to override most people's commitment to a cause, in the face of boring, dirty assignments cut off from any obvious connection with a motivating cause, or in the case of alienation about the utility of the mission. These arguments do not guarantee that the professional motive is ubiquitous in competent military action. I am not re-describing motives by fiat. My point is that there are theoretical grounds for claiming professional motivation is ubiquitous in competent military action, in contrast to other non-professional motives.

A theorist can assume the same professional motive for personnel on opposite sides of a conventional war. A theorist cannot then assume conventional combatants are motivated by the war's cause or subsidiary collective action to which they proximately contributed since they presumably have the same professional

110 *The foundations of the moral equality of combatants*

motive but different ends are associated with their actions. The theorist then lacks a unique marker of liability connecting collective and contributory actions one could potentially use to asymmetrically inculpate service personnel on the unjust side of a war.

Yet, one might object, service members do not shed their personal motives upon enlistment; we can imagine that many are personally motivated to win the war they prosecute. Might not a personal motive to achieve a bad end override the "aloof" professional motive? A doctor with a fully formed character would be driven both by a professional motive and a motive to halt any person's suffering, but we can expect the combatant's professional motive to wholly supplant a personal motive in many cases since desiring another person's death is rarely if ever morally appropriate in civilian life. The combatant should not *personally* want to kill the enemy in the way that a serial killer wants to kill his victim (Walzer 2015: 35–36, 39–40). An individual combatant might be a sociopath who is aroused by killing people, but we have no grounds to assume all service members are depraved in this way.

In this section, I argued the motive theorists can assume is ubiquitous in competent military action is a professional military motive to achieve whatever apparently lawful military objective is ordered. It cannot then be assumed that the particular lawful but unjust content of a particular war or operation reduces down to the individual motive of the participating service personnel since the ubiquitous motive is aloof of the particular end the relevant action advances. A bad motive is not a potentially inculpating marker of liability the theorist can assume is ubiquitous in service members' military actions.

Military actions are actions animated by an irreducible corporate intention even when carried out by individual persons. While the isolated soldier in a trench does something that looks like an individual action, he is usually doing it in service of the military's corporate intention of winning the war due to some political motive such as defending a treaty partner. He would not be in that trench, equipped, trained, and supported as he is, attacking enemy troops, absent that corporate intention and motive. Sub-section IV.ii discussed difficulties of reducibility based on combatants' fractional causal responsibility for, and limited knowledge of, the collective actions they advance. It has been important to emphasize intentional factors in sub-sections IV.iii and IV.iv since these factors usually distinguish military actions from violent individual actions even in the rare instances when a combatant is directly involved in kinetic activities with complete knowledge of the end of his action.

V Conclusion

This chapter showed how it is possible that contributions to thoroughly unjust collective actions by responsible actors are not unjustified. The chapter also showed how it is that combatants on opposite sides of a war (where one side is unjust) could be performing identical actions, distinct from any normative connections with their downstream effects. These two

Responsibility, justification, and liability in war 111

arguments are necessary to show how the moral equality of combatants is even possible. What remains, in Part III, is to show how two actions that are identical in an action-theoretic sense can both be justified even though they are advancing different sides in the war.

Culpable contributions to unjust irreducibly corporate actions are unjustified. One can divide moral responsibility for collective actions among group members provided detailed information about their knowledge and intentional states with respect to the collective outcomes. Practically, this analysis would be of most use in courts martial or war crimes tribunals where responsibility for specific collective crimes could be assessed. A culpability standard of liability allows us to potentially hold marginal actors responsible for grave outcomes and deem conspiracy members responsible for specific outcomes they enabled through their participation in the group even absent specific knowledge of a particular operation consistent with the group's *raison d'être*. However, outside a judicial setting, a theorist usually lacks the grounds to claim that a strategic number of combatants on the unjust side are performing unjustified actions on account of their culpable orientation toward the proximate or ultimate collective actions. The same normative structure that allows unjust irreducibly corporate actions to not necessarily be composed of unjustified actions also blocks typical organizational actors from having the markers of culpability for proximate or ultimate unjust collective actions.

A further purpose of this chapter is to advocate against reductivism and individualism in just war theory. Military action is only military action in a collective context. Civilians bent on impersonating service personnel, committing acts of violence in stolen uniforms, are not performing military actions. They are outside of a military chain of command and acting of their own volition rather than due to a professional motivation. Moral insights derived from analysis of civilian self-defense scenarios do not necessarily transfer to military contexts where personnel act in a collective, epistemically deprived institutional setting where their intentions are the compelled internalization of other people's intentions.

Finally, this chapter has provided support for the traditional moral division of labor between service personnel and political leaders, with the former being held responsible for complying with *jus in bello* and the latter for complying with *jus ad bellum*. The traditional arguments for absolving service personnel of *ad bellum* decisions is that they lack the power to launch wars, they lack the knowledge of the geopolitical exigencies involved in an *ad bellum* decision, and they may lack the wisdom to make the relevant judgment. Revisionists typically reject the latter two arguments as outmoded in most modern contexts. On the first point, regardless of whether or not service personnel can launch wars, revisionists stress that they can choose whether or not to fight in wars. The main force of their arguments is to show how combatants can be held accountable for participating in unjust operations or wars because, counter to the traditionalist view, combatants are performing unjustified actions by participating in unjust operations or wars. Service personnel must then take on the responsibility of

112 *The foundations of the moral equality of combatants*

considering the *ad bellum* criteria in order to see if the actions they are being ordered to do will be unjustified.

I have nothing to add to theorists who argue that it is expecting a lot of a 19-year-old to make a moral decision about the justice of a war, particularly taking into account how much information is required to credibly calculate the last-resort and proportionality elements. We have seen that the structure of military operations makes gathering information, especially about operations within war, very difficult. Most importantly, this chapter shows how contributing to the main strategic thrust of an unjust operation or war does not necessarily mean that a combatant is performing unjustified actions. So the *ad bellum* criteria do not pertain to a state of affairs that determines whether a combatant's actions are justified. By contrast, *jus in bello* pertains to the sort of individual contributory actions for which combatants are responsible and can perform.

Notes

1 Though they are individualists, Emerton and Handfield argue that people's rights cannot be evaluated outside the institutional settings that help protect those rights (2014: 62).
2 For other critiques of descriptive individualism, see Kutz (2005) and Walzer (2006).
3 McMahan seems to have a similar dynamic in mind when he writes that a mother could not be held liable to defensive harm under the following circumstances. An innocent victim has no other way to defend herself but to harm an innocent woman in a moment when the victim is under attack by the woman's son. Even though, decades earlier, the mother could have foreseen a slight risk of her unborn son becoming a criminal in the future, she ought not to be held liable for his deeds on account of her giving birth to him, because child-bearing is not connected in the right causal way to a future unjustified attack by the grown child (2005: 395).
4 The phrase is Kutz's.
5 See Skerker (2010: chapter 6).
6 For a critique, see Dill and Shue (2013).
7 Fabre sometimes refers to real historical cases.
8 For example, note how many specific conclusions Lazar draws based on his assumption that the armed pedestrian frequently invoked by McMahan is armed with a grenade—though McMahan never specifies the armament (McMahan 2009).
9 While Miller thinks joint mechanisms produce collective actions, he rejects the notion of corporate intentions. His depiction of how joint mechanisms work is nearly identical though to French's description of CID structures.
10 The balance of good effects of his action could potentially create all-things-considered reasons to perform the repairs.
11 Though perhaps a logical trap would not suffice. Frowe and McMahan have indicated in conversation that they reject neo-Kantian moral theories rooted in alleged first principles simply because these starting points are not intuitively satisfying. There is no non-arbitrary ground to disabuse revisionists of a reflective equilibrium method if they rely on their own intuition to prefer reflective equilibrium to other methods.
12 Fabre argues for why individuals alone have independent moral status in the normative, rather than action-theoretic, realm (2012: chapter 1).
13 Frowe and McMahan have indicated this to me in conversation.
14 Lazar and Dill and Shue briefly make similar points (Lazar 2012: 38; Dill and Shue 2013: 9).

Responsibility, justification, and liability in war   113

15 Lazar also discusses how militaries are collective agents (2012: 37). His article illustrates an expression of the larger dynamic this chapter discusses.

16 This is a common position for nearly all revisionists.

17 I and others have argued that point elsewhere (Skerker 2014: 78–79; Lazar 2015: 94, 2014: 24, 27–28; Dill and Shue 2013: 6, 9).

18 Revisionists can and do respond that their work is not necessarily supposed to be action-guiding (though see McMahan 2006). That combatants cannot always know that their actions are unjustified does not change the fact that these combatants lack objective justification. Due to the minimal modes of liability reductive individualists use, such non-culpable actors can still be liable to defensive violence. If the violence necessary to fight a just war usually exposes non-kinetic actors to more harm than they are liable to suffer (Dill and Shue 2013: 6), the just side's winning justifies the extra violence as the lesser evil (McMahan 2014: 139). I have therefore criticized reductive individualists' action and liability theories, rather than the feasibility of their recommendations.

19 Lazar also makes this point (2015: 131).

20 For a full critique of Kutz on this point, see Skerker (2014), Isaacs (2011: 126–127).

21 Lazar uses different terminology, but agrees with this concept (2012: 37).

22 Many have adopted McMahan's terms. Narrow proportionality considers whether the good done in forestalling a person's attack can justify the harm done to him. Wide proportionality considers whether the good done in stopping some injustice justifies the foreseen harm done to innocent bystanders.

23 Others make the same point (Lazar 2009: 191; Dill and Shue 2013: 3).

24 She has the ability to direct her actions toward unlawful targets like hospitals.

25 The technical terms come from Bratman.

26 Drone pilots engaged in targeted killings typically do amass detailed knowledge about their targets as they surveil them for long periods of time. This sort of knowledge would not be forthcoming when drone pilots support ordinary combat operations because of the speed and exigency of combat.

References

Arnold, D. (2006) "Corporate Moral Agency," *Midwest Studies in Philosophy*, 30: 279–291.

Bazargan, S. (2013) "Complicitous Liability in War," *Philosophical Studies*, 165: 177–195.

Bratman, M. (2006) "Dynamics of Sociality," *Midwest Studies in Philosophy*, 30: 1–16.

Cooper, D. (1991) "Collective Responsibility," in May, L. and Hoffman, S. (eds), *Collective Responsibility: Five Decades of Theoretical and Applied Ethics*, Lanham, MD: Rowman & Littlefield.

Copp, D. (2006) "On the Agency of Certain Collective Entities: An Argument from "Normative Autonomy," *Midwest Studies in Philosophy*, 30: 194–221.

Crawford, N. (2007) "Individual and Collective Moral Responsibility for System Military Atrocity," *Journal of Political Philosophy*, 15(2): 187–212.

Davidson, D. (1980) "Actions, Reasons, and Causes," in *Essays on Actions and Events*, New York: Oxford University Press.

Dill, J. and Shue, H. (2013) "Limiting Killing in War: Military Necessity and the St. Petersburg Assumption," *Ethics & International Affairs*, 26(3): 311–333.

Emerton, P. and Handfield, T. (2014) "Understanding the Political Defensive Privilege," in Lazar, S. and Fabre, C. (eds), *The Morality of Defensive War*, Oxford: Oxford University Press.

Erskine, T. (2003) "Assigning Responsibilities to Institutional Moral Agents: The Case of States and 'Quasi-States'," in Erskine, T. (ed.), *Can Institutions have Responsibilities?*, New York: Palgrave Macmillan.

114   *The foundations of the moral equality of combatants*

Fabre, C. (2012) *Cosmopolitan War*, Oxford: Oxford University Press.

Fain, H. (1972) "Some Moral Infirmities of Justice," in French, P. (ed.), *Individual and Collective Responsibility*, Rochester, VT: Shenkman Books.

Flores, A. and Johnson, D. (1983) "Collective Responsibility and Professional Roles," *Ethics*, 93: 537–545.

French, P. (1987) "The Corporation as a Moral Person," in May, L. (ed.), *The Morality of Groups*, Notre Dame, IN: Notre Dame University Press.

Fishback, I. (2016) "Necessity and Institutions in Self-Defense and War," in Coons, C. and Weber, M. (eds), *The Ethics of Self-Defense*, Oxford: Oxford University Press.

Frowe, H. (2014) *Defensive Killing*, Oxford: Oxford University Press.

Handfield, T. and Emerton, P. (2009) "Order and Affray: Defensive Privileges in Warfare," *Philosophy and Public Affairs*, 37(4): 382–414.

Harbour, F. (2003) "Collective Moral Agency and the Political Process," in Erskine, T. (ed.), *Can Institutions have Responsibilities?*, New York: Palgrave Macmillan.

Isaacs, T. (2011) *Moral Responsibility in Collective Contexts*, Oxford: Oxford University Press.

Kutz, C. (2005) "The Difference Uniforms Make," *Philosophy and Public Affairs* 33(2): 148–180.

Kutz, C. (2010) *Complicity*, Cambridge: Cambridge University Press.

Lazar, S. (2009) "Responsibility, Risk, and Killing in Self-Defense," *Ethics*, 119(4): 699–728.

Lazar, S. (2012) "Necessity in Self-Defense and War," *Philosophy and Public Affairs*, 40(1): 3–44.

Lazar, S. (2015) *Sparing Civilians*, Oxford: Oxford University Press.

May, L. (2006) "State Aggression, Collective Liability, and Individual Mens Rea," *Midwest Studies in Philosophy*, 30: 309–324.

McMahan, J. (2005) "The Basis of Moral Liability to Defensive Killing," *Philosophical Issues*, 15: 386–405.

McMahan, J. (2009) *Killing in War*, Oxford: Clarendon Press.

McMahan, J. (2014) "What Rights may be Defended by War?" in Fabre, C. and Lazar, S. (eds), *The Morality of Defensive War*, Oxford: Oxford University Press.

McMahan, J. (2015) keynote address, The Future of Just War Theory Conference, October 7, Monterey, CA.

Miller, S. (2001) *Social Action: A Teleological Account*, Cambridge: Cambridge University Press.

Narveson, J. (2002) "Collective Responsibility," *Journal of Ethics*, 6: 179–198.

Pitkin, H. (1966) "Obligation and Consent—II," *The American Political Science Review*, 60(1): 39–52.

Pettit, P. (2003) "Groups with Minds of Their Own," in Schmidt, F. (ed.), *Socializing Metaphysics: The Nature of Social Reality*, Lanham, MD: Rowman and Littlefield.

Rodin, D. (2002) *War and Self-Defense*, Oxford: Oxford University Press.

Runciman, D. (2003) "Moral Responsibility and the Problem of Representing the State," in Erskine, T. (ed.), *Can Institutions have Responsibilities?*, New York: Palgrave Macmillan.

Sadler, B.J. (2006) "Share Intentions and Shared Responsibility," *Midwest Studies in Philosophy*, 30: 115–144.

Skerker, M. (2010) *An Ethics of Interrogation*, Chicago, IL: University of Chicago Press.

Skerker, M. (2014a) "An Empirical Defense of the Moral Equality of Combatants," in Ellner, A., Robinson, P., and Whetham, D. (eds), *When Soldiers Say No*, Surrey: Ashgate.

Skerker, M. (2014b) "Seeking a Variable Standard of Individual Moral Responsibility in Organizations," *Ethical Theory and Moral Practice*, 17(2): 209–222.

Walzer, M. (2006) "Response to Jeff McMahan," *Philosophia*, 34(6): 43–45.

Walzer, M. (2015) *Just and Unjust Wars* (5th edn), Philadelphia, PA: Basic Books.

Zupan, D. (2008) "A Presumption of the Moral Equality of Soldiers," in Rodin, D. and Shue, H. (eds), *Just and Unjust Warriors*, Oxford: University Press.

Part III

The moral equality of combatants

5 The foundations of military norms

I Introduction

Combatants contributing to the main strategic thrust of just and unjust sides of a war do not have asymmetrical privileges and liabilities by virtue of their performing justified and unjustified actions, respectively. Non-culpable combatants on opposing sides performing the same physical behaviors (e.g., firing mortars) are performing actions that are normatively identical, distinct in action-theoretic and moral senses from the collective actions or outcomes they casually advance. It remains in Part III to defend the moral equality of combatants by explaining how each side can be objectively justified in performing these actions. The scope of the symmetrical privileges and liabilities obtaining between non-culpable combatants must also be explained. Finally, these last chapters will advance a collectivist, exceptionalist approach to just war theory as an alternative to the individual-based approach criticized throughout this book.

Part III will articulate a conditional defense of the moral equality of combatants. If modern militaries cannot efficiently function while also permitting selective conscientious objection, then combatants have equal belligerent privileges and liabilities in conflicts between basically just states, between basically just states and privileged non-state groups, or between privileged non-state groups in a stateless zone. Basically just states secure environments relatively free of rights violations for their inhabitants through security-standard-compliant methods, including legal mechanisms equally applied to all inhabitants (more below). Selective conscientious objection refers to a service member's principled refusal to participate in a conflict on the perceived grounds that it is unjust. Service personnel in basically just states have duties to obey all their lawful orders, including deployment orders, as a professionally specified way of meeting collective moral responsibilities to deliver security to their communities. If affording service personnel a right of selective conscientious objection in basically just states is practically untenable, then the duty of obedience is not voided when the deployment is to an unjust war. This duty amounts to a positive agent-neutral moral reason justifying deployment to either a just or unjust war. This positive moral reason is not overridden by reasons linked to the rights of the people potentially harmed by their actions because the combatants on both sides of a conflict have *ex*

120 *The moral equality of combatants*

ante permission granted to them by all affected parties, including noncombatants, to obey all their lawful orders, including deployment orders.

The moral equality of combatants will be defended according to the following construal of the phrase. Service personnel on both sides of a conflict are objectively justified in deploying and fighting regardless whether the collective action they further is just or unjust. To say that service personnel are justified in obeying their lawful orders is not to say that there are no weaker countervailing moral reasons for disobedience. All the service personnel enjoying equal moral privileges and liabilities have positive moral reasons stronger than countervailing reasons for disobedience but not necessarily so strong that the service personnel are morally required to act. It follows that one service member could have slightly stronger or weaker reasons than his enemy and the pair would still have equal belligerent privileges and liabilities. As a component of their belligerent privileges, each side can act in compliance with *jus in bello* norms in international waters/airspace, cyberspace, or in the basically just enemy state without wronging affected noncombatants and combatants there (noncombatants may be wronged by just behavior in unjust or failed states). As a component of their liability, neither side is wronged when detained, interrogated, harmed, or killed by enemy combatants acting in compliance with *jus in bello*.

I will not claim that the relevant political leaders launching the relevant military campaigns are performing actions of equal moral value, that personnel contribute to equally good collective actions, or that the service personnel are equally virtuous. I therefore will not make a potentially broader claim that the relevant service personnel have "equal moral status" since that could be construed to include one of these latter two constituents.[1]

To outline Part III, Chapter 5 will develop a theory of professional ethics that presents properly constituted professional duties as institutionally mediated expressions of collective moral responsibilities. Chapter 6 uses this model to articulate military norms, including the norm of obedience. Chapter 7 refers to the duty of obedience to offer a conditional defense of the moral equality of combatants.

The purpose of this chapter is to develop the foundation of military norms. Section II of this chapter explains the moral foundations of social institutions and the subsequent moral weight of professional norms. Section III focuses on the foundations of military norms, articulating a model that can be used to articulate norms for all state agents. This section also defends the role of militaries in basically just states. Finally, section III defends collectivized targeting rules, a first step to clarifying how the military norms of necessity, discrimination, and proportionality should be applied.

II The moral foundations of institutions

i Rights, needs, and institutions

I will rely in sub-section i on technical work done by Seumas Miller to explain the moral foundations of institutions. I do not claim that this method is the only

The foundations of military norms 121

way to account for the moral weight of military norms in a way congenial to a conditional thesis of combatant moral equality.

By virtue of natural properties, human beings have positive and negative claim-rights. These rights impose reciprocal positive and negative duties on all others. One person can meet her positive duties toward another by delivering morally required goods and services in circumstances when positive rights are apt and the duty-bearer is in the position to deliver those goods and services. One can meet her negative duties by deferring to others' negative rights. For example, many argue that all humans have a positive claim-right to the basic goods for a decent life such as food, shelter, and medical care. If this is true, it follows that a very poor person without the means of providing for herself (perhaps because of disability or scarcity in the local environment) may demand assistance from a well-off person with the power to help her. All humans also have negative claim-rights against being murdered, assaulted, robbed, raped, deceived, and so on, which all others (not merely those in her proximity or those with certain means) can meet by refraining from such rights violations and by protecting her from them. We can speak of any group of people as having an aggregation of individual rights in the sense that one encountering a group of five has a duty to respect the rights of five people.

Individuals also have joint moral rights insofar as they are members of certain groups. These are rights that attach to individuals but only as group members, for example, a right of national determination or a right to secede (Miller 2010: 68). A joint moral right of special relevance to this chapter is the right to security, a right to live in an environment that is free of rights violations to a degree that people are not unduly inhibited from pursuing different personal and joint projects. The right to security is a joint right since it can be unmet even when a particular person's relevant individual rights to life, bodily integrity, and property are unthreatened. We can see this unmet right on the part of, say, a wealthy person, who lives in a secure compound in a violent city, who is nonetheless unduly limited on account of being unable to collaborate with other people or embark on joint projects. The right to security will be unfulfilled in most complex societies absent institutions to deter, investigate, and punish rights violations.

The aggregation of individual rights, joint moral rights, and aggregated human needs creates collective moral responsibilities to protect and address those rights and fulfill those needs. Collective moral responsibilities are moral responsibilities of groups to attend to these rights and needs because only groups can effectively meet them. Groups are not supra-individuals with special group-sized responsibilities. Collective responsibilities attach to individuals but only if they are members of certain types of groups. For example, collective moral responsibilities are not incumbent on a hermit living in an isolated patch of wilderness because he does not have the capacity to act on such responsibilities.

Typically, these collective moral responsibilities are acquitted by creating and supporting institutions to address the relevant rights, like schools, hospitals, businesses, churches, and militaries (Miller 2010: 57, 77, 80; see also Camenisch 1983: 52–55). Governments are meta-institutions tasked with

122 *The moral equality of combatants*

coordinating the activities of institutions. These institutions are essentially teleological (ends-oriented), set up to foster, create, and protect the collective moral goods (e.g., health, education, security) that protect rights and fulfill morally important needs (Camenisch 1983: 54–55). I will use the term "moral goods" to refer to aggregated individual rights, joint moral rights, and aggregated needs.

The collective moral responsibility of society is largely, though not completely, transferred to the professionals who work in morally vital institutions. For their part, laypeople should support the work of these institutions (subject to certain limitations, below) by cooperating with institutional actors, supporting the institutions though tax payments or charity, and refraining from attempts to undermine them. They might also be morally required to directly assist institutional actors in cases when they cannot cope with exigent circumstances, like helping clean debris after a natural disaster. These institutions are created to acquit collective moral responsibilities and the end of these institutions are collective goods. Therefore, professionals have a joint moral duty to comply with their properly constituted professional imperatives (a joint moral duty is a moral duty to do something that can only be done in a group) (Miller 2010: 80). Thus professional imperatives are not simply like the obligations of a member of a club, instrumental to the club's end, but moral duties, with the weight to compete with other moral duties, since they meet others' positive rights, protect negative rights, and produce the goods to meet morally important needs.

This inclusion of professional duties (for professions securing morally important goods) among moral duties is a point of contrast with the reductive individualists' approach to role responsibilities. Reductive individualists argue that the same morality applies to all people in all facets of life.[2] They allow that professionals may pursue role responsibilities to a point, but must defer to ordinary moral principles in a conflict. Miller's view is not that there are two moralities. Rather, morality encompasses some duties applying to most (i.e., able-bodied, sane adults) and some duties that only apply to members of certain communities. The latter might include duties applying to members of affluent states *vis-à-vis* members of poorer states (but not vice versa), duties of former colonial powers *vis-à-vis* members of their ex-colonies, and duties that apply to members of certain institutions. There are both individual moral responsibilities and collective moral responsibilities, the latter of which can best be met by participating in institutions or by supporting their work. The following sections will develop two elements from this discussion in order to undergird the argument about combatant moral equality. We need to discuss further how professional duties can be moral duties (sub-section III.i) and how laypeople's duty to support just institutions means that their rights can be infringed by professionals without their being wronged.

ii Governmental institutions

Most people do not collaborate in the creation of the institutions that help deliver the collective goods everyone needs for a decent life. Since these needs and associated needs-based rights are ubiquitous, it cannot be the case that

The foundations of military norms 123

institutional actors only have moral duties to perform their institutional tasks when there is a kind of active and conscious transference of collective moral responsibility from a community to a formal institution. Rather, most institutional actors inherit these duties when they accept a role in an extant institution. The dependency of professional morality on the collective moral responsibility to deliver collective goods means there is a kind of "free market" for potential institutional actors looking to meet their collective moral responsibilities. Institutional imperatives take on the status of moral duties if the extant institution best meets collective goods (in the sense to be detailed below). For example, a police officer and a vigilante both may provide some security to a community, but the former may do such a superior job compared to the latter that, of the two, only the professional imperatives of police become duties. So not every job's professional imperatives are moral duties and not every entity in a particular professional field like education, healthcare, or security can say that its internal imperatives are moral duties.[3]

The possibility of non-governmental entities delivering tangible collective goods many governments deliver like education, health, and protection suggests that the constitutive role of government is the formal task of making and enforcing fundamental law—law that, among other purposes, provides the framework for all other rule-making institutions. This governmental entity could in theory be a tribal chief or chiefs, a warlord, militia, or even a private company instead of a state in the modern sense (Rodin 2002: 159; Norman 1995: 146). In cases of contested legitimacy such as civil wars and insurgencies, the entity that best meets the joint moral rights, aggregated rights, and aggregated needs of people in the area over which that entity claims jurisdiction is morally legitimate.[4] The institutional imperatives of the morally legitimate governmental institution (and sub-institutions) are moral duties and people interested in helping to deliver governmental services ought to join it rather than its competitor(s). The sense of "best" meeting joint moral rights *et al.* will be discussed in the section on the security standard, below.

A key responsibility of a government is to meet the collective right of security for the people in its jurisdiction. Threats to collective security can come from internal threats including ordinary criminality, from the government itself, and from external state or non-state-based threats. The second type of threat will be excluded in what follows, since we will focus on explaining the moral standard a government should follow in trying to meet the security needs of the people in its jurisdiction, specifically with respect to police and military services.

Given the present absence of a global government and absence of enforcement arms for international bodies like the United Nations, the institutions best able to meet the collective right to security posed by extra-territorial violent actors are national militaries. It is a contingent matter whether every state or state-like entity needs a military or whether a small, resource-poor, or geographically protected state can go without one for lack of threats or due to a client relationship with a nearby military power. More work will be done in

124 *The moral equality of combatants*

sub-section III.iv to defend the military as a legitimate institution whose imperatives can become moral duties.

iii The international order

The argument for the legitimacy of rights-respecting governments and their enforcement of domestic laws also indirectly creates the possibility of an anarchic international order. A government is properly concerned with rights protection from both internal and external threats. The contractualist model I am developing endorses an orderly system when it comes to law enforcement, encompassing enforcement, prosecution, and punishment via impartial and consistent procedures that themselves meet contractualist standards. The parties who can be modeled as consenting to the system are the same people protected by the system if they are law-abiding and punished by it if they break the law. People are modeled as consenting to whatever rights-protecting and rights-respecting entity effectively exercises power over the area where they live. This foundation provides no particular specification for the size of the state. If there is more than one state in the world, there is the possibility that external threats to a given state's inhabitants will come from other states. So the contractualist justifies an arrangement in which multiple states attempt to protect their inhabitants by enforcing domestic laws on their territory and mustering military and intelligence personnel to guard against external threats.

The anarchic order *per se* is not consent-worthy in the sense that we might expect express consent to accrue to adversarial legal or business arrangements. Whereas those adversarial systems can be consent-worthy for producing optimal outputs, there is no guarantee that the (morally) best government will triumph in conflict with another. By endorsing local effective governance, the contractualist model effectively endorses a self-help scheme in which states each try to secure their national security. To this end, states could work in concert, in opposition to each other, or without interacting with one another. A rights-respecting global government is probably rationally preferable to an anarchic international order. Such a just global government is consent-worthy if it exists. Diplomatic efforts toward establishing one would then be consent-worthy without de-legitimating extant states since consent accrues to extant arrangements best meeting the consenters' needs.

Thus, the contractualist model endorses war-making meant to protect a state's inhabitants as a function of government. There is no guarantee of justice in an anarchic or partly anarchic (i.e., partly governed by treaties and characterized by multilateral alliances) international order in which each state ideally acts in the interest of its inhabitants. As in domestic society, not every actor is a good actor and not every good actor will avoid mistakes. At best, under the self-help scheme characterizing the international order, citizens will be spared from major individual and collective rights violations from external aggressors.

III The foundation of military norms

i Professional morality

It is necessary to explain in general how it is possible for service members to have special agent-relative obligations and duties to do things normally forbidden to civilians prior to detailing the contractualist model's military norms. I will develop an account of military norms in the context of a theory about the norms for all security-seeking state agents and so will frequently refer to police and judicial norms in what follows in order to contextualize and de-mystify the privileges and liabilities of service personnel.

For a professional working in a morally vital institution, professional duty is a moral duty because of the professional activity's fulfillment of the collective moral responsibility to deliver, create, and foster moral goods. Professionals have professional duties to adhere to their properly constituted professional norms when performing their jobs. Put another way, a professional's duty explains why he must behave in a certain way and the norms describe what he must do. Professional norms have moral power because they are what guide the professional's actions to the institutions' morally vital ends. Professional norms tend to be chiefly teleological, directing the professional to educate children, heal the sick, protect the innocent, and so on, but they are also constrained by deontological concerns reflecting *ex ante* rules winning the hypothetical consent of all affected by the professionals' actions. These constraints specify how the institutional imperatives are to be met, guided by consenters' presumed aversion to being grossly wronged in some areas while being assisted in others. The teleological orientation toward collective goods and deontological concerns about the means of attaining them are the ingredients of professional norms, and so, the content of professional duty.

Broadly speaking, the facilitation of moral goods explains why professionals are morally permitted or obliged to sometimes act differently from laypeople in similar situations. Unlike norms pertaining to laypeople, these norms are meant to facilitate collective moral goods through institutional mechanisms, delivering moral goods to a wide number of people impartially, consistently, over time, regardless of the particular composition of the institution's staff. This institutional frame can even direct professionals to act in an opposite manner of a layperson confronting a similar situation. For example, a soldier may shoot a sleeping person he believes will threaten him in the future whereas pre-emptive self-defense is usually forbidden for civilians.[5] The divergence of action-guiding norms for laypeople and professionals who both have individual duties to act justly and collective moral responsibilities to facilitate justice and security stems from the following differences in their aims and capabilities. Professionals are seeking mainly to protect joint moral rights and aggregated goods, which the layperson usually cannot directly protect. Professionals usually protect individual rights indirectly through institutional mechanisms and protocols, whereas the

126 *The moral equality of combatants*

layperson can usually only protect those rights in an *ad hoc*, direct, and temporally limited manner. For example, police do much to meet the joint moral right to security by patrolling, conducting speed traps, responding to complaints, adjudicating disputes, managing crowds, engaging in investigations, and contributing to the remediation and punishment of crime as parts of the criminal justice system. Beyond these actions, citizens' mere knowledge that the police engage in these activities contributes to a feeling of security. Private individuals are usually not in the position to do more than contribute to collective goods like security and justice in an *ad hoc* and non-systematic manner affecting a small number of people. Absent coordination with others, it would often be a matter of luck if an individual could even temporarily contribute in a meaningful way to collective goods and joint rights, such as when a commuter spots an unattended bag that turns out to have a bomb in it. Non-coordinated action might just as often turn out to violate rights when vigilantes and nosy neighbors act on their own.

The professional duties of police do overlap with laypeople's individual duties when police are in a position to halt a rights violation to a specific person, such as halting a mugging, but the institutional context of their actions will still direct them to act differently than a private citizen. Whereas the private citizen only has the prospect of halting the immediate rights violations, the police officer, as state agent, is initiating a whole process of codified interactions between the suspect and the state, so must interact with the suspect with an eye to his becoming a subject in the criminal justice system. For example, the officer has to a) gain control of the apparent mugger with the minimum amount of force, b) warn the suspect about his right not to answer self-incriminating questions and to have an attorney, and c) not use force, threats, or promises in questioning the suspect.

ii Hypothetical consent

Thus far, I have explained how the professional duties of state agents are moral duties and can in principle direct them to act differently than laypeople confronted with similar situations. However, a professional duty to meet the collective moral right of security is too vague to be action-guiding for professionals like police and service personnel. Many security-seeking tactics could be unacceptable to the community supposedly benefited by them for reasons ranging from brutality to ineffectiveness. I propose we take advantage of the criterion of universalizability inherent in most schemes of rights and duties to further delineate relevant professional duties. One way of working out the scope of schemes of rights and duties is through universalization tests since a key component of deontological morality, on most construals, is the equality of human persons. In order to identify rights and their scope of legitimate exercise, philosophers imagine everyone in the world who is capable of bearing rights as having the putative right under discussion and potentially planning to act or actually acting on the putative right to the proposed degree. Plans or actions that cannot be

The foundations of military norms 127

logically universalized or practically universalized, or rules for actions or permissions to act that cannot win actual or theoretical consent by those potentially affected by the action, are morally impermissible. Non-universalizable rights-candidates fail and thus lack correlatives of duties.

The contours of state agents' duties to deliver security can be specified by imagining professional behavior that would win the hypothetical consent of all the parties affected by the agents' action. I will refer to this understanding of professional morality as the contractualist model. Modeling hypothetical consent cannot give the agent a wide range of action-guiding directives since it will be limited to actions geared toward protecting generic human interests or moral qualities. The agent has rational grounds to think that anyone would consent to proportionate actions taken to save the consenter's life, limb, and property and to protect her rights (without violating other people's rights) because every person has rational grounds to demand and seek the preservation of these interests and rights. An actual person might not want to live or have anyone harmed on her account, but has rational grounds to demand the opposite. She cannot blame a stranger for assuming she wanted her rights met and defended absent some express sign.

Philosophical discussions of hypothetical consent sometimes idealize the consenters and/or the context for consent in order to screen out biases, idiosyncrasies, and immoral views actual people have, and non-ideal factors characterizing actual debate on moral issues such as ignorance, limited time, and intimidation. These thought experiments are conducted in an effort to identify a fundamental framework for all of interpersonal morality or for identifying just political institutions. My use of hypothetical consent will be less ambitious than both of these projects, using it instead to identify the contours of extant professional duties.[6] As argued above, I agree with Miller that the properly constituted professional duties of morally vital institutions are moral duties. Hypothetical consent is one way—not necessarily the only way—of working out the proper constitution of professional duties of morally vital institutions. To be clear, I am not using hypothetical consent to ground professional norms, but rather, as a tool to work out the unvarying norms entailed by professional duty and the derived professional tactics, which will vary with context.[7] Professional morality is ultimately grounded in the collective moral responsibility to protect, foster, and create moral goods.

I will refer to the hypothetical consent of all affected by potential state actions below without specifying which notion of hypothetical consent discussed in the social contract literature is being invoked: the consent of idealized consenters operating according to ideal communication rules, of actual people following ideal communication rules, or of actual people unconstrained by ideal communication rules.[8] It is unnecessary to devote space here to defending one theory for a couple of reasons. First, collective moral responsibility grounds the relevant professional norms instead of hypothetical consent. The difference between consent models makes a difference when the theorist wishes to use them to ground norms. Second, I suspect all contractual starting

128 *The moral equality of combatants*

points would yield the same results regarding the contours of state agents' duty to facilitate a community's security. A large group of actual people unconstrained by communication rules as well as a group of actual people so constrained might well endorse the same security-seeking tactics identified by the theorist based on a thought experiment involving idealized contractors and ideal communication rules since the options for professional duties for police and service personnel are fairly limited. Further, the proper choices, whether one engages in egalitarian moral reflection or self-interested calculation, are clear. Whereas the duty to assist the needy, respect people's privacy, or respect people's autonomy might be executed in many different ways in different contexts, inhibiting consensus on the constitution of such duties, the sorts of options we might put before real or idealized consenters regarding police or military norms are less numerous and less sensitive to cultural differences. Military norms, for example, turn on broad questions designed to produce clear action-guiding norms about the use of force, like "May military targets that are not vital to the attacker's strategy be attacked?" "May military targets be attacked if there are risks to noncombatants?" "How should a comparison of the value of the target with the risk to noncombatants factor into targeting decisions?" We can readily predict how idealized or actual people would respond to questions involving their physical safety and so will not expect gaps between the anticipated consensus of a large group of people unconstrained by communication rules, people bound by egalitarian communication rules, and idealized consenters whose hypothetical consent is based on axiomatic preferences for the full enjoyment of their rights, and the like. In this arena, we can be fairly confident that consensus decisions reached through unconstrained (non-ideal) dialogues based on actual persons' raw interests and desires will match rationally indicated choices revealed through ideal contractualist constructions and so we can use a rationalist model of consent for the purpose of identifying morally legitimate professional norms (see Chapter 6, sub-section II.i) (see Waldron 1987: 144). In a dynamic to be explained in the following section, we can deem rationally consent-worthy professional norms and tactics morally legitimate even if some actual people affected by the relevant professionals' behavior object to them.

We need to engage in some kind of philosophical construct to model what large numbers of people would endorse since referenda on professional ethics are neither feasible nor necessarily morally salient. The duties of police and service personnel need to be considered in reference to large numbers of people—namely, all the people in the world. Combatants' actions can benefit all the inhabitants of their states and of allied states and potentially pose threats to the combatants and noncombatants of any state threatening their state or allies or any state or region hosting irregular militants or pirates. While police jurisdictions are much smaller than the "jurisdictions" of the military, any person in the world could in principle move to, or pass through, a police department's jurisdiction and so be subject to local laws and police powers.

The foundations of military norms   129

iii The security standard

The contractualist model utilizes hypothetical consent to expose the contours of professional norms and tactics by way of a formal framework I call the security standard. The security standard will be introduced in a general way here and be used to articulate military norms in Chapter 6. The framework can be used to expose the contours of the professional norms of all morally vital institutions, but I will here focus on governmental institutions tasked with maintaining the security of the state. The security standard endorses norms and tactics. Within the professions, professional norms are general rules for institutional actors that are largely rule-consequentialist in their logic. The norms lead to the morally vital collective goods the institutions are designed to meet when all or most institutional actors adhere to the norms. The norms are morally rich as they deal directly with core human rights or moral goods. They are general, capacious, and communicative to practitioners and outsiders regarding the values of the profession. The norms are enforced by internal, and sometimes external, sanctions. Finally, they are communicated and reiterated within the profession with a degree of gravity such that professionals are socialized to see these norms as deeply important, constitutive of their professional roles, and perhaps on par with non-professional norms.

Tactics are instrumental applications of norms. For example, the military norm of discrimination might lead to military units choosing lighter munitions or prohibiting indirect fire when confronting insurgents in densely populated areas. Discriminate tactics will depend on the physical environment, available technology, enemy behavior, and the like. Viewed the other way, the underlying and unifying principle of conscientiously chosen tactics is expressed in a norm.

The security standard is composed of two first-order rules for picking norms and tactics—two rules for expressing the contours of security-seeking state agents' professional duty. First, we can see that a rule would win the consent of all affected that directs state agents to adhere to norms and tactics reliably, efficaciously, proportionally, and efficiently leading to the institutions' goal of security instead of norms and tactics unreliably, inefficaciously, disproportionately, and inefficiently doing the same. Since security-oriented norms and tactics ranking favorably in these four practical categories may infringe on people's rights, we can imagine consent accruing to a second rule selecting the most rights-respecting among the most reliable, efficacious, proportional, and efficient norms and tactics.

Guided by these two first-order rules, the security standard endorses norms and tactics surviving a three-stage winnowing process. The standard: (1) canvases possible norms aimed at meeting a joint moral right like security; (2) isolates the most reliable, efficacious, proportional, and efficient norms; and (3) endorses the most rights-respecting among the norms meeting the practical metrics of 2. Once norms are relatively settled, the winnowing process is repeated for potential locally available tactics applying the approved norms. The practical elements of 2 are aimed at achieving the collective good of security while the

130 *The moral equality of combatants*

deontological element of 3 acts as a brake, excluding practically effective norms and tactics that come at too high a moral cost. Essentially, the security standard is a way of balancing affected parties' interests in the effective and efficient delivery of certain moral goods by institutional actors with the parties' interests in protecting other goods and rights potentially jeopardized by institutional actors' behavior.

While I will refer to the "practical elements" of the security standard (reliability, efficacy, proportionality, and effectiveness), it should be noted that these elements are also morally rich. For example, the proportionality element may compare goods like lives saved with evils like lives lost. Further, all the practical elements are indirectly morally significant in leading to morally valuable goods like security. Thus, an officer who selects an unreliable tactic in defending a town is committing a moral, and not just a prudential, wrong.

Norms and tactics can "score" better or worse according to the security standard. It is more natural to think about the practical elements of the security standard applying to tactics, insofar as tactics are instrumental actions. Yet norms, as general rules for action or, in this case, rules for picking tactics, can also be judged by the four practical elements in terms of their conducing to the relevant collective goods over time. Tactics can usually be measured according to the four practical elements more precisely than norms since the former often involve discrete technological or technical changes to standard operating procedure. Yet norms still admit of general assessment along these four elements, especially when compared with alternatives, in terms of the sort of tactics they prescribe and general practitioner dispositions they cultivate. For example, a norm rooted in ethnic or racial superiority prescribing the extermination of rival groups as the proper solution to political challenges will chronically lead to disproportionate responses. Further, the casual attitude toward murder the norm would cultivate among practitioners would likely create domestic problems when morally deranged service personnel return home.

A norm or tactic with no conceivable causal connection to the end sought is imbued with zero justificatory weight. Some norms are so insensitive to human rights, and some associated tactics so brutal, that the negative portion of a proportionality calculation can be assumed to outweigh any good done. Such tactics occasionally arising in national security situations, including ethnic cleansing, mass rape, and genocide, are never legitimate tactics of policing or war, even if they may have some brute, short-term efficacy. A norm or tactic that is sometimes, but rarely, reliable or efficacious similarly fails the security standard. Such a low score on any of the criteria disqualify the norm or tactic. In such a case, the state agents adhering to the norm or employing the tactic are not acting within the scope of their duties. A promising norm or tactic has to be at least more efficacious and reliable than not (>50%), and must be proportionate. A tactic is proportionate if the harm done does not exceed the good accomplished or preserved through the action. Efficiency is context-dependent and so does not lend itself to a categorical or scalar assessment. The efficiency element has to be compared across different tactics and

The foundations of military norms 131

can potentially be a significantly lower-scoring element than the other three without disqualifying the norm or tactic.

The rights-respecting element of the security standard is weighted greater than the combined practical elements, so a norm or tactic that is reasonably successful in the practical sense can be excluded if it infringes on rights to a great extent. The basic calculation is that people cannot be modeled as consenting to a cure that is worse than the disease afflicting them. These are situations where the norms or tactics meant to protect rights actually harm rights to a greater degree than they were being harmed or were likely to be harmed when the tactics were designed. This is obviously going to be an inexact comparison since one needs to consider the impact of a security-seeking tactic, like compelling plane passengers to pass through metal detectors and have their luggage screened, with the product of the calamity hopefully forestalled (terrorist attack) multiplied by the likelihood of its occurring. The implication here is that a given tactic might be consent-worthy in one environment but not in another, as the likelihood of certain kinds of rights violations changes.

Given a competitive total score, a contending norm or tactic has to be compared against others. A lower-scoring norm or tactic is not consent-worthy if an agency can engage in a better-ranking tactic. The security standard provides moral grounds for people to constantly press for better tactics on the part of state agents, comparing their state's tactics with those used by agents of other states. State agents fail in their duty in they persist in using outmoded tactics that are less practically effective or more rights-infringing than available alternatives.

The security standard can endorse extant phenomena best meeting its criteria, giving legitimacy to security-standard-compliant tactics already in use if they score well and cannot readily be replaced with much better ones given the relevant agency's resources.[9] It might also completely reject extant tactics in a particular jurisdiction and prescribe better tactics in abstract (e.g., if the "state-of-the-art" tactic still scores dismally low) or in use in other areas. Again, state agents have a moral duty to perform their properly constituted professional duties because these duties are institutionally mediated expressions of collective moral responsibilities. Security-standard-compliant norms and tactics are those "properly constituted" professional duties. They are worthy of the consent of all affected parties because they take into account those parties' rights twice; the norms conduce to state agents' protection of affected parties' rights through means that also maximize deference to affected parties' rights. Properly constituted norms strike an optimal balance between these two concerns. So professionals are performing moral duties by engaging in security-standard-compliant tactics but not if their tactics fail this standard. Legitimate tactics, then, are tactics expressive of state agents' professional duties, which do not wrong the affected parties even when infringing their rights (this dynamic will be explained from the affected parties' perspective in sub-sections II.ii and iii of Chapter 7) provided that state agents engage in these tactics in an upright manner.

132   *The moral equality of combatants*

In sum, the security standard answers the question for state agents: in what does my professional duty consist? State agents should use the security standard in assessing which norms to cultivate and which tactics to use. They should also constantly seek norms and tactics that are more reliable, efficacious, rights-respecting, etc. Again, while it may at first seem more natural to think about reform in reference to tactics, sometimes institutions are so out-of-sync with their clients that the problem requiring reform is the basic culture and outlook of institutional actors. Legislators should hew to this standard when crafting laws meant to reform security agencies. The internal counsel for such agencies should interpret the letter of existing laws according to the spirit of the security standard. The public has a duty to use this standard to oversee the protocols of state agents dealing with foreigners (discussed below). Tactics falling short of this standard, given economically and technically feasible alternatives available to the government, can be reasonably criticized and targeted for reform.

iv Military service

We have already seen how it is possible for professional norms to have moral weight in terms of the moral principles that apply to everyone. Prior to detailing the composition of military norms, a defender of the moral equality of combatants must explain why the *military* profession enjoys this distinction and therefore why military norms have special agent-relative weight for a service member over non-professional norms. At the same time, the defender has to avoid any argument that could also grant, say, gangsters permission to obey their group "norms."[10]

Military enlistment for the purpose of protecting the national security of a state is generally a good. This is the case even when military protection for someone in state A comes at the expense of the security of someone in state B. The same moral foundation by which military A is permitted to protect state A permits military B to protect state B. The cosmopolitan base prevents military enlistment from being like enlistment in the mafia, whose interests and actions are generally contrary to those of the rest of society. The mafia's "norms," indexed to the mafia's ends, are not institutionally mediated expressions of ordinary moral principles since the mafia does not produce morally valuable goods like health, education, or security. Mafia "norms" then have no special agent-guiding weight for mobsters.

Militaries have a legitimate role in securing the national security of states, including collective security secured through service to allies. The rights of inhabitants are protected indirectly by securing the national security of states so military and intelligence personnel will less commonly halt rights violations in the immediate sense a policeman can. Military and intelligence personnel have a broader remit than police, playing more of a prophylactic role than domestic law enforcement personnel, including the protection of the territorial integrity and territorial waters of a state, the security of bordering ally states, and international shipping lanes on which the state's economy depends. The broader remit is

The foundations of military norms   133

dictated by the contractualist model since the wider zone of security is necessary both for protection against violations of negative rights (e.g., posed by pirates in international waters and enemy craft with long-range weapons) and for fostering inhabitants' positive freedom, which depends on a reasonable belief in a peaceful and stable future.

Militaries can play this role by deterring external threats by their mere presence on patrol or in garrison. Further, modern militaries can hardly compose themselves overnight from conscripts or recruits in response to some exigent threat. Thus *standing* militaries have a legitimate role. It follows that enlistment in militaries is a morally good action inasmuch as it involves volunteering to protect others' rights in a legitimate institution. One's presence contributes to this end even if one enlists for wholly self-interested actions.

Military norms have agent-relative weight for service members since the military is a necessary institution, military service is permissible, and military enlistment is good. These norms are weighty enough to contest with the norms that guide people in ordinary life.[11] In order to show that they can override non-military norms that perhaps would direct a service member to refuse his lawful orders, I need to do more than show that they conduce to morally valuable goods like national security. I have to show, first, that they do not wrong the targets of normatively prescribed action. Second, I have to show that the professional norms are overall justified, meaning there are stronger moral reasons for hewing to these norms than to non-military norms that would otherwise govern the actor's action. I will take up the former challenge in Chapter 6, section II, and the latter in Chapter 7, section III.

An exception to seeing military service as a generically good activity is in situations where the state in question is gravely unjust to its own people (Mapel 1998: 184; Thomas 2007: 516; McMahan 2009: 72). In this context, the military is not securing the rights of the state's inhabitants and so can confer no special agent-guiding norms. Not even the potential defensive use of the military on behalf of the internally repressive state would justify enlistment since the government's falling to an aggressive but non-rapacious neighbor would be an improvement over the present state of affairs. The comments that follow regarding the military norms and moral equality of combatants will not apply to these sorts of militaries but only to conventional militaries serving basically just states and *in bello*-compliant irregular militants serving basically just states or distinct sub-state communities. Basically just states secure environments relatively free of rights violations for their inhabitants through security-standard-compliant methods, including legal mechanisms equally applied to all inhabitants. "Basically just" is a relatively low threshold for the legitimacy of a state's police, military, and intelligence actions. The importance of protecting people's core rights from violations by fellow inhabitants or external enemies means that some illiberal policies do not make the state's security-seeking actions illegitimate. Another way of putting this is that it is possible for some institutions in a state (like the repressive secret police or corrupt bureau of mining) to be illegitimate, conferring no moral sanction to

134 *The moral equality of combatants*

its members to act on institutional imperatives, without making all the state's other institutions illegitimate.[12]

This approach is helpful to make sense of the state that is a paradigmatic state actor in a modern war and at the same time an outlier: Nazi-era Germany. No useable just war paradigm can fail to apply to the Second World War and yet the practice of the Nazi regime was so baroque and horrible as to challenge every paradigm of military ethics and political theory. Nazi-era Germany was not a basically just state because it did not apply the law equally to all its inhabitants; it strove to murder a substantial portion of its population. Yet even amidst the horror of euthanasia and genocide directed at certain groups, the institutions of the German state worked more or less normally for ethnic Germans. Thus, the argument in this chapter about moral equality would apply to non-culpable members of the *Wehrmacht* (e.g., who believed they were defending their state against conventional adversaries), but not to members of the *Waffen-SS, Einsatzgruppen*, or staff at concentration camps.

Broadly, the revisionist critiques successfully apply to someone considering enlistment in a military in a state that is gravely unjust to its own people. He ought not to enlist; he is at least partially liable for unjust wars the leader launches after the soldier's enlistment; he is not permitted to kill enemy service members; his tactical goals do not count as goods in a proportionality calculation. Drawing on the theory of culpability for goal-oriented collective action in Chapter 4, we can view a knowing enlistee in such a military like someone entering into a criminal gang. The same holds true in the less likely event that the state is basically just but the military is independently corrupt, preying on the state's own resources and launching external attacks on its own initiative.

IV Conclusion

This chapter introduced the moral foundation for my contractualist approach to just war theory. People partially fulfill their collective moral responsibilities to meet joint rights by creating just institutions, including governments, which serve as meta-institutions. Collective moral responsibility is largely transferred to institutional actors whose properly constituted institutional imperatives take on the status of moral norms because of their role in protecting joint rights. Institutional actors have a duty to execute their institutional norms. I appealed to the hypothetical consent of all affected by professional actions as a way of exposing the norms constituting institutional or professional duties, the logic being that the affected parties will endorse an optimal balance of actions facilitating the protection of joint rights with a minimum of rights infringement.

Notes

1 McMahan denies an "equal moral status" because at least one side contributes to an objectively unjust collective action (2009: 57).
2 Michael Walzer, Henry Shue, and Noam Zohar argue that peace-time self-defense and war just are different activities with different rules (Shue 2008; Walzer 2006: 43).

The foundations of military norms 135

Zohar asserts that human existence has a dual character: we are both individuals interacting with one another and nations interacting with one another through their service personnel. The rules of war give some deference to both modes of existence. While Zohar seems to have irreducibly corporate actions in mind, he does not produce an argument for his position (2004: 738–739).

3 Some collective goods could conceivably be met by multiple competing or complementary institutions (e.g., the needs of the poor might be met by non-governmental and governmental institutions) in which case all the relevant actors have moral duties to acquit their institutional imperatives.

4 Discussed in Skerker (2010: chapter 6).

5 Thomas Nagel and Alan Gewirth have similar approaches to professional morality (Nagel 1978; Gewirth 1986). Richard Wasserstrom argues in a similar vein regarding criminal defense attorneys (1988: 63). My argument serves as a refinement and critique of Camenisch's related argument that professional morality is a different embodiment of non-professional morality (1983: 61).

6 I lack the space here to refine the political contractualist model I developed in Skerker (2010: chapter 2).

7 For an overview of the debate about hypothetical consent's ability to ground norms, see Southwood (2010: 135–137).

8 "Contractualists" hold for certain initial moral constraints about dialogue while "contractarians" do not place such restrictions on dialogue partners. Contractarians include Hobbes (1971), Gauthier (1987), and Morris (1996: 215–243). Contractualists can be further divided into those who conduct thought experiments involving idealized contractors operating according to ideal communication rules and those who argue that interpersonal morality is constituted by actual people debating according to ideal communication rules. The former group includes Kant (1991a–c), Rawls (1971), Harsanyi (1982), and Nagel (1991). The latter group includes Scanlon (1998) and Habermas (1985). The benefit of the unconstrained nature of the contractarian dialogue is that dialogue partners are imagined to reach agreements that are in the parties' interests to respect regardless of the parties' level of desire to behave morally.

9 Benbaji and Statman have a similar idea (2019: 63). While this "automatic legitimacy" might seem odd, clashing with intuitions regarding the (express) consent we give to commercial service providers, hypothetical consent is a compelling way of explaining how people can be expected to comply with laws of a state they did not consciously join (including the orders of state agents) and how legislators and state agents should proceed given the impossibility of garnering the express consent from every person affected by legislation and law enforcement (Waldron 1987: 133, 138; Nagel 1978: 36; Rawls 1971: 337). This construction will seem odd to Hobbesians and Lockians with "strong" construals of natural rights (complete in a state of nature) (see Pitkin 1965: 46; Scanlon 1975).

10 Kutz's position is vulnerable to critique on this point (2005). See Rodin (2008: 65) and McMahan (2009: 82–83).

11 To this point, Benbaji, Statman, and I share a broadly similar view (Benbaji 2011: 50–52, 2008: 487; Benbaji and Statman 2019). My argument concerning military norms differs in two ways from Benbaji and Statman. First, rather than asserting that the laws of war are moralized by virtue of their fairness and mutual benefit to all participants, I argue that military norms are institutionally mediated expressions of collective moral responsibilities (cf. Benbaji 2008: 600, 2011: 50). Military norms exist prior to law, serving as a potential moral foundation for the formation of just laws. Second, and relatedly, Benbaji argues that enlistees tacitly accept the privileges and liabilities of service personnel articulated in international law, regardless of whether or not all subjectively understand or agree with these terms (2011: 45). Benbaji's and Statman's reliance on tacit consent to justify the entire war convention

136 *The moral equality of combatants*

exposes their arguments to the standard critiques of Locke's notion of tacit consent, namely that it is dubious to base X's real obligations on arrangements he ought to consent to. I will argue that the moral dimensions of soldiering are set forth by the contractualist model via hypothetical consent; they adhere to the profession and provide grounds for critique or praise of service members regardless of a particular service member's subjective understanding of his role. Hypothetical consent only articulates the dimensions of the role. Service members are bound to obey because of their duty to support just institutions. Space limitations required omitting an entire chapter criticizing Benbaji's and Statman's method of moralizing the laws of war; I hope to publish it separately as an article titled "Moralizing the War Convention" (unpublished).

12 On the duty to obey unjust laws in a basically just state, see Skerker (2010: 35–38), Rawls (1971: 351–354), Locke (1983: 48), Kant (1991a: 59, 1991b).

References

Benbaji, Y. (2008) "A Defense of the Traditional War Convention," *Ethics*, 118: 464–495.

Benbaji, Y. (2011) "The Moral Power of Soldiers to Undertake the Duty of Obedience," *Ethics*, 122: 50–52.

Benbaji, Y. and Statman, D. (2019) *War by Agreement*, Oxford: Oxford University Press.

Camenisch, P. (1983) *Grounding Professional Ethics in a Pluralistic Society*, New York: Haven.

Gauthier, D. (1987) *Morals By Agreement*, Oxford: Oxford University Press.

Gewirth, A. (1986) "Professional Ethics: The Separatist Thesis," *Ethics*, 96(2): 282–300.

Habermas, J. (1985) *The Theory of Communicative Action*, Boston, MA: Beacon Press.

Harsanyi, J. (1982) "Morality and the Theory of Rational Behavior," in Sen, A. and Williams, B. (eds), *Utilitarianism and Beyond*, Cambridge: Cambridge University Press.

Hobbes, T. (1994) *The Leviathan*, Indianapolis, IN: Hackett Press.

Kant, I. (1991a) "What is Enlightenment?" in Reiss, E. (ed.), *Political Writings*, Cambridge: Cambridge University Press.

Kant, I. (1991b) "On the Common Saying, 'This May be True in Theory, But it Does Not Apply in Practice," in Reiss, E. (ed.), *Political Writings*, Cambridge: Cambridge University Press.

Kant, I. (1991c) *The Metaphysics of Morals*, in Reiss, E. (ed.), *Political Writings*, Cambridge: Cambridge University Press.

Kutz, C. (2005) "The Difference Uniforms Make," *Philosophy & Public Affairs*, 33(2): 148–180.

Locke, J. (1983) *A Letter Concerning Toleration*, Indianapolis, IN: Hackett.

Mapel, D. (1998) "Coerced Moral Agents? Individual Responsibility for Military Service," *Journal of Political Philosophy*, 6(2): 171–189.

McMahan, J. (2009) *Killing in War*, Oxford: Clarendon Press.

Miller, S. (2010) *The Moral Foundations of Social Institutions*, Cambridge: Cambridge University Press.

Morris, C. (1996) "A Contractarian Account of Moral Justification," in Sinnott-Armstrong, W. and Timmons, M. (eds), *Moral Knowledge?* Oxford: Oxford University Press.

Nagel, T. (1978) "Ruthlessness in Public Life," in Hampshire, S. (ed.), *Public and Private Morality*, Cambridge: Cambridge University Press.

Nagel, T. (1991) *Equality and Partiality*, New York: Oxford University Press.

The foundations of military norms 137

Norman, R. (1995) *Ethics, Killing and War*, Cambridge: Cambridge University Press.

Pitkin, H. (1965) "Obligation and Consent–I," *The American Political Science Review*, 59(4): 990–999.

Rawls, J. (1971) *A Theory of Justice*, Cambridge: Cambridge University Press.

Rodin, D. (2002) *War and Self-Defense*, Oxford: Clarendon Press.

Rodin, D. (2008) "The Moral Inequality of Soldiers: Why *jus in bello* Asymmetry is Half Right," in Rodin, D. and Shue, H. (eds), *Just and Unjust Warriors*, Oxford: Oxford University Press.

Scanlon, T. (1975) "Nozick on Rights, Liberty, and Property," *Philosophy and Public Affairs*, 6(1): 3–25.

Scanlon, T. (1998) *What We Owe to Each Other*, Cambridge, MA: Belknap Press.

Shue, H. (2008) "Do We Need a 'Morality of War'?" in Rodin, D. and Shue, H. (eds), *Just and Unjust Warriors*, Oxford: Oxford University Press.

Skerker, M. (2010) *An Ethics of Interrogation*, Chicago, IL: University of Chicago Press.

Southwood, N. (2010) *Contractualism and the Foundations of Morality*, Oxford: Oxford University Press.

Thomas, W. (2007) "Unjust War and the Catholic Soldier," *Journal of Religious Ethics*, 35(3): 509–525.

Walzer, M. (2006) "Response to Jeff McMahan," *Philosophia*, 34(6): 43–45.

Wasserstrom, R. (1988) "Lawyers as Professionals: Some Moral Issues," in Callahan, J. (ed.), *Ethical Issues in Professional Life*, New York: Oxford University Press.

Waldron, J. (1987) "Theoretical Foundations of Liberalism," *Philosophical Quarterly*, 37(147): 127–150.

Zohar, N. (2004) "Innocence and Complex Threats: Upholding the War Ethic and the Condemnation of Terrorism," *Ethics*, 114: 734–751.

6 Military norms

I Collectivization in military ethics

i Introduction

For service personnel, military duty is the institutionally mediated expression of the collective moral responsibility to provide security for a community. This collective moral responsibility explains *why* military duty is morally binding on service personnel. The hypothetical consent of all affected by military operations can be modeled to detail the norms constituting military duty for all service personnel, wherever they may serve. These norms detail *what* any service member, anywhere, is supposed to do. Sections I and II of this chapter will articulate those norms. Section III will explain how norm-compliant actions do not wrong the targets of military violence.

ii Collectivization in jus in bello

Revisionists radically challenge traditional construals of *jus in bello* targeting. The traditional moral and legal view is that all uniformed enemy personnel are potentially targetable with lethal violence anytime during a conflict anywhere on the globe except when they are surrendering, gravely injured, or already detained by the agent military. It is their membership in the military rather than any kind of variable, personal quality of liability that makes them targetable in wartime. While some revisionists make practical concessions when it comes to targeting groups of personnel on the unjust side (McMahan 2006: 48, 2008: 32; Kutz 2008: 69; Coady 2008: 162) or argue that the importance of defeating unjust aggression permits the disvalue of killing some non-liable or less liable enemy personnel, revisionist just war theory argues that the "deep morality" of war prefers targeting based on individual liability. For example, McMahan argues that the just side should make targeting decisions based on reasonable presumptions about enemy troops' individual moral liability when it can do so and still meet its tactical goals, such as when such goals would be equally met by targeting an elite enemy unit or a unit of conscripts (McMahan 2006: 47). Further, according to the revisionists, the moral restrictions on defensive violence in civilian life also apply in war so the just military defender is in principle

Military norms 139

limited to using only that amount of violence that is subjectively necessary for him to use to neutralize the liable party's imminent threat and that is objectively proportionate in terms of the damage it inflicts compared to the harm it forestalls (some scholars discount the value of the harm inflicted on liable targets) (see, e.g., McMahan 2006: 48–49).

It is important to consider which parties are targetable before discussing the main components of *jus in bello* since the principle of necessity restricts the killing of members of the targetable group, discrimination requires exclusive direct targeting of the targetable group, and proportionality compares the value of incapacitating members of the targetable group with the disvalue of harming members of non-targetable groups. The arguments in Parts I and II of this book undercut the moral basis of individualized targeting. A positive defense of the received views of *jus in bello*, and ultimately of the moral equality of combatants, has to begin now with a defense of collectivized targeting.

The security standard prefers collectivized to individualized targeting rules. The standard also endorses norms incorporating collectivized versions of the limits on defensive force rather than construals of necessity, imminence, and proportionality referencing the individual. Broadly speaking, the security standard endorses norms and tactics leading to effective security operations. These operations have to reach a minimum deontological threshold and be more rights-respecting than near-equally effective alternatives, but there is no point in considering the deontological merits of norms and tactics that do not conduce to profession's legitimate ends. It will therefore benefit us in a discussion of targeting rules to consider military commanders' perception of the collective nature of their enemy's threatening posture. These practical concerns are morally relevant because of their role in the prosecution of just wars.

The enemy military as a whole represents an imminent threat to the agent military since all able-bodied service personnel are part of a joint enterprise directed via corporate intention to threaten the agent military.[1] It can be assumed that combatants presently uninvolved in operations threatening to the other side (at a rear base, for example) will be involved in the future.

The collectivized version of imminence leads to a collectivized version of the necessity criterion. The enemy military as a whole is not always a threat to a given opposing service member. Rather, it is a threat to the opposing military as a whole. Whereas there is a very low likelihood during a war that the enemy will attack a particular, say, logistician, at a rear base, in any given moment there is a very high likelihood the enemy military will attack *some* portion of the adversary in any given moment. It thus is necessary for a military to defend itself and its state's interests as a whole by neutralizing enemy targets causally integral to that mission. It may be necessary to kill support personnel—whom a civilian defender would rarely need to kill in an analogous situation to avert an imminent attack (e.g., a mobster's mechanic)—because of the role they play in the enemy military force, directly supporting the lethal work of the kinetic operators.[2]

The temporal span of a war suggests thinking about the good done in a collectivized proportionality calculation in the following manner. The good

140 *The moral equality of combatants*

of neutralizing a given target can be calculated by considering the neutralization's role in the agent military's overall strategy—its role in forestalling the overall harm of the enemy's war effort—rather than with respect to the parties immediately benefited.[3] For example, sinking a destroyer when it is still out of cruise missile range of the agent's coastal targets is disproportionate in the moment of the sinking since no agent combatant or noncombatant lives are protected from imminent harm. Yet the sinking is proportionate if the entire span of the war is viewed as a single temporal unit. Doing so permits the agent to consider the lives that would be endangered days after the opportunity for the pre-emptive attack arises on the positive side of the proportionality calculation. A commander is incentivized to consider the war as a temporal whole and attack any causally relevant parts of the enemy military whenever they are exposed, because the enemy is also scouting and attacking her force's vulnerable points. The commander has a responsibility to her troops and to her state to avoid needlessly sacrifice troops by eschewing relatively easier targets and missions, say, in the days before they become an imminent threat.

Let us now turn to the targeting rules preferred by the security standard with these practical concerns in mind. Regarding targeting permission, self-defense paradigms depending on the attacker's posing of a direct threat[4] to justify a defensive response lack the resources to target support personnel, limiting defensive violence to the riskiest tactics of engaging the less than 10% of service members engaged in kinetic activities. This restriction would likely fail the reliability, efficacy, and efficiency elements of the security standard as it would preclude the kind of opportunistic targeting preferable from tactical, operational, and strategic points of view. A targeting rule based on individualized direct threats would also fare poorly with respect to the security standard's proportionality standard. A conventional force committed to targeting direct threats alone would seem to have to wait until enemy forces point weapons at them or begin firing before they can respond.[5] If the enemy did not see him coming, the agent would have to expose himself so the enemy could decide if he wanted to become a direct threat, surrender, or flee. Obeying a targeting rule limited to direct threats would therefore entail the agent exposing himself to the highest level of lethal risk every time he engaged the enemy. The ratio of benefits to harms following such a rule is far inferior to the ratio associated with a rule permitting the agent to attack his enemy opportunistically.

The minimal models of liability many revisionists propose for *indirect* threats *would* permit the just side's opportunistic targeting since almost all service personnel are indirect threats. The agent can then proceed almost exactly as he would with a collectivized targeting rule. Yet Part I of this book argued against those models of liability and Part II showed that strategically significant numbers of enemy personnel cannot be deemed individually liable for the unjust war with a culpability standard of individual liability nor with less demanding individual models relying on participatory intention. Thus,

Military norms 141

rules for fighting just wars where the just side was limited to targeting individually liable personnel could not competitively meet the practical elements of the security standard.

Regarding limits to just self-defense, in most individual self-defense paradigms, a defender is only permitted to respond to an imminent unjust attack with the amount of force necessary for her to ward off the attack. The response must also be proportionate. Tactical difficulties would ensue in war if combatants could only incur proportionate damage on enemies when it was personally necessary for them to do so in response to imminent attacks. Barring occasions when they were trapped or surprised, it would not be necessary for mobile combatants to use defensive violence because they would be able to reposition ahead of enemies before they posed an imminent threat. The necessity criterion would seem to preclude attacking the unjust side on account of past wrongs (e.g., a cross-border raid, the seizing of territory, or the sponsoring of a terrorist attack) or counter-attacking after an initial unjust attack had been repulsed.[6] The proportionality limitation would make certain opportunistic attacks difficult since little harm is being immediately prevented by killing sleeping, retreating, or traveling troops.[7]

The abstemious warfare that would seem to follow an individualized defense paradigm would fail the security standard for not efficiently and efficaciously executing national security goals. The limitations would also seem to promise to extend the duration of wars for lack of definitive engagements between the opposing forces, exposing combatants and noncombatants to more risk while also allowing the unjust situation that perhaps initiated the war to persist.

The practical elements of the security standard suggest a preference for granting service personnel the flexibility of targeting any combatant causally relevant to the enemy's defensive or offensive posture, in keeping with the agent's tactical, operational, and strategic considerations, rather than only those troops involved in direct action or those liable according to some construal of individual responsibility. Assuming the agent is a competent tactician, it is self-evident why targeting the enemy according to the agent's tactical and operational desiderata is a more reliable, efficient, and efficacious way to win a war than to target the enemy according to any other criteria. A rule of collectivized targeting is a more proportionate way of winning the war than a rule insisting on individualized targeting since the agent can choose opportunistic or asymmetric engagements where the net good done (the number of allied lives protected minus the number of allied lives lost in the effort) will likely greatly exceed the net good done after an operation limited to individualized targeting. It is important to clarify that I am collectivizing the type of proportionality invoked in individual self-defense (i.e., narrow proportionality) rather than in *jus in bello*.[8] In the former type, the good is the harm averted for the defender and the disvalue the harm defensively inflicted on the attacker.

A rule permitting collectivized targeting would *prima facie* seem less rights-respecting than any rule geared toward individual liability. Nonetheless,

142   *The moral equality of combatants*

a collectivized targeting rule extended to all combatants meets the rights-respecting element of the security standard better than individualized targeting rules (or alternate collective targeting rules) if we take into account the rights of both combatants and noncombatants. To explain this point, first, it needs to be made clear that we will consider the right to life as the most inclusive right of those that might be infringed by military operations. Second, we will model combatants' and noncombatants' consent to various levels of lethal risk rather than an infringement on their right to life, since X's toleration of a tactic presupposes X's continued life to enjoy the tactic's benefits. Rules for the use of tactics projecting the lowest numbers of casualties will be considered the most rights-respecting in that they will promise *ex ante* to pose the lowest lethal risk to a given person in the target group.

An individualized targeting rule closer to civilian self-defense rules, only permitting attacks on imminent threats, benefits service members on the tactical defense since there are fewer times when defenders pose risks to attackers than attackers pose risks to defenders. Further, this proposed rule also gives combatants greater control over the risk to which they are exposed since poorly supervised individuals or whole units could continually retreat and/or take cover so as not to pose a direct threat to others. Combatants on the offense[9] would be benefited by a targeting rule permitting collectivization since they would be permitted to choose advantageous times to attack enemy combatants such as when they are sleeping, in transit, or otherwise unsuspecting (e.g., in ambushes). Further, they could nullify the potency of a fighting force by attacking support staff rather than the more dangerous kinetic operators.

In each tactical exchange, there will be varying numbers of attackers and defenders. Over the course of many wars or sets of wars, we can expect the advantages of collectivized or individualized targeting rules to even out. Thus, we do not have abstract grounds to say that a collectivized targeting rule would be considered the most rights-respecting if the hypothetical consent of service personnel alone was modeled. However, collectivized targeting of combatants would be preferable if we take into consideration the consent of both combatants and noncombatants. First, collectivized targeting of all combatants to the exclusion of noncombatants obviously benefits noncombatants. Second, collectivized targeting of combatants would promise to end wars sooner, perhaps benefiting noncombatants by accomplishing their state's national security goals faster and, at any rate, exposing them to collateral risk for a shorter period of time. Combatants as a whole are benefited by shorter wars for the same reason,[10] though, as just mentioned, there will be an asymmetry of benefit in a given war for the side that is more frequently or more successfully on the offense. Since, *ex ante*, one might just as likely be a combatant on the tactical offense or defense, the asymmetrical advantage for those on offense drops out as a theoretical consideration, and we are left with noncombatants' reasons for preferring collectivized targeting of all combatants.

II Five military norms

i Preliminaries

I argued in Chapter 5 that it was gratuitous to defend a particular construal of hypothetical consent since we should not expect different construals to yield different military norms. It is worth exemplifying this consensus now to underline the optimization of consequentialist and deontological aims that security-standard-compliant military norms seek to forge. We can imagine two preferences guiding actual people in a dialogue (whether governed or ungoverned by ideal communication rules) to subsequently endorse a pair of rules for military action. First, in a given war or in the run-up to a war between states A and B, we can imagine the noncombatants of state A wanting their combatants to prosecute their state's legitimate national security causes against state B. Both the combatants and noncombatants of state A presumably would prefer combatants B to simply surrender or stay home. Meanwhile, noncombatants B want their combatants to prosecute state B's interests and both the noncombatants and combatants of state B presumably would prefer combatants A to quit. Second, we can assume that none of the noncombatants or combatants want to be killed. Given that the first set of preferences are contrary to one another—a rule only allowing one military to prosecute its goals would be rejected by everyone in the target state—the only mutually acceptable rule to all involved would be to allow each military to try to accomplish its goals. Bearing in mind the two preferences, for the prosecution of military goals and the avoidance of death, we can imagine there would be consent to a second rule regarding use of force that strikes an optimal balance between maximizing each sides' ability to achieve its goals while minimizing the risks to all.

We will not see the canceling out of preferences witnessed in the non-ideal versions of hypothetical consent if we start with a version idealizing both the consenters and the communication rules they abide, but we will nonetheless end up with the same kind of rules for military behavior. Consenters operating behind a veil of ignorance or with some other kind of mechanism to ensure impartiality can be modeled as endorsing a rule(s) for military action with the following two features. The rule(s) permit any basically just political entity to pursue its legitimate national security interests while minimizing risk to all affected. These features characterize the rule(s) since the model consenters could in principle be either the party benefited or threatened by military action.

The security standard is that set of rules, identified by hypothetical consent, optimizing the maximization of the morally important benefits of military action and the minimization of risk to all affected.[11] The military norms detailing the contours of military duty are the security standard's vehicles for seeking the efficient attainment of morally relevant military goals with a minimal amount of negative moral side effects. Upon isolating the most efficient, effective, reliable, and proportionate norms and tactics to the relevant military goals among available options, the standard then seeks the most rights-respecting norms and tactics among the practically sound options. The security standard is guided by a

144   *The moral equality of combatants*

principle of reciprocity since the modeling group on whose behalf norms and tactics are considered is all people potentially affected by military action. So the beneficiaries of security-standard-compliant norms and tactics could also be the targets of the relevant norm-guided actions.

Security-standard-compliant military norms are not limited to the following five, but I will restrict my comments to necessity, discrimination, proportionality, a prohibition on gratuitous suffering, and obedience. These norms emerge as we apply the security standard to military actions affecting three logical groupings: combatants, noncombatants, and groupings in which combatants and noncombatants are mixed. Necessity and a prohibition on gratuitous suffering are the only relevant norms applicable to an agent military facing combatants alone. Discrimination is relevant when noncombatants are physically near combatants or when infrastructure used by both is targeted. Proportionality is relevant when noncombatant casualties appear unavoidable because of their proximity to crucial military targets.

Military norms place limits on the collectivized targeting rules discussed in the last section. We learned that individual liability does not matter from a standpoint of military practicality. Only the causal relevance of targeted service personnel to the enemy military's threatening posture is relevant. This causal rationale for collectivized targeting does not require targeting all enemy service personnel. Rational assessments of a military's needs serve as the basis of the military norms of *jus in bello*. For example, assessment of a military's needs indicates that the enemy military should be viewed as a collective threat, but that only a certain number of enemy personnel need to be attacked in order to achieve a tactical objective. It violates the norm of necessity to attack personnel in excess of that number.

A final note: the contractualist model will produce versions of familiar military norms. This should not be surprising. Late medieval *jus in bello* is an expression of natural law-based morality, which sees national security as a key moral good necessary for human flourishing and which limits the means pursuant to security out of equal respect for all human beings. In early modern times, *jus in bello* was codified in international law, which assumes state sovereignty and adopts the cosmopolitan perspective on the treatment of combatants and noncombatants necessary to win international agreement on treaties. Thus, the contractualist model shares with mature *jus in bello*'s historical roots a cosmopolitan perspective that has the resources to treat agent and adversary alike as well as a respect for political entities' national security imperatives. The natural lawyer derives cosmopolitan norms from the foundational view that humans are equal by virtue of their common species membership or status as creatures of God. The contractualist produces cosmopolitan norms that logically should win the consent of all the people in the world. The international lawyer writing treaties does in concrete form what the contractualist does abstractly; the treaty writer drafts laws that can win the actual consent of adversaries and that therefore must both facilitate, if not optimize, a balance between the pursuit of adversarial parties' interests along with their mutual protection from harm.

Military norms 145

ii Necessity

We can identify the norm of necessity when we apply the security standard to actions affecting combatants alone. The unnecessary use of force is inconsistent with the security standard. Killing enemy troops or destroying materiel or infrastructure when it is not tactically necessary exceeds what in the abstract would be a reliable and effective means of defeating the enemy. The unnecessary use of force is not an efficient way of waging war since weapons and personnel are being wasted in excessive attacks. Attacks involving unnecessarily large amounts of lethal force will often be disproportionate since the tactically unnecessary damage done to the enemy may well exceed the harm prevented by the agent. A norm encouraging or permitting unnecessary force will likely lead to more disproportionate actions over time. Even in cases when such a great harm is prevented by the action that it remains proportionate, the security standard disfavors relatively disproportionate actions when more proportionate actions are possible.

The failure of wanton killing to meet the practical elements of the security standard means that tactics breaching the norm of necessity violate an institutional right of service personnel. Institutional rights have moral content but only exist in the context of a particular institution (Miller's usage); these rights have moral content insofar as the relevant institutional norms are institutionally mediated expressions of ordinary moral principles. Wanton killing is not a violation of service members' natural right against being attacked. Volunteer service personnel expressly join a profession whose parameters are dictated by security-standard-compliant norms. By enlisting, they accept a role in which they can be directly targeted by enemy conventional combatants or privileged irregulars in war (explained in sub-section III.iii), but only when the attacks occur according to military norms. Service personnel have natural and institutional claim-rights against being attacked by their comrades and by noncombatants, and institutional rights against being wantonly killed by enemy combatants since using force leading to unnecessary casualties is impermissible according to the rules characterizing the profession. To draw a partial comparison, boxers cede their claim-rights against being attacked but only to their opponents—not to fans or ring officials—and only via certain blows. While combatants' permission to enforce their institutional rights are moot since they are already fighting their enemy, the enemy can be criticized, shamed, and punished for war crimes *post-bellum*.

iii Discrimination, proportionality, ban on unnecessary suffering

A clarification is in order prior to discussing the norm of discrimination and the proportionality element of the security standard. I will invoke three different proportionality-related concepts in what follows: the proportionality limitation to justifiable self-defense, the security standard's proportionality standard, and

146 *The moral equality of combatants*

the *in bello* norm of proportionality. First, there is the proportionality limitation invoked in individual self-defense—"narrow proportionality"—where the good is the harm averted for the defender, and the disvalue (weighed against the good) is the harm defensively inflicted on the attacker (McMahan 2009: 20). Second, sub-section I.ii discussed the collectivization of this sort of proportionality, so that benefits to the agent military were compared to harm to the enemy military. The proportionality element of the security standard refers to this type of collectivized proportionality when combatants alone are targeted. Third, when the target is mixed, the disvalue of noncombatant casualties is included and the *jus in bello* norm of proportionality becomes relevant. This norm, which McMahan calls wide proportionality,[12] compares the value of all lives protected on the agent's side to the disvalue of noncombatant lives lost on the enemy side. The lives of enemy combatants do not factor into the equation as a disvalue.[13]

Targeting differentiated groups of combatants. The norm of discrimination states that combatants are morally required to *distinguish* between combatants and noncombatants and to engage in operations in a *discriminate* fashion, directly targeting combatants alone and choosing weapon systems and tactics conducive to the discriminate delivery of force (Haque 2017: chapter 5). How is this norm defended by the security standard? Directly targeting combatants and their materiel is obviously a generally reliable, efficacious, and efficient method of winning a war. Regarding proportionality, consider a discriminate and indiscriminate attack on the same concentration of enemy troops in an urban environment using the same weapon system, say, a 500-lb bomb.

Discriminate attack

Each military has 1,000 combatants. One enemy casualty preserves two agent military lives over the course of the war. All troops are equally important to the war effort. The first military to lose 20% of its manpower will surrender. The discriminate attacker draws on intelligence, surveillance, and reconnaissance (ISR) to pinpoint the target's location and then uses a laser designator to guide the bomb to the target. The indiscriminate attacker engages in no ISR and simply drops the bomb from an airborne platform. The discriminate attack kills ten enemy soldiers and the indiscriminate attack kills one soldier (it largely misses the concentration of troops).

The discriminate attack reduces enemy strength by 1% and preserves 20 agent lives, 2% of the agent force. The indiscriminate attack eliminates 0.1% of the force and preserves 2 agent soldiers, 0.2% of the force. While the discriminate attack has greater benefit to the agent military than the indiscriminate attack, the proportionality ratio of good for the agent compared to disvalue to the enemy across the two attacks remains the same. However, the military employing similarly discriminate attacks (holding other variables the same) will force its

Military norms 147

enemy to surrender sooner, in an average of 20 bombing sorties rather than 200 indiscriminate sorties. The briefer campaign holds numerous benefits for the discriminate attacker in terms of cost and lives likely preserved (pilots endangered during sorties, other troops endangered by the otherwise-incapacitated enemy troops, and agent noncombatants endangered by the enemy's actions) while the harm to the enemy military remains the same. Thus, discriminate attacks on differentiated groups of combatants scores better than indiscriminate attacks according to the security standard's proportionality element.

Targeting combatants alone is more rights-respecting than targeting noncombatants alone or a mix of the two groups since only combatants have expressly consented to a regime in which they will be unilaterally targeted by enemy combatants (see below). Revisionists have attempted to show that some noncombatants are liable to being killed, and so, on this line of thought, targeting combatants alone would not necessarily be more rights-respecting than alternatives. Since I largely eliminated their minimal modes of liability, we can focus on combatants' hypothetical and express consent to an efficacious regime of only targeting combatants as making the relevant difference between combatants and noncombatants in terms of rights.

The contractualist model's norm of discrimination is not an absolute norm as a liability-based discrimination norm might be. The current legal view is that factories producing military materiel and dual-use facilities like power stations are targetable, provided that the number of foreseen noncombatant deaths and amount of suffering associated with the attack is not disproportionate to the concrete military value of the target. Yet the civilian employees of these facilities are not legally targetable *per se*. Under most circumstances, the contractualist model would also reject targeting defense industry workers in their homes on account of failing both deontological and practical elements of the security standard. The deontological (rights-respecting) concern with attacking noncombatants is clear: they have not joined a profession characterized by a rule permitting lethal targeting. Regarding the practical elements, low-skilled workers can usually be easily replaced and less fungible personnel like aircraft engineers make minor causal contributions to an overall war effort that usually take years to bear fruit. It would thus be foolish to ignore frontline troops, attack engineers, and then wait for the tactical effects of subsequent supply chain problems.

Modern militaries often employ large numbers of civilian contractors to work alongside military personnel in support roles. These are not munitions workers toiling in stateside factories but technical experts filling ordinary military billets (because of manpower shortages) or providing vital specialized technical or analytical assistance to support military operations in stateside or forward bases. Assuming they are unarmed, they are in a curious position. Unlike factory workers who build materiel in peace-time as well as in war, they are an integral part of the military operations; unlike secretaries, janitors, and cooks on bases, they fulfill a uniquely military role, but unlike members of the military (except chaplains and sometimes doctors) they are not provided offensive training and arms. The fact that they are an integral part of the collective threat facing the

148 *The moral equality of combatants*

enemy suggests that they may be counted as combatants in proportionality calculations when bases and defense installations are attacked from long range. Inasmuch as all attacks on targetable persons are governed by necessity, though, their non-threatening nature considered individually suggests that they should not be directly targeted by infantrymen in a close-quarters fight.

Targeting differentiated groups of noncombatants. Revisionists reject the traditional construal of discrimination since noncombatants may be more liable than combatants on the unjust side to defensive violence. Targeting noncombatants could also lead to a quicker end to the war, in some instances, saving lives on the just side. Though I have shown how targeting combatants alone meets the security standard, it will be helpful to use the security standard to respond to the revisionists on external grounds and answer questions some might have regarding possible exceptions to the norm of discrimination.

When combatants and noncombatants are clearly differentiated, targeting noncombatants and their possessions in lieu of combatants is neither an efficacious nor efficient way of blunting the enemy's military force. It is true that targeting a state's economic base could eventually deprive the military of supplies as well as the government of income. Targeting medical facilities could also prevent the return of service personnel whose injuries would not otherwise preclude a return to the battlefield. Yet this tactic is indirect, taking time to catch up with the military. Directly attacking noncombatant targets initially exposes the attacker to less risk, but the attacker will engage in this approach at his peril if he does not first defeat the enemy's military.

Directly attacking a clearly differentiated group of noncombatants usually fails the proportionality element of the security standard because little good is likely being accomplished for the agent military with such an attack. Noncombatant casualties can count as a good to the extent that the killing of civilian workers in defense industries can indirectly aid the military campaign, though usually not as much as combatant deaths. The low proportionality score, along with low efficiency and (obviously) deontological scores, will usually preclude the tactic. The minimal benefit gained in targeting noncombatants is germane to security-standard-construal proportionality because the agent typically exposes himself to risk in attacking a target. Thus, the benefit derived from destroying a militarily valuable target has to be discounted by the number of agent casualties incurred in the attack. For example, if destroying a tank is estimated to save ten agent combatants over the course of the conflict, but it is estimated that on average one agent is lost in each attack, then the proportional benefit of destroying the tank, excluding other consequences, is a net nine lives. Military agents are endangered to varying degrees by the defensive measures arrayed around their targets. Both military and civilian sites may be guarded, say, with anti-aircraft systems. It is reasonable to think that defenses would be shifted to civilian areas if the agent military shows a propensity to attack those areas. Assuming a steady average agent casualty rate over time attacking both military and civilian areas/targets, discriminate attacks on combatants alone will fare better in terms of proportionality than alternate targeting schemes since attacks on purely military

Military norms 149

targets can be expected to have greater benefit to the agent than indiscriminate attacks or attacks directed at noncombatants.

Targeting mixed groups of combatants and noncombatants. To continue with the discussion of discrimination, in counter-insurgent warfare, the conventional or more powerful military force might resort to a modern variation of *chevauchée* in order to force concealed, dispersed, and highly mobile enemy fighters to come meet the attackers *en masse. Chevauchée* was a common medieval tactic of laying waste to the countryside and civilian settlements in order to goad a reluctant group of knights to meet for a decisive pitched battle. It is not hard to imagine a counter-insurgent force attacking a civilian area in the hope that dispersed insurgents return to defend their families. *Chevauchée* suffers in terms of the efficiency, proportionality, and deontological elements of the security standard.

Indiscriminately attacking mixed groups of combatants and noncombatants due to a failure to distinguish, or to use indiscriminate tactics following distinction, may be more efficient and reliable than carefully hunting down combatants mixed among noncombatants. Partly for this reason, counter-insurgent campaigns often amount to, or devolve into, general counter-population attacks. Yet a caveat-free norm (not requiring discrimination) governing attacks on mixed enemy targets might score poorly with respect to the security standard's proportionality element because the agent may impose little damage on enemy combatants and therefore achieve little good. Since the target group is mixed, the *in bello* norm of proportionality (i.e., wide proportionality) is also apt to negatively judge the action even if the results are not disproportionate in the security standard sense of proportionality (i.e., collectivized narrow proportionality). This follows because an attack that incurs significant losses to the enemy at low cost to the agent may still be disproportionate because of the disvalue of noncombatant deaths. Whatever the verdict regarding proportionality, indiscriminate attacks on mixed groups will usually run afoul of the security standard's deontological element.

Proportionality. The traditional military norm of discrimination perhaps comports more with people's intuition than the norm of proportionality since the former more closely tracks the norms surrounding self-defense. As in typical civilian self-defense scenarios, discrimination only permits targeting those directly posing a threat with violence, or (departing more from the civilian comparison) those engaged in a threatening enterprise. The legal and conventional just war construals of *in bello* proportionality are more puzzling. The norm does not demand an intuitively satisfying absolute ban on harming noncombatants. It considers both sides' tactical goals goods worthy of objective respect in a proportionality calculation. Recall, revisionists argue the unjust side's tactical goals cannot be considered goods because they are objectively contributing to an unjust strategic end. Contrary to the conventional view, neither preventing harm to combatants (and sometimes, noncombatants) on the unjust side nor the killing of combatants on the just side should be considered a good since those groups are liable and non-liable to harm, respectively (see McMahan 2009: 25, 27, 30).

150 *The moral equality of combatants*

Even apart from revisionist concerns, it seems perverse, given the moral value the norm of discrimination places on noncombatants, that a military is permitted to knowingly kill a number of noncombatants that is limited only by its tactical ambitions. For example, a unit may be proportionally justified in collaterally killing one noncombatant pursuant to destroying a tank, but justified in killing 100 noncombatants if seeking to destroy a nuclear weapons lab.

A defense of the symmetrical legal and conventional just war construals of *in bello* proportionality must explain why each side's subjective valuation of its tactical goals is considered objectively valid in a proportionality calculation and each side's possible subjective *devaluation* of its enemy's noncombatant population is supplanted by an egalitarian assessment of the equal worth of all noncombatants. The contractualist model is able to defend a version of proportionality permitting all sides in a war to pursue their tactical goals while at the same time minimizing noncombatant casualties. The norm permits attacks that should not cause a greater number of noncombatant casualties than the number of allied combatant and noncombatant lives preserved through the action. It also requires the actor to modify the attack so as to minimize noncombatant casualties to the greatest extent possible consistent with successful engagement of the target.

A planned discriminate attack on a mixed target can promise collateral noncombatant casualty figures grossly disproportionate to the projected number of lives protected by the target's destruction, equal to the number protected, favorably low compared to the number protected, or anywhere on a spectrum between these three points. Proportionality projections are highly speculative for two reasons: there are challenges in estimating noncombatant casualties, especially in exigent circumstances, and even steeper challenges in estimating the number of lives protected by destroying a particular target like a tank. This second figure includes those immediately threatened by the tank and those protected by the troops who would have been killed by the tank. Given the uncertainty of this calculation, an action-guiding proportionality norm that is actually usable would likely need to distinguish impermissible from permissible actions on the above-mentioned spectrum at a point separating extremely disproportionate actions from all the other actions on the spectrum instead of the 1:1 protected/harmed "midpoint." Given the uncertainty about noncombatant casualties and the fact that the agent can make a reasonable case that the destruction of each of her targets will protect dozens of lives over the course of the war, only flagrantly disproportionate estimates "shocking the conscience" will likely and reasonably appear disproportionate to the agent, such as destroying an apartment building to kill one sniper. (The next chapter will explain why all affected can consent to service members hewing to action-guiding norms with reasonable subjective thresholds for action rather than objective thresholds.) Thus, going forward, we will understand the contractualist version of *in bello* proportionality to guide service personnel to refrain from attacks promising extremely disproportionate outcomes.

A norm directing service personnel to attack tactically significant targets without a proportionality restriction is a norm permitting extremely disproportionate

Military norms 151

attacks. Such a norm indicates that collateral noncombatant deaths need not factor into agents' calculations about whether or how to engage a target. Let us consider such a norm with the security standard in order to contextualize proportionality norms. A targeting norm without proportionality restrictions might well be more reliable than a norm restricting agents to using proportionate force. Imagine 20 snipers firing from the roofs of 20 apartment buildings. The caveat-free norm would permit destroying the buildings from long distance with stand-off weapons as a means of neutralizing the snipers. Since counter-sniper teams can miss or be killed by the snipers they seek, destroying the buildings from a safe distance is a more reliable tactic than maneuvering counter-sniper teams into position where they can attempt to shoot the snipers. A tactic that is 100% reliable is also obviously efficacious. The absence of a proportionality restriction would also lend itself to efficacious operations in the sense that a commander would not to need to call off an otherwise-efficacious strike foreseeably causing a disproportionate level of harm or damage. A caveat-free targeting norm can pass the security standard proportionality element, if, for example, ten allied troops are saved by killing a two-man scout-sniper team.

Yet a caveat-free norm is disqualified because of low efficiency and deontological scores. Assuming the same weapon system in both cases, it is obviously more efficient to scout, maneuver, and to fire one tank shell at a sniper's position than to destroy an entire building with 100 tank shells. While there will be some variation given the nature of the targets and weapon systems, overall, we can expect more proportionate tactics to be more efficient since tactics improving the proportionality calculation (achieving the objective while killing a smaller, strictly necessary number of enemies) will likely involve better target research, more accurate targeting, less ordnance delivered, and smaller blast radii. Finally, a caveat-free norm will obviously be less rights-respecting than an alternative directing the agent to take collaterally threatened noncombatants into account.

A proportionality norm for attacking mixed targets requiring agents to refrain from extremely disproportionate attacks will likely be somewhat less reliable and efficacious than a caveat-free norm regarding mixed targets. A proportionality norm will likely direct service personnel to take more risk in attacking. The norm might require aiming with more care, from a closer range, with smaller-caliber weapons or smaller munitions, and after spending more time to confirm target details. There could be situations where the only way to avoid extremely disproportionate attacks would be to avoid attacking at all or taking on so much risk that it would be suicidal for the agent to proceed. A caveat-free norm for mixed targets, again, will effectively permit the agent to use as much firepower as she wishes from whatever range with whatever targeting research she wishes to complete, so long as she is aiming at a military target. However, in proportionality's favor, from a practical standpoint, given the significant good plausibly achieved in terms of lives protected by destroying military targets, a norm prohibiting extremely disproportionate attacks will likely rarely completely prohibit attacks. Also, the amount of targeteering and weaponeering necessary to avoid extremely disproportionate attacks will likely lead to targeted strikes that

152 *The moral equality of combatants*

are nearly as efficacious as disproportionate saturation attacks. More targeted strikes will also save munitions that might have been wasted in disproportionate strikes. These extra munitions are then available to use in other militarily necessary strikes.

An attack will likely be more rights-respecting, proportionate, and efficient the more favorable the ratio between expected lives protected and noncombatant lives lost in the preceding proportionality calculation. The first element is self-explanatory. A planned attack promising a favorable wide proportionality ratio between military benefit and noncombatant casualties likely entails a favorable security-standard-construal proportionality ratio between the harm done to enemy combatants and harm prevented to the agent military. If an attack on an airfield meets the norm of proportionality (wide proportionality) due to expected 10:1 ratio of enemy combatants to noncombatant casualties, it will also likely score favorably regarding security standard proportionality for delivering a great benefit to the agent military compared to the risk incurred by the agent. While it will depend on contingencies regarding the target, the weapon system, and tactic for its use, an attack's wide proportionality will likely vary directly with its efficiency since the steps needed to make an attack more proportionate will likely involve more careful targeting, more targeting research, and the use of more accurate weapon systems. Thus, while a proportionality norm fares slightly worse than a caveat-free targeting norm in terms of reliability and efficacy, it scores much better on the other three metrics and its lower scores are not so low as to inhibit effective military operations over time.

The security standard indicates further specifications of the proportionality norm. I argued above that the only salient, action-guiding distinction for attacking mixed targets is between actions that are "extremely disproportionate attacks" and "not extremely disproportionate attacks." The latter category is clearly superior to the former by the lights of the security standard. Yet the security standard demands more of the agent than merely refraining from extremely disproportionate attacks. The deontological element of the security standard makes the contractualist model's proportionality norm more restrictive than some philosophical characterizations of it as well as more restrictive than the legal standard of proportionality. Say a given target's destruction is estimated to save 50 lives on the agent's side. Different available tactics/weapon systems provide commanders with three strike options with estimated collateral damage estimates of 15, ten, and five lives. Taking into account political sensitivities and the projected media impact, it is judged that ten casualties is proportionate to the destruction of the target. A norm only prohibiting disproportionate attacks lacks mechanisms for selecting the least harmful of the latter two proportionate attacks (five casualties). International law requires commanders to do more than refrain from disproportionate actions, also taking "precautions" to minimize noncombatant casualties. The contractualist version of the proportionality norm effectively combines the legal construals of proportionality and precaution. The deontological element of the security standard indicates that the norm or tactic best protecting the rights of affected parties among practically

Military norms 153

sound candidates is the most consent-worthy. So a proportionality norm with a secondary step directing the agent to select the action minimizing noncombatant casualties among those actions that are not extremely disproportionate is more consent-worthy than a proportionality norm without this secondary step.

The contractualist version of *in bello* (i.e., wide) proportionality is symmetrical like the legal and conventional just war construals of the norm. Both sides in a war may consider their tactical aims as goods in a proportionality calculation and must count foreign noncombatants as disvalues of equal (dis) value to their own noncombatant casualties. The contractualist model offers a simple, compelling explanation for this counter-intuitive symmetry. The contractualist model permits all sides to pursue their tactical goals subject to proportionality restrictions because this rule strikes an optimal balance between permitting protection for the agent's in-group and limiting risk to out-groups. This optimal balance between in- and out-groups is indicated by the hypothetical consent of those potentially affected by military operations. *Ex ante*, the consenters do not know which group they will populate, but can be modeled as consenting to a rule calling on all to respect each side's subjective valuation of tactical goals and an objective assessment of all noncombatants as morally equal. Considering the agent perspective, consenters want the rules to permit their pursuit of sound military strategy as a means of realizing their legitimate national security goals. Considering the noncombatant perspective, consenters want the rules to offer maximum protection to noncombatants consistent with military efficacy.

Revisionists argue that this symmetrical form of proportionality is impossible. The unjust side's tactical goals do not count as goods in a proportionality calculation since the goals' moral value is informed by the strategy the goals' advance and the liability of the potential casualties. The conventional view of a target's destruction by the unjust side would count the number of lives on the agent's side saved due to the target's destruction plus any enemy combatant deaths as positives and the number of foreign noncombatant casualties as negatives. The revisionist would only, at most, put some of the unjust agent's protected noncombatants on the positive side of the equation and treat the military advantages to the unjust side and all the *in bello*-compliant combatant and noncombatant casualties on the just side on the negative side (see McMahan 2009: 57). I have argued against the revisionists' linkage of the macro injustice of a war with the contributing actions performed by individual combatants, removing the grounds for revisionists counting some combatants' deaths differently on the basis of liability. It remains that tactical goals of the military on the unjust side objectively contribute to an unjust outcome. I have just explained how it is possible for both sides to accept, say, the bombing of the bridge by the unjust side as a good in a proportionality calculation and accept that the attack is permissible, provided a disproportionate number of noncombatants are not killed as a side effect of the bombing. The contractualist approach explains how each sides' tactical goals can be universally considered goods and how harm to each sides' noncombatant populations can be universally considered a disvalue.

154 *The moral equality of combatants*

Now explaining why a norm has certain equitable features—and so can permit reciprocal behavior among those covered by the norm—is not the same thing as showing that it is a part of a coherent account of the moral life. What I have done here is provide an account of symmetrical *in bello* proportionality that is not "morally absurd" (McMahan 2009: 30). I have not shown that this account is right. As mentioned above, some gangsters may have "norms" involving elements of reciprocity and may also expressly consent to being exposed to lethal risk without being justified in their criminal behavior. In section III, I will make the contractualist elaboration of the contours of professional duty more plausible by showing how combatants and noncombatants are not wronged when they are attacked, exposed to risk, or protected according to the terms of *jus in bello* articulated here. Chapter 7 will explain how the agents hewing to these norms can be justified regardless of the cause they advance.

Prohibition on unnecessary suffering. The causing of harm is the military's stock-in-trade. Yet the security standard prohibits using tactics or weapon systems that cause more pain than available alternatives in the course of incapacitating enemy personnel. Such tactics or weapons may be just as reliable, efficacious and efficient as less harmful weapons, but fail the security standard's deontological element when less harmful alternatives exist. A tactic or weapon system causing more pain than alternatives infringes on a service member's natural and institutional rights against gratuitous suffering.

iv Obedience

The norm of obedience to lawful orders is not simply an institutional rule regarding agent-principal behavior, but a norm with special agent-guiding status. As we will see, the norm of obedience, like the *in bello* norms, is crucial to a military's fulfillment of its institutional role of delivering security to its state. That obedience is a military norm means that it is an institutionally mediated expression of collective moral responsibility to deliver security with the weight to decisively guide service personnel in actions not conflicting with the other military norms. To anticipate the argument to follow in Chapter 7, the norm of obedience will do much of the work supporting a thesis of moral equality of combatants since it has the power to override countervailing norms directing people to avoid contributing to unjust collective actions. All concerned, including noncombatants of adversary states, can be modeled as consenting to all combatants in basically just states and all privileged irregulars obeying their superiors' lawful orders. This unusual result follows first, because the efficient and effective functioning of the consenters' own military requires obedience. Second, consent to a rule of obedience for one's own military cannot be modeled without consent also being extended to combatants in other states.

Combatants promptly obeying lawful orders is a reliable, efficacious, and efficient way for the military to prosecute its goals. Regarding proportionality, obedience can lead to trouble if service personnel carry out immoral or foolish orders, but clearly more harm than good would be done if militaries lacked

Military norms 155

hierarchies and combatants were all allowed to make independent decisions about when to deploy and what to do in theater. Even putting aside the prospect of war crimes, it is difficult to see how wars could be effectively waged without coordinated military action facilitated through a chain of command that can demand obedience to all lawful orders (Benbaji 2009: 609–615; Statman 2014: 353, 358).

The norm of obedience does more than establish a causal chain facilitating coordinated military action. The cultivation of a strong norm of obedience and the punishment of disobedient personnel will give personnel the impression that military rules are widely followed. Each combatant can then more likely be confident that his orders are genuine ones passed faithfully down the chain of command from superiors as opposed to being merely the superiors' caprices. Personnel can also be confident that subordinates and peers will obey the orders they are given, reducing coordination problems. We can imagine the dysfunction of a military in which officers cannot trust subordinates to comply with their orders, the veracity of orders received through the chain of command, nor that peers will follow their orders. The efficient accomplishment of military operations is morally important to serve the legitimate purposes of militaries.

The deontological element of the security standard is addressed by the caveat of obedience being to lawful orders. The contractualist model prefers institutions to *ad hoc* groups meeting joint moral rights for the reasons detailed in sub-section I.i of Chapter 5. While it is conceivable that an institution can be enduring and its actions regular and predictable without being subject to state law, legal compliance makes it more likely that the institution functions in a morally acceptable manner, allows citizens to exercise a measure of control over its quasi-independent functioning, and makes the members more accountable in that they can be punished for violating state laws and not merely for disregarding their superiors' contingent orders. (It should be borne in mind that laws governing the military are internally as well as externally oriented, banning actions decreasing a military's effectiveness like nepotism, hazing, corruption, and shirking of civilian oversight.) Apart from the particular noncombatant protections in international law, the regularity and predictability of a law-compliant military's behavior also makes it easier for noncombatants to avoid the military's violence.

By definition, laws in basically just states protect basic rights equitably. All can be modeled as consenting to service personnel hewing to orders consistent with such laws given the consent-worthiness of equitable rights-protecting laws. Basically just states will also have military law and/or will be party to international laws expressing security-standard-compliant *in bello* laws. There might be cases where the military's own rules will be more rights-respecting than those of the larger society, such as was the case regarding anti-discrimination rules in the US during the Truman administration. *Ex ante*, however, it is reasonable to think that a military bound to the larger society's laws will be more rights-respecting that a military in which commanders have *carte blanche* to give orders without legal review. Even in

156 *The moral equality of combatants*

basically just non-democratic states, a law-governed military has to take a broader perspective on its operations, including the effect on noncombatants, making it more likely that noncombatant concerns about unnecessarily destructive tactics would be taken into account. An arrangement in which the military is accountable to civilian law is also likely to score better with respect to the deontological element since law-compliant military actions will less likely provoke reprisals on the agent military's noncombatant population to the extent that it is more rights-respecting than the alternative.

It follows that the norm of obedience does not apply to unlawful orders. While *ad hoc* orders issued by commanders out of compliance with a larger legal code might happen to score well with respect to the security standard, as we have just seen, a rule permitting *ad hoc* rule-making is not consent-worthy. So an obedient service member is not performing a moral duty—meeting her institutionally mediated collective moral responsibility to deliver security—when she obeys an unlawful order.

A thesis of moral equality is more promising if obedience is a norm all affected parties would find consent-worthy, including combatants and noncombatants in unjustly attacked states. Consent-worthy norms are consent-worthy for incorporating all affected persons' rights. If there is a military norm to obey all, or virtually all, deployment orders, then we are well on our way to being able to support a thesis of moral equality since it would appear to cover deployment to (at least some) unjust as well as just wars. One might object that launching an unjust war is an illegal action and so the norm of obedience should no more extend to obedience to deployment orders to unjust wars than obedience to unlawful *in bello* orders. One can grant that there should be a norm of obedience to all *in bello*-compliant orders, for all the above reasons, but draw a distinction between tactical and deployment orders. A significant part of a possible defense of the moral quality of combatants is undercut if service personnel on the unjust side are not duty-bound to deploy. We will turn to that discussion in Chapter 7. First, however, in order to conclude this chapter, I have to defend my broader characterization of military norms by showing how affected parties are not wronged by norm-compliant service personnel even when they are harmed by those actions.

III The effect of military norms

In sub-sections I.i and ii of Chapter 5, I explained how professional norms can be institutionally mediated expressions of universal moral duties. I argued that the military profession is an instrument for a society to meet its collective moral responsibility to provide security and, thus, the military profession's properly constituted norms are expressions of universal moral duties. A skeptic can still wonder, first, if this characterization is a genuine moral phenomenon, such that properly formulated professional norms could really be morally binding on professionals. Even if this concern is satisfied, the skeptic can still object that my particular formulation of military norms is faulty.

Military norms   157

This section and the next chapter will be devoted to meeting these two challenges. First, in this section, I will show how the targets of norm-compliant military action are not wronged. A convincing account for why combatants and noncombatants are not being wronged even if they are maimed or killed, will go a long way to confirming that both skeptical challenges can be met.

i Harming without wronging in domestic situations

Generally, one is violating rather than acquitting a moral duty if one wrongs Y in order to benefit X. For example, one cannot claim to be meeting a positive duty by murdering Y in order to transplant Y's heart into X. There are multiple ways to explain why the negative characterization of the action takes precedent over the positive. Negative duties are absolute and so trump non-absolute positive duties; positive duties can only be acquitted through permissible means; a patient's positive claim-rights to be saved are weaker than another patient's negative claim-rights not to be used as a means, etc.[14] So assuming the numbers of people benefited and wronged are roughly the same, a service member from state X would seem to be violating negative duties toward members of state Y rather than performing a moral duty on behalf of the inhabitants of state X if she was wronging the combatants and noncombatants of state Y to benefit the inhabitants of X.[15]

I will outline the claims to be defended in this section. Noncombatants are not necessarily wronged by rights-infringing actions performed by enemy combatants (conventional combatants and/or privileged irregular militants) because the military action is in the context of an adversarial enterprise protecting the affected parties' joint rights. Noncombatants in one political entity have positive joint rights to security so they can demand their service personnel act on their military duty in accordance with military norms to protect them. Since everyone in the world has this right, everyone also has the reciprocal duty to support just institutions in deference to the rights-holders, including the militaries of basically just states. This duty entails ceding claim rights against militaries of basically just foreign states to operate according to their military norms. This ceding of rights gives foreign state agents liberty-rights, creating the space for them to perform their duties without wronging the citizens of basically just adversary states. Volunteer combatants are not wronged by being directly targeted by enemy troops according to the rules of *jus in bello* because they expressly consent to joining a profession constituted by the consent-worthy norms described in this chapter.

It will be helpful to start with domestic parallels in this section to explain how people are not necessarily wronged when threatened, hurt, or killed by another state's military. A detailed account developed on familiar terrain will enable more rapid application to the contested and unfamiliar military context in the following section. The same model of professional ethics can be used in criminal justice or military contexts. People are not wronged by their own state agents when those agents competently engage in security-standard-compliant

158 *The moral equality of combatants*

actions designed to protect the affected parties' rights.[16] One or more of four reasons account for this dynamic. Each reason will be explained in the paragraphs to follow.

First, people are not wronged by domestic state agents any more than they would be by a layperson engaging in an objectively proper (necessary and proportionate) action to directly protect patients' threatened individual or joint rights, even if the person is somewhat harmed in the process. For example, a drowning person is not wronged if she suffers abrasions as she is roughly hauled into a boat by either a police officer or layperson. Second, inhabitants are not wronged when their joint rights are indirectly met by state agents engaging in security-standard-compliant actions generally contributing to a secure environment, such as when police perform bag inspections in the subway. This is the case even when inhabitants have their liberty or privacy infringed in the process. Third, innocent suspects are not wronged when police act coercively with them according to security-standard-compliant norms because this behavior is a reflection of a general enterprise meant to protect innocent suspects' joint and individual rights. Fourth, criminals are not wronged when police act coercively with them consistent with their professional norms. By violating or threatening others' rights, criminals have ceded the otherwise-legitimate expectation that others will fully respect their rights pursuant to necessary and proportionate actions meant to restore the just *status quo ante*.[17]

The first reason the patient is not wronged by state agents is most apparent: her positive rights are being met by the agent's action. Yet it is too simple to say that one is never wronged when one is objectively being helped. Rights and duties are not dependent on consent (Stark 2000: 318), but negative rights can be waived by a patient's express consent and positive rights can be waived by express dissent. An agent risks wronging the patient who has dissented to action meant to meet her positive rights.

For example, a layperson has a duty to render assistance to others in need and a duty to defer to other's autonomy—a duty, broadly, to leave other people alone and give them a wide berth to make their own decisions. These positive and negative duties may be in tension when an agent sees a stranger in apparent distress. The agent might want to help but also be unsure if the stranger needs or wants help, especially if the assistance would require doing what she is usually not permitted to do, such as manhandling a stranger. The agent can act on her positive duty to render assistance when she models the hypothetical consent of an incapacitated or inebriated stranger, but should probably desist if the stranger explicitly objects to assistance. If the stranger seems to have her wits about her, she is in the best position to know if she needs assistance and also has the authority over her own body in cases where her body or behavior is not threatening to others. Thus, the agent may learn from the objecting stranger that she really does not need help (and so the agent's positive duty to render aid is not operative) or, even if the stranger could benefit from assistance, that she does not want it, in which case the agent's negative duty to defer to other's autonomy

Military norms 159

may override her duty to render aid. This issue of dissent to ostensibly helpful actions will have special relevance to military operations, below.

Regarding the second reason, a patient is usually indirectly aided by state agents who are engaged in a general enterprise meant to protect the patient among others. More so than the patient being directly aided, the patient indirectly aided—say, standing in line at airport screening—might feel aggrieved because she is suffering some mild harms and inconveniences for the sake of a benefit that is diffused among many other recipients in response to a remote threat. While there might be a case for the directly, individually aided patient (e.g., given first aid) being wronged when she is aided over her dissent, the dissent of the indirectly aided patient benefited by actions in keeping with a broad prophylactic effort does not mean she is wronged by the effort. Her dissent does not alone have agent-guiding weight. First, dissent does not play the role in this case it plays with a directly and individually aided person, alerting the agent that the patient does not think she needs assistance. In the airport case, the patient is not well suited to judge how much she is being objectively benefited compared to airport security personnel. Second, while individually, directly aided people objectively benefited (usually) have the authority to refuse self-beneficial aid, the airport passenger has no right to halt security-standard-compliant measures taken to protect a group of which she is a part. She can opt out (in this case, by not flying), but cannot refuse to participate due to her duty to support just institutions, and through them, the rights of other people.

The duty to support just institutions comes from one's collective moral responsibilities to meet certain joint moral rights.[18] One must support just institutions when they are the most effective instruments to protect others' joint and individual rights. One supports institutions by complying with the rules of the institutions and refraining from attempts to subvert them (Waldron 1993: 8–10; see Stark 2000: 324). By supporting just institutions that adjudicate disputes, prevent and deter crime, regulate commerce, license businesses, etc., one helps to protect one's own rights as well as respects the rights of fellow inhabitants in the territory the institutions govern. The duty to obey the rules of a just institution, including the laws of a just state and the contingent orders of state agents, is a moral duty.[19] (The duty can be overridden if the law is egregiously unjust.) As with other duties, compliance respects others' rights but also contributes to a reciprocal system ultimately protecting the rights of the duty-bearer. One can think about this duty from the opposite direction as an expression of the reciprocal aspect of the positive right to security. One cannot begrudge one's neighbor's enjoyment of the same right that one may demand be protected on one's own behalf. Since the duty to uphold just institutions is a moral duty, it is independent of promise-grounded obligations or particular affirmations or predilections (Stark 2000: 318; cf. Walzer 1998: ix–xvi, 7–10, 18–21). One has to observe one's duties even if one did not promise to do so or if one prefers to breach them.

A duty to deliver X to Y means one cedes a claim-right for X to Y. One owes a duty to uphold just institutions to the inhabitants of a state and directly

160 *The moral equality of combatants*

expresses the duty to the government employees who are those inhabitants' agents. A duty to uphold just institutions means ceding claim-rights against state agents in basically just states competently pursuing their security-standard-compliant professional obligations and duties when insisting on those rights would prevent state agents from serving their principals. This ceding of claim-rights gives the state agents liberty-rights in turn, creating the space for them to perform their security-standard-compliant actions without wronging the affected parties. So, regarding the third reason mentioned above, innocent people are not wronged when their rights are infringed by state agents acting in consent-worthy, norm-compliant ways. Refusing to comply with state agents' security-standard-compliant tactics, including their contingent orders, are violations of negative duties one owes to one's fellow state inhabitants.

If all potentially affected by policing operations can be modeled as consent-ing to certain security-standard-compliant policing norms, neither innocent sus-pects nor (mentally sound) criminals can complain of being wronged when they are accosted by police, arrested, interrogated, detained, and so on. The rights of all persons to security are met when police competently act on security-standard-compliant norms. Police are broadly acting to protect rights when they take steps to improve a community's security; the hypothetical consensual aspect of the security standard tailors their actions to make them more tightly in line with affected parties' rights. Hypothetical consent is permissive of police actions when it comes to the justification of police norms and tactics meant to keep the (actual or model) consenter safe. Considerations of how to protect the consenter's security justifies a series of actions aimed at rights violators or sus-pected rights violators. At the same time, a principle of reciprocity urges restraint of police tactics since the principle justifies police behavior targeting the consenter if she is suspected of perpetrating or planning rights violations. So the consent that we imagine a consenter extending to domestic security-seeking tactics takes into account that the consenter might also be the target of those tactics. Thus, for example, if the security standard justifies police arresting a suspect given x-level of evidence that the person has committed a crime, the suspect is not wronged when x-level of evidence implicates her, even if she is innocent. *Ex ante*, she can be modeled as consenting to a rule directing police to arrest people implicated by x-level of evidence. She cannot reasonably claim to be wronged, much less fight police (say, when they serve an arrest warrant) when she is actually innocent for the same reason she cannot renege from general prophylactic measures when she finds them inconvenient. She has a duty to support just institutions. These institutions would fail at their protective man-date if police could be halted by the unilateral directives of citizens. There is no way to only investigate people who are actually guilty. The norm-indicated investigative procedures are what police use to *determine* who is guilty.

Regarding the fourth reason, criminals also have a duty to support just institu-tions. Apart from whatever duties they have already breached, they breach duties to other state inhabitants if they violently resist (norm-compliant) police in addition to wronging police officers personally. There are two additional reasons (mentally sound) criminals are not wronged when police interact with them in a dutiful manner. Whereas innocent suspects may not have consciously done anything to appear suspicious to a police officer (they may just happen to match a fugitive's description), criminals consciously choose to act as the party whom they, and everyone else, knows will be the target of certain kinds of police actions. Even if a person has some subjective justification for breaking the law, he usually cannot claim to be ignorant of the fact that he is breaking the law and inviting police response, at least for crimes that are also major rights violations. Further, one cannot generally complain of being wronged when they are prevented by *anyone* from perpetrating crimes or escaping punishment for them, though they could complain if they are halted by a private citizen using disproportionate force or a police officer violating her professional norms.

ii Wronging and non-wronging of noncombatants

These four reasons are in play in international armed conflicts. The duty to support just institutions is not restricted to institutions of one's own state, but extends in different ways to foreign institutions. The duty to support just institutions is based on the duty to aid and protect the rights of other human beings—a cosmopolitan duty unrestricted by contingent factors like national identity. Foreign citizens, just as much as a visiting tourist, need the protection of state institutions. So one cedes claim- and liberty-rights to the state agents of a foreign state one visits as a tourist when insisting on those rights would prevent foreign agents from permissibly performing their duties to protect their own citizens, residents, and guests. So as a tourist, one is morally bound to not interfere with the just operations of local police or other officials; to not flout local laws that are consistent with basic human rights; to not refuse to pay sales or hotel tax; and to not otherwise subvert local just institutions (e.g., interfere with local elections).

Normally, the duty to support just institutions imposes few demands on a person in her home state for the benefit of people in other states. Yet in war, the duty to support just institutions owed foreigners entails ceding claim-rights against foreign agents acting according to their professional duty. Assuming that war-making without causing unintended noncombatant casualties is usually impossible, noncombatants cede claim-rights against being exposed to just collateral risk when a necessary military target is attacked by the enemy military subject to an accurate proportionality calculation. A just risk in this case is one associated with an attack conforming to the standards of *jus in bello*. One is then not wronged when the enemy exposes him to proportional risk in the course of this sort of attack. One usually *is* wronged if directly targeted since directly targeting noncombatants usually violates military norms. These norms are universally consent-worthy articulations of combatants' duty to meet the joint right to security via the facilitation of the security of all basically just political entities in a manner minimizing harm unrelated to that goal. The hypothetical consensual articulation of the duty incorporates deference to the rights of all affected,

162   *The moral equality of combatants*

balancing respect for rights to security requiring certain consequentially oriented actions with rights to life requiring omissions and curtailment of those actions.

If noncombatants A retained the relevant claim-rights, then the enemy military B could not permissibly engage in the same protective function noncombatants A have a right to demand of (their own) military A. This is to say that noncombatants B would not have the same moral right to security—the same right to demand protection of their government—that noncombatants A enjoy by virtue of being human beings.

Effectively, the duty to support just institutions means everyone living in a basically just state has a right to military protection. Citizens of one state cannot demand citizens of another state forgo military protection—which would be the effect if combatants were not permitted to engage in military operations. Similarly, domestically, one cannot demand that police investigate suspicious people but then claim to be wronged by a norm-compliant investigation when evidence implicates oneself.

Domestic noncombatants are also benefited by this reciprocal scheme of rights and duties obliging support for just foreign institutions. Rights infringements or threatened rights infringements by foreign state agents are part of a general adversarial enterprise meant to protect domestic noncombatants' rights. When noncombatants A are indirectly threatened by norm-compliant military B, this threat comes in the context of an adversarial scheme also permitting military A to generally protect the rights of noncombatants A (and pose risks to noncombatants B). So while military B does not directly benefit noncombatants A in the way that noncombatants A are benefited by their own police force, military B's threat is a necessary cost of military A's protection in the absence of a just global government.

We cannot acknowledge a right to military protection for the inhabitants of one state based on universal human rights without extending the right to all other persons. Collective moral duties lead to people forming and maintaining states and state institutions. If contingent factors lead to a multiplicity of non-allied states, these moral duties create the grounds for just war as governments, rightly pursuing their state's security, will ultimately have to rely on their own judgment and power to secure their states. Ideally, no state would aggressively attack another and all disputes would peaceably be resolved with diplomacy. However, absent a global government or coordinating multi-lateral body with enforcement power, this system creates the conditions for manifestly unjust wars and mistaken wars in which the instigator believes his cause to be just.

Here, one might object that noncombatants on the just side should indeed have a right to protection, but that there should be no such right when one's military is engaged in an unjust campaign. This significant objection will be addressed in Chapter 7.

Noncombatants also cede liberty-rights to join the fight against foreign troops alongside their own combatants, lest they lose the *jus in bello* protection prohibiting direct targeting of them. However, they may defend themselves if they are directly targeted by enemy personnel, in violation of *jus in bello*. The attackers'

Military norms 163

breach of their norms release the targeted noncombatants from the duty of deference that depended on the combatants' forbearance.

Noncombatants may also defend themselves if they are in imminent danger of being harmed as a side-effect of a legitimate military attack (when taking shelter is impossible). This claim would seem to go against my argument that noncombatants are not *wronged* if exposed to a just collateral threat consequent to an accurate proportionality calculation by enemy combatants. Let us consider a domestic scenario where a layperson feels she risks being harmed by a state agent. Clearly, someone could defend herself against a policeman trying to rape her. Yet consider the more common case where an innocent person's rights are materially infringed by a police officer—say, she is questioned, order to move her car, or arrested, in the absence of any obvious reason—and it is unclear if the officer is acting within the scope of his duties or harassing the person. Usually, people in basically just states should defer to their state agents in the moment, rather than, say, fight back. Someone who feels she has been poorly treated can file a complaint with the police department, launch a lawsuit, conduct a peaceful protest, alert the media, and complain to her political representatives. The accountability mechanisms she can access for local law enforcement—and which police know they will face—can give a citizen of a basically just state some confidence that her police are adhering to security-standard-compliant norms when she is exposed to risk or inconvenienced by police actions. She has another reason for deference even when she feels she is being wronged in that she knows she has a decent chance of gaining restitution (so long as she is not about to be killed or tortured by a police officer).

Properly constituted military norms strike an optimal balance between the interests of the agent and the target but, unlike in domestic situations, there is no neutral authority accountable to the affected party determining the proper expression of a norm in local contexts. The enemy military (ideally) tries to minimize collateral damage in multiple attacks in pursuit of their strategic aims while the agent military tries to stop the enemy. Given the independence of the two sides (hopefully) engaging in proportionality calculations for multiple attacks and continually trying to frustrate each other's plans, there is no guarantee for any given noncombatant that an imminent attack exposing him to risk is the product of a correct execution of a military norm. There is also a far lower chance that she can gain restitution from a survivable rights violation or infringement given the extremely non-stringent, delayed, and inconsistent application of international law. So the noncombatant may defend himself given the reasonable possibility that the attack is not proportionate or necessary.

Can a noncombatant opt out of this adversarial, reciprocal regime providing for his security but also exposing him to reciprocal risk? The fact that these people's claim-rights are ceded to local agents in accord with a duty means that state inhabitants' express consent or dissent is immaterial to the moral legitimacy of state agents' norm-compliant actions. Police could hardly do their jobs if suspects' objections to being questioned, arrested, interrogated, investigated, etc., meant the police action was morally impermissible. Similarly, combatants

164   *The moral equality of combatants*

could not protect their states if their otherwise-norm-compliant military action was prohibited by virtue of the express dissent from the affected parties in the adversary state or even some members of their own state. A person of sound mind can perhaps refuse non-emergency medical treatment—and complain of being wronged if the first responder proceeds against her clearly expressed and unambiguous refusal of care—but one cannot inhibit a professional from caring for others even if one is part of the affected group. So a pacifist or someone objecting to a particular war can object to her state's military actions, but that dissent itself does not revoke the military's permission to proceed.

iii *Wronging and non-wronging of combatants*

All potentially affected parties can be modeled as consenting to the above military norms as expressions of military duty to contribute to a political entity's security. The norms specify different treatment of combatants and noncombatants to that end. The collective moral responsibility to protect joint rights like security also manifests differently for these two groups. Both combatants and noncombatants have duties to support just institutions but only combatants have a duty to observe military norms.

Similar to noncombatants, combatants are not wronged when targeted in an appropriate way by norm-compliant enemy combatants representing basically just political entities. They benefit from the adversarial practice of which these actions are a part and they have a duty to support just institutions. Combatants can be modeled as ceding claim-rights against being directly targeted with lethal violence according to the terms of the above-described military norms. The norms of necessity and prohibiting unnecessary cruelty benefits them compared to alternate schemes insofar as they are targeted with violence. They are benefited by the adversarial practice of which they take a direct part because the practice permits their political entity to secure its legitimate national security goals.[20] They are benefited by the collectivized targeting regime described in section I, because it allows them to more efficiently wage war, opportunistically choosing advantageous engagements, and likely ending the war sooner.

Like all persons, combatants also have duties to support just institutions, both in their own state and in others. Since all people depend in various ways on just institutions to protect their joint rights, combatants have duties even in foreign theaters to respect the foreign government institutions not involved with national security. For example, invading combatants should not interfere with ordinary local law enforcement, healthcare delivery, education, and so on. Combatants' duty to support just institutions extends to supporting foreign citizens' right to military protection by ceding claim-rights against enemy military forces performing *their* duties. If combatants A did not cede claim-rights against being directly targeted by norm-compliant enemy personnel representing a basically just political entity, these personnel would be wrong to serve their political entity in the same way military A serves its basically just political entity. *Ex ante*, there is no base from which to model one group of combatants' duty to

Military norms 165

protect their political entity while withholding permission to another group performing the same duty. Chapter 7 will explain how, if selective conscientious objection is untenable, this symmetrical service includes obedience to all (*in bello*) lawful orders, including deployment orders, no matter the character of the proposed war.

Military norms are institutionally mediated expressions of ordinary moral principles—in this case, the collective moral responsibility to deliver security to one's community—and moral duties and liabilities are independent in the first instance (i.e., prior to special waivers) of express consent. So service members' duty to observe their professional norms and their liability to being the direct target of norm-compliant enemies is not based on their express consent. By voluntarily enlisting, enlistees accept the role of service members and take on the norms constituting that role in an adversarial system. Service members cannot be modeled as waiving their rights to life per that role—as this would permit anyone to kill them. They do not cede claim-rights to be killed by their enemies (cf. Hurka 2007: 210) in the manner expressly endorsed by euthanasia applicants, but have to be modeled as ceding claim-rights to being directly *targeted* by combatants representing basically just political entities with lethal action conforming to military norms.[21] They can be wronged by being wantonly killed, killed in ways that impose unnecessary levels of suffering, killed by unprivileged irregular militants, or killed by non-combatants who are not directly threatened. Combatants can also be wronged by foreign combatants if attacked when the two relevant states are not at war. Combatants are not left defenseless by this rights-ceding because they gain reciprocal liberty-rights to directly target their enemies in turn.[22] This permission creates the moral space for them to perform their duties in service of their political entities without wronging their combatant targets.

Combatants' designation as combatants is dependent on their express consent. They are not wronged when they are directly targeted by enemy troops, but non-combatants are wronged by being directly targeted. By voluntarily enlisting, enlistees agree to play the role of lawful target in wartime at the hands of any combatant from a basically just state according to the use-of-force guidelines in *jus in bello*.[23] Express consent does not give adversary troops permission to kill enlistees in the sense that express consent might give a doctor *ad hoc* permission to kill someone joining a pool of terminally ill patients who will be euthanized according to some "death with dignity" program. When a particular enlistee joins the military, adversary troops already had a duty to directly target enemy troops in any future war and the personnel the enlistee joins already had a liability to being targeted in any future war. By enlisting, an individual expressly identifies himself to adversary armed services as one of those people who can be targeted in a future war according to military norms.[24] His express consent to join the military does not cede a claim-right against being directly targeted to his enemy—that ceding is linked to his norm- and liability-laden role as combatant. Instead, he is ceding a claim-right noncombatants retain not to be considered a combatant. He can no longer claim to be wronged if he is treated according to military norms as a

166 *The moral equality of combatants*

combatant, including by being directly targeted in wartime. By partial analogy—since boxing is constituted by a conventional rather than a moral framework—the socially approved (in some cultures) role of boxer includes a permission to strike one's opponent in certain ways and a liability to being struck in turn. One's stepping into the ring during a bout with boxing gloves cedes a claim-right (the officials, trainers, and spectators retain) not to be treated as a boxer by the awaiting boxer and targeted accordingly. Since the practice of boxing and the role of boxer—with its privileges and liabilities—are already established, the ring entrant cannot tell his opponent "Right. I was planning to 'box' by hitting you without conceding any right to be struck in return."[25] Similarly—in this respect—a sane and rational person contemplating commission of a crime should know that he is considering an action that will assign him a role in the criminal justice system with well-known liabilities. He cannot claim that he is being wronged if he is investigated and arrested by norm-compliant police.

My argument does not depend on the empirical question of whether all enlistees actually know that the role of the service member is characterized by these norms and liabilities.[26] They are bound to the duties and liabilities attached to the role because the duties and liabilities are moral qualities rather than mere descriptions of the role. Like all duties and liabilities, military norms are independent of dutyholder's promises or desires and are binding on a person so long as he occupies the duty-linked role and has the mental capacities for exercising duties. Other people reasonably expect and depend on professionals or other role actors like parents to uphold role-linked duties, so it is incumbent on role occupants to meet those duties even if they were unexpected or unwelcome. (I have not discussed conscripted combatants due to limitations of space. Justifications of their being targeted would rely on the liability-laden role they are compelled to adopt. One would have to argue they are not being wronged by their state by being pressed into service.)

The dynamic exposing combatants to danger is different than the one exposing police to danger. Police are duty-bound to expose themselves to risk in order to spare risk to laypeople. Yet their voluntary service does not give criminals permission to behave violently toward police (McMahan 2009: 52). By contrast, all service personnel in basically just states occupy the same role with the same constitutive moral dimensions, including the obligation to defend their state's national security interests and the liability to being targeted by enemy personnel in wartime. Thus, military enlistees join a profession where their adversaries will be professionals adhering to the same norms, but working for different principals. In this respect, they have more in common with professional athletes (in team sports) or lawyers than police.[27] Sub-section III.iv of Chapter 5 explained why the military profession is a necessary one and enlistment in a basically just state a good action. The legitimacy of the military role partly answers the question of why adherence to this possibly counter-intuitive bilateral contract is worthy of moral respect. It still remains to explain why the bilateral contract and the rest of the security-standard-approved norms are morally justified in cases when countervailing moral concerns suggest adherence to military norms is inappropriate (McMahan 2009: 57).

Military norms 167

So all combatants in basically just states are given liberty-rights by adversary combatants and noncombatants to interact with them on the basis of properly constituted military norms. Since the norms direct actions consistent with the targets' ceded claim-rights, neither adversary combatants nor noncombatants are wronged by the *in bello*-compliant military action of the enemy. This is a significant result. In Part I, I argued that the revisionists did not have a good foundation for their argument that the agents of the unjust cause were liable for the unjust cause. Yet one could still perhaps assert the asymmetry thesis by focusing on the non-liable target and arguing that there is an objective asymmetry between the non-liable target who will be wronged by an attack, on one hand, and his attacker, on the other, even if the attacker is not liable for the collective injustice he causally advances. Indeed, Frowe argues that kinetic actors on the unjust side are still unilaterally targetable, since directly threatening innocents gives the innocent parties permission to defensively respond regardless of responsibility or any other agent quality. I am blocking this method of asserting the asymmetry thesis by arguing the following. Non-liable service personnel on the just side are not wronged by *in bello*-compliant service members on the unjust side because of the permission all conventional combatants and noncombatants in basically just states extend to their conventional adversaries. They are not innocent in the sense of people who would be wronged by being lethally targeted.

This concludes my critique of Frowe's tripartite defense of the asymmetry thesis. Recall, Frowe argued first that all direct threats to innocents can be defensively targeted, regardless of their liability. Second, indirect threats and causes of threats can be targeted if they are liable. Third, they can also be targeted if non-liable, to prevent them from violating duties that can even be violated inadvertently. The critique against agent-responsibility advocates' reliance on luck made in Chapter 2 applies to Frowe's second argument about the liability of indirect threats and causes of threats. Her first and third arguments, about direct threats and duty violators, respectively, depend on the patients being wronged by the agents' violence. I showed how neither combatants nor noncombatants are wronged by either side's agents' norm-compliant actions, nullifying these two arguments for the asymmetry thesis.

The argument in this section furthers the defense of an equitable version of the proportionality norm, begun in sub-section II.iii, in which both sides' tactical goals are seen as equally good in a proportionality calculation. This section explains how one side's tactical goals are not made disvalues on account of their leading to actions that wrong affected noncombatants. Noncombatants are not wronged when they are harmed as a side effect of proportional and necessary military actions.

IV Summary

The purpose of this chapter was to use the security standard to identify major military norms. The argument in the second half of the chapter, showing how combatants and noncombatants are not wronged by norm-compliant military action, can potentially mollify a skeptic who thinks that there are no special military norms or that my articulations of them is not apt. My formulation of the norms is more plausible for not wronging affected parties.

168 *The moral equality of combatants*

Notes

1 Walzer espouses this view in all his work, but it is hardly unique to him.
2 Lazar has a similar idea (2012: 24).
3 For an individualist take on how temporal scope can affect proportionality, see Emerton and Handfield (2009: 388).
4 Frowe's stronger argument relies on the attacker being a direct threat.
5 Indeed, counter-insurgency often requires conventional troops to wait until insurgents in civilian clothing raise weapons before they can engage them—much to the danger of conventional troops.
6 Humanitarian interventions would still be permissible with an individual self-defense paradigm.
7 Civilian self-defense paradigms can sometimes make unusual allowances for the killing of a sleeping or retreating villain who has promised future violence or has a history of violence against the defender. The paradigm example would be when the defender is a battered spouse who cannot fight her husband toe to toe. This allowance for non-synchronous defense in asymmetrical power situations is not germane in the case of similarly armed and armored service personnel.
8 The collectivized versions of imminence, necessity, and proportionality are functionally similar to the concepts invoked in limiting self-defensive violence, but are not derived from them.
9 Note, I am speaking of combatants rather than a military on offense since an entire military would not necessarily only be fighting in a tactically defensive or offensive manner.
10 Benbaji makes the same point that permissions to fight efficiently and efficaciously benefit combatants insofar as this regime provides their states a means of just defense against aggression (2011: 50–51).
11 Benbaji and Statman have a similar idea about the justification of *jus in bello*, justified on their account through tacit consent (2019: 136).
12 McMahan thinks narrow proportionality has a place in wartime, but uses the term "wide proportionality" to refer to the type of proportionality most scholars invoke with respect to *in bello* contexts (2009: 20–22).
13 The contractualist model explains this omission in the following manner. The norm of proportionality is germane when mixed groups of combatants and noncombatants are endangered by the agent military's actions. The hypothetical consent of noncombatants as well as combatants is therefore included in the abstract specification of military duty. Noncombatant deaths *per se* are not consent-worthy goals because these deaths normally do not have utility for combatants. Noncombatants obviously do not wish to die, therefore both combatants and noncombatants can be modeled as endorsing norms and tactics minimizing such deaths. By contrast, combatant deaths have generic military utility and so norms and tactics reducing combatant deaths are only consent-worthy to the point where an excess would come at the expense of concrete military advantage. Neither combatants nor combatants can be modeled *ex ante* as endorsing norms or tactics reducing combatant deaths as much as possible since military goals would then not be attainable.
14 The latter two explanations can accommodate wronging some to save many. The final explanation comes from Walen and Wasserman (2012).
15 Thus I am leery of the move Fabre and Lazar make, justifying military service by deeming it a case of legitimate transfer of agent-relative preferences from noncombatants to the service personnel of their state (Lazar 2013; Fabre 2014: 62–63; see Frowe's critique, 2016).
16 So professional norms are not merely an "intensification" of ordinary moral norms, as Camenisch argues (1983), nor a simple "application" of them, as Nagel argues (1978: 88).

Military norms 169

17 I am here assuming a "criminal" is breaking a law that also protects a core human right.
18 Miller, Rawls, Waldron, and Stilz derive the duty differently (Miller 2010: chapter 2; Rawls 1971: 351–354; Waldron 1993; Stilz 2014; Nozick 1974: 102, 110).
19 Rawls (1971: chapter 51). Scanlon has a similar idea (1998: 265–266). I explain why there is a moral duty to obey even seemingly minor laws in Skerker (2010: 36–38).
20 Benbaji has similar views (2011).
21 McMahan challenges a subtly different characterization of belligerent liability: that what is at stake is granting one's enemy the right to *kill* oneself (2009: 51–58). Ceding a claim-right against being directly *targeted* with lethal action means a combatant is not wronged by his enemy when his enemy shoots at him, drops bombs on him, etc., so given the efficacy of weapon systems, a combatant is ultimately not wronged by being threatened, harmed, or killed. Yet it seems important to assert in the first instance that a combatant is ceding a claim-right against being *targeted* rather than a claim-right against being *killed* for three reasons. First, military norms have to be action-guiding and a norm involving directions to kill a particular class of persons is not usually feasible on a dynamic battlefield (whereas it is in a controlled setting where the victim is defenseless such as in a prison or a hospital). So military norms do not direct combatants simply to kill enemy combatants and refrain from killing noncombatants but to directly target the former and avoid directly targeting the latter. Second, military norms do not simply direct the killing of enemy troops but only the militarily necessary targeting of troops, with methods that minimize unnecessary suffering. Third, ceding a right to be killed wrongly suggests that the enemy enjoys a unilateral right to kill—as though they can demand ceding personnel present themselves for execution.
22 Benbaji characterizes part of the moral landscape between just and unjust sides in the following manner. The unjust side poses an unjust threat to the just side so combatants on the unjust side lose a right against being attacked. However, they retain the right to defend themselves if they are non-culpable for the unjust war. Benbaji concedes this analysis does not justify the legal permission culpable combatants on the unjust side have to kill and the legal liability of non-threatening (e.g., sleeping) combatants. As a result, he proposes an additional contractual framework (2008: 486). Benbaji's addition also points to a shortcoming in Hurka's characterization of enlistees ceding their rights against being attacked but retaining their rights of self-defense. Overall, it is best to abandon attempts at characterizing equal belligerent rights as involving ceded rights to being attacked and retained rights of self-defense. It is not always clear if authors mean self-defense in a tactical or moral sense—whether one can defend oneself only when facing an imminent threat or whenever one wishes provided one has an unjust adversary. The former construal is inadequate to justify the sort of equal belligerent privileges that would be tactically desirable since it would limit the entitled party to fighting only when it had no option of retreat. The latter construal would permit military units on the just side to hunt, ambush, and pursue the unjust side. Yet it is unclear how a right enjoyed only by the just side helps justify equal belligerent privileges.

Emerton and Handfield take a similarly individualist approach to Benbaji and Hurka, though in a way that addresses the potential unclarity about what is meant by defensive violence (2009). The typical combatant can engage in defensive violence—construed broadly to include tactically offensive operations (since these actions will defend the relevant combatants or their peers in the long run)—regardless of the justice of their cause. Nearly all combatants may fight to survive because they are non-culpable for the war and trapped in a dangerous situation created by their government's, and the enemy's, actions. The authors' defense of the moral equality of combatants is vulnerable to revisionists' critiques to the effect that non-culpable

170 *The moral equality of combatants*

combatants are still liable for the unjust collective action they perpetrate because of the minimal standards of liability the revisionists use. Those reductive individualists using the agent-responsibility standard specifically would argue that combatants on the unjust side are liable since they chose to enlist or accept conscription. Moreover, contra the authors, combatants are not forced to choose between surrendering or fighting to survive; in many cases, they could desert.

23 Walzer makes a similar argument that service personnel voluntarily enter a profession involving attacks from adversaries (2015: 37). McMahan argues enlistees clearly consent to the risk of being attacked but this acceptance of risk does not equate to their consent to being attacked (2009: 52). It is true that someone's accepting that he will be subject to certain practices does not mean that he gives permission to the opposing agent of that practice or accepts a norm permitting the agent's action. A policeman understands that a criminal might fight back while being arrested but does not accept that this is permissible behavior. By contrast, a boxer accepts both that his opponent will attack him and that this attack is permissible. All rational enlistees know, or should know, that as a matter of fact they can be directly targeted in wartime by enemy troops. The question is whether they endorse the practice as well. My argument is that soldiering has a profile constituted by norms that can be worked out *ex ante*. These norms are not conferred by express consent so McMahan's critique is not germane to my argument. This response also succeeds against McMahan's argument that accepting that X is permitted to kill oneself is not the same thing as granting permission to X to kill oneself (2009: 54).

24 McMahan and Steinhoff object to the boxing analogy used by some to justify counter-force violence in part by saying a combatant on the just side of a war is more like someone thrust into the boxing ring against his will and then told he must abide by the rules of boxing (McMahan 2009: 56; Steinhoff 2007). (Remarkably, Benbaji and Statman think that coerced consent still counts as consent; 2019: 127.) I am arguing that enlistees agree ahead of time to be targetable by enemy forces in wartime so the combatant in question is more like a boxer who is paid by the champ's managers to attend his training camp as a potential sparring partner. The boxer may or may not get called into the ring. This argument meets McMahan's objection to Benbaji that, even if combatants waive rights against one another, the unjust aggressors force defenders into waiving their rights (McMahan 2011: 147). Rather, the waiver occurs ahead of time, before any unjust aggression.

25 By the same token, the result is not boxing if Smith accosts Jones on the street and invites him to strike him.

26 Hurka defends the moral equality thesis by arguing that service personnel freely take on a role characterized by symmetrical belligerent privileges and liabilities. He argues that the role is symmetrically characterized since states insist on absolute obedience to deployment orders and enlistees in all states accept this account of their role as involving privileges and liabilities unaffected by the nature of the cause they advance (2007: 210). McMahan objects to the contention that service personnel actually accept this characterization of their role (2009: 53–54). My position is not dependent on enlistees' empirical views, so avoids McMahan's critique on this score.

27 Privileged irregulars are not professional, but by definition adhere to the same code.

References

Benbaji, Y. (2008) "A Defense of the Traditional War Convention," *Ethics*, 118: 464–495.

Benbaji, Y. (2009) "The War Convention and the Moral Division of Labour," *The Philosophical Quarterly*, 59(237): 593–617.

Military norms 171

Benbaji, Y. (2011) "The Moral Power of Soldiers to Undertake the Duty of Obedience," *Ethics*, 122: 43–73.

Benbaji, Y. and Statman, D. (2019) *War by Agreement*, Oxford: Oxford University Press.

Camenisch, P. (1983) *Grounding Professional Ethics in a Pluralistic Society*, New York: Haven.

Coady, A. (2008) in Rodin, D. and Shue, H. (eds), *Just and Unjust Warriors*, Oxford: Oxford University Press.

Emerton, P. and Handfield, T. (2009) "Order and Affray: Defensive Privileges in Warfare," *Philosophy and Public Affairs*, 37(4): 382–414.

Fabre, C. (2012) *Cosmopolitan War*, Oxford: Oxford University Press.

Frowe, H. (2016) "Authorisation and Agent-Relative Reasons," unpublished manuscript.

Haque, A. (2017) *Law and Morality at War*, Oxford: Oxford University Press.

Hurka, T. (2007) "Liability and Just Cause," *Ethics and International Affairs*, 21(2): 199–217.

Lazar, S. (2012) "Necessity in Self-Defense and War," *Philosophy and Public Affairs*, 40(1): 3–44.

Lazar, S. (2013) "Associative Duties and the Ethics of Killing," *Journal of Practical Ethics*, 1(1): 1–30.

McMahan, J. (2006) "Killing in War: A Reply to Walzer," *Philosophia*, 34: 47–51.

McMahan, J. (2008) "The Morality of War and the Law of War," in Rodin, D. and Shue, H. (eds), *Just and Unjust Warriors*, Oxford: Oxford University Press.

McMahan, J. (2009) *Killing in War*, Oxford: Clarendon Press.

McMahan, J. (2011) "Duty, Obedience, Desert, and Proportionality in War," *Ethics*, 122(1): 135–167.

Miller, S. (2010) *The Moral Foundations of Social Institutions*, Cambridge: Cambridge University Press.

Nagel, T. (1978) "Ruthlessness in Public Life," in Hampshire, S. (ed.), *Public and Private Morality*, Cambridge: Cambridge University Press.

Nozick, R. (1974) *Anarchy, State, and Utopia*, New York: Basic Books.

Kutz, C. (2008) in Rodin, D. and Shue, H. (eds), *Just and Unjust Warriors*, Oxford: Oxford University Press.

Rawls, J. (1971) *A Theory of Justice*, Cambridge: Cambridge University Press.

Scanlon, T. (1998) *What We Owe to Each Other*, Cambridge, MA: Belknap Press.

Skerker, M. (2010) *An Ethics of Interrogation*, Chicago, IL: University of Chicago Press.

Stark, C. (2000) "Hypothetical Consent and Justification," *Journal of Philosophy*, 97(6): 313–334.

Statman, D. (2014) "Fabre's Crusade for Justice: Why We Should Not Join," *Law and Philosophy*, 33: 337–360.

Steinhoff, U. (2007) *On the Ethics of War and Terrorism*, Oxford: Oxford University Press.

Stilz, A. (2014) "Territorial Rights and National Defence," in Fabre, C. and Lazar, S. (eds), *The Morality of Defensive War*, Oxford: Oxford University Press.

Waldron, J. (1993) "Special Ties and Natural Duties," *Philosophy and Public Affairs*, 22(1): 3–30.

Walen, A. and Wasserman, D. (2012) "Agents, Impartiality, and the Priority of Claims over Duties," *Journal of Moral Philosophy*, 9: 545–571.

Walzer, M. (1982) *Obligations*, Cambridge, MA: Harvard University Press.

Walzer, M. (2015) *Just and Unjust Wars*, Philadelphia, PA: Basic Books.

7 The moral equality of combatants

I Questions about the norm of obedience

The consent-worthiness of the norm of obedience is key to defending the moral equality of combatants. Service personnel must obey deployment orders if service personnel are duty-bound to obey all their lawful orders. The last chapter made the moral equality thesis more plausible by showing how combatants and noncombatants are not wronged in the course of security-standard-compliant military operations. In Chapter 6, sub-section II.iv, I introduced an objection about deployment orders to unjust wars nullifying the norm of obedience. I put off a similar question in sub-section III.ii, asking why persons harmed in unjust wars are not wronged: why the permission all combatants and noncombatants extend to adversary militaries to look after their state's security is not voided when the state's leaders order an unjust war. I will address these concerns over the next two sections.

One might object that there is something categorically different about a deployment order compared to orders *in* war. Order-following is justified according to the contractualist model because it is necessary for the effective and efficient execution of war aims. War is paradigmatically justified to defend or secure the rights of a state's people. Absent a threat to these rights, there should be no cause for war. Unlawful *in bello* orders—to murder noncombatants, for example—lack normative power because the contractualist model only extends cosmopolitan justification to norms and tactics consistent with the security standard. These are norms and tactics anyone could consent to because they protect joint rights everyone needs protecting without imposing intolerable costs on their targets. The objection continues, deployment orders to unjust wars should not have any more normative weight than immoral orders running afoul of *jus in bello* since they do not secure genuinely threatened joint rights. Service personnel should be permitted, if not required, to opt out of unjust wars. A way to insist on this point while also allowing that *standing* militaries are necessary institutions requiring obedience is to advocate for a right to selective conscientious objection.

Selective conscientious objection refers to a service member's refusal to participate in a particular operation or war because she believes the conflict to be

The moral equality of combatants   173

unjust. The objector is not a pacifist and is willing to serve in just conflicts. Many of the revisionists' arguments about moral asymmetry have traction if selective conscientious objection is practically tenable, in which case, service personnel can leave the service or opt out of a particular operation without greatly damaging the efficient functioning of the military. If selective conscientious objection is tenable, one can accept my arguments about the necessity of the military, the general moral weight of military norms as institutionally mediated expressions of collective moral responsibilities, and the consent-worthiness of the norm of obedience, without allowing that the norm of obedience extends to deployment orders to unjust wars. Obedience to all deployment orders would not be essential to a military's effective and efficient functioning. The military that can permit selective conscientious objection might be able to do so because of structural similarities with a large law firm, which can bear refusals by some attorneys to work on certain cases because of the ample supply of similarly trained replacements. The military might also be like a grocery store that can continue functioning despite unplanned resignations of staff because of the short training time for replacements. Since deployment to all wars is unnecessary for the proper functioning of the military in fighting just wars, the argument continues, the duty to support just institutions does not mean ceding claim-rights against being threatened or attacked by service personnel on the unjust side— who are doing what they must in supporting a necessary, but fallible, institution. If selective conscientious objection is tenable, we could then demand that service personnel consider the justice of the war and refuse deployment orders to most unjust conflicts. Combatants might be culpable or partly culpable for fighting in an unjust war if they knew it was an unjust war, without a service duty mitigating their liability.

In this chapter, I will extend a conditional endorsement of the moral equality of combatants, and with it, a traditional symmetrical understanding of *jus in bello*, in the event that selective conscientious objection is practically untenable. It is a full defense of the traditional doctrine, even justifying the military service of combatants waging an aggressive war. As such, my argument goes farther than some reductivist traditionalists who defend a moderate moral equality between combatants on the just side and those on the unjust side defending their states against the just sides' counter-attack (Hurka 2005; Steinhoff 2008; Lazar 2017: 11–12). The relevant authors' reductivist commitments lead to their arguments' limited scopes. Unlike some traditionalists' arguments, mine does not appeal to the extant law extending equal belligerent privileges and liabilities to conventional combatants (Benbaji and Statman 2019; Dill and Shue 2012), a move vulnerable to revisionist rejoinders that a) revisionism identifies the "deep morality" of war (regardless of the law) and b) perhaps the law should be reformed.

Unlike all other authors who have addressed the topic, I see the debate about moral equality as turning in part on an empirical question. The empirical state of affairs regarding the tenability of selective conscientious objection is relevant because hypothetical consent accrues to the symmetrical privileges and

174 *The moral equality of combatants*

liabilities of service personnel if militaries cannot actually achieve their purpose while also permitting selective conscientious objection. We saw above how the contractualist model endorses certain tactics because hypothetical consent accrues to extant practices best complying with the security standard.

II Selective conscientious objection

It is important to grasp the implications and scope of selective conscientious objection prior to assessing its fit with the security standard. What would it mean for selective conscientious objection to be practically untenable? Selective conscientious objection would be untenable if the military could not meet the goals it is morally obliged to carry out. I will use the practical elements of the security standard to assess if a rule permitting selective conscientious objection would still permit militaries to efficiently, effectively, reliably and proportionally fight just wars and if such a rule would also permit states to effectively engage in other national security actions such as diplomacy, war-planning, and deterrence. Attention will be paid to the effects of granting service personnel a legal right of selective conscientious objection and the effects of personnel actually invoking it. The former set of effects would be significant even if the state never went to war or if no service personnel ever invoked the right.

i The effects of legalizing selective conscientious objection

We will have to engage in some educated speculation in order to address these questions because no state currently grants a right of selective conscientious objection.[1] Military planners would need to assess if they could plan for military contingencies and effectively engage adversaries in deterrence or combat if service personnel were granted a right of selective conscientious objection. In the counterfactual case of states that have newly instituted a right of selective conscientious objection, actuaries might be able to estimate the rate of selective conscientious objection invocation based on surveys of personnel or examples of peer states that already grant a right of selective conscientious objection. Historically based estimates would be available for states that have offered a right of selective conscientious objection for a significant period of time. In either the counterfactual situation or the current world without legal selective conscientious objection, planners would need to consider the fungibility of troops in different specializations, the availability of troops in different duty stations around the country or the world, and the possibility of technological solutions for personnel shortages. Planners would then need to consider if they can fight after losing a certain percentage of their personnel or lose percentages in particular specializations.

In a state that newly authorizes selective conscientious objection, policymakers would likely need to assume deployments to all conflicts will be less reliable than in the absence of selective conscientious objection because of the uncertainty about selective conscientious objection invocation rates and

The moral equality of combatants 175

uncertainty about the time it might take to replace departed service members. This concern would be especially pressing for troops already forward-deployed at overseas bases and engaged in routine sea tours since it would be easier to replace a stateside objector when his unit was given significant lead time for a deployment. Even large militaries do not have potential duplicates for every service member. The expense and training time of combatants dictate this scarcity. For example, in the US, it takes 13 weeks to produce a Marine rifleman, six months to produce a Marine officer, 1–1.5 years to produce a Navy SEAL (Hunt 2008: 46), and around two years (and $1.5–2 million) to produce a pilot. Combatants are mostly non-fungible for specializations more complex than infantry rifleman and even at that, a sailor handed a rifle is not going to be of the same quality as a full-time member of the army or marine infantry. It is worth noting that even without a legal right of selective conscientious objection, the US Defense Department currently struggles to fill billets given *roughly* estimable future manpower needs, attrition rates, and recruitment class sizes.

Training time and expense, the opportunity costs of training one recruit over another, and the non-fungibility of many service members prompt the contractual nature of modern volunteer military service. The point some make that claiming selective conscientious objection would not entail breaking one's contract because militaries could shift personnel to domestic billets misses the relevant point. The military war-games, anticipating it will have x number of submarine officers and y number of submarine school instructors, not $x-10$ officers and $y+10$ instructors. One is not really fulfilling one's contract if one contracted to be a submariner, but ends up performing domestic duties during wartime instead.

The knowledge that military deployment is unreliable will obviously limit political leaders' foreign policy options. Diplomats would need to assess whether their state's traditional adversaries would respond to the same logic of deterrence or states would be willing to form alliances, if both the granting state and other states knew that future deployments would be hampered by an uncertain rate of selective conscientious objection invocation.

Military leaders also need to assess whether a legal right of selective conscientious objection would negatively impact discipline given that deployment to war is the paradigmatic activity of service personnel. One might object that modern militaries inform their members of a duty to refuse immoral (*in bello*) orders and this does not seem to undercut good order and discipline (Gross 2010: 31). One response would be that there is probably less likelihood of error and less room for conflation of political preference with moral reasoning (Wing 1999: 38) when it comes to *in bello* violations the combatant directly witnesses than with *ad bellum* decisions potentially involving complex diplomatic, legal, and intelligence analyses.

Still, one can imagine tactical orders that are morally hazy, so a stronger response to this objection is to point out that service personnel have a duty to disobey unlawful orders, but do not have the right of summary judgment in this regard (at least in the US). Instead, they must submit to a court martial or

176   *The moral equality of combatants*

non-judicial punishment hearing in which they must prove the unlawfulness of the order and defend themselves against charges of disobedience. The built-in oversight of the hearing process and service members' likely caution, given the knowledge they will have to defend themselves against possible felony conviction for disobedience, compensates for the fallibility of individual judgment. Further, the fact that it is the court martial tribunal rather than the service member definitively determining the lawfulness of an order shows that service members lack a general right to disobey orders. By contrast, apart from proposed hearings to assess avowed conscientious objectors' *sincerity* (more below), the putative right of selective conscientious objection is summary and complete, up to the service member's own judgment, and without a substantive institutional check. It is therefore a far more weighty and potentially destabilizing power than the one implied by the duty to disobey unlawful orders.

ii The effects of invoking selective conscientious objection

Let us turn to issues associated with the actual invocation of selective conscientious objection. Advocates for selective conscientious objection think that granting a right of selective conscientious objection would not disrupt a military's legitimate activities because not many service personnel would claim it,[2] private contractors could be hired to fill gaps (Garren 2007), and it would be a good thing, anyway, if so many service personnel claimed it prior to an unjust war that a military's prosecution of the war would be hobbled (ibid. 2007: 1).

On the first point, a right of selective conscientious objection could lead to more personnel losses and more disruption than perhaps imagined (Ryan 2011: 34) because of the broader opportunities for invocation and increased willingness for personnel to invoke it. The moral rationale undergirding a putative right of selective conscientious objection would apply to more than objections to major wars, but also to special operations, targeted killing programs, punitive raids, humanitarian interventions, peacekeeping, and perhaps even joint exercises with dubious regimes. Apart from garrisoned and reserve troops given days' notice of a deployment, a right of selective conscientious objection would also apply to navy and marine personnel on ordinary sea tours and other personnel in overseas bases who are sent to participate in hostilities. It should be noted that invocation by troops deployed abroad could create particularly destabilizing disruptions in readiness and operations since invocations of selective conscientious objection could prevent or inhibit non-invoking personnel from participating in a controversial operation. For example, imagine that a conscientious aircraft carrier helmsman, already at sea, is ordered to re-direct his carrier toward what he considers an unjust war. If he invokes selective conscientious objection and refuses to drive the carrier, he (temporarily) prevents all 100+ strike aircraft from participating in the war.[3]

Regarding the disposition to claim selective conscientious objection, some suggest that there is not much harm in permitting the putative right because few service personnel would actually invoke it given the culture of service in

The moral equality of combatants 177

the military and reluctance to "betray" one's comrades by refusing to deploy, or to fight, if one is already forward-deployed (Wing 1999: 38; Robinson 2009: 34). First, it is an odd form of moral argument to defend a right by suggesting that most people will not have the perspective or courage to exercise it. There is something wrong with the putative right if society cannot tolerate widespread exercise of it.

Second, recent American evidence suggests that the American military at least is not some kind of cult for modern personnel, inculcating all with blind loyalty to the group. Junior officers in all the services have left the US military in droves following 9/11 (Shanker 2006); the intelligence and special operations community in particular has been desperate to retain trained analysts and operators leaving for higher-paying private-sector jobs. Even subtracting the contingent stressors of serial deployments and the incentives of higher pay, it is instructive to note the attrition rates after the minimum five to seven years of service for Marine and Navy officers graduating from the US Naval Academy (1984 to 2004) is significant, ranging from 15–21%. The rate climbs to between 47 and 59% after ten years of service for the period between 1980 and 1999.[4] The average attrition rate for US Military Academy alums after five years in the 1990s was 28% (Kolb 2008). Of course, this data cannot be interpreted to suggest that a certain percentage of service personnel would invoke selective conscientious objection before their contracts expires, if provided the chance. Instead, the relatively high attrition rate even before 9/11 suggests that scholars are wrong if they think all service personnel have a kind of cultish devotion to the military such that they would fight even if they believed the war was unjust, especially if they had the legal option of refusing.

Few combatants from Coalition or NATO countries invoked selective conscientious objection in the post-9/11 conflicts. Yet it is fallacious to estimate future legal selective conscientious objection invocation rates based on current invocation rates when it is illegal. Invoking selective conscientious objection now requires not only moral maturity and moral courage, but the willingness to face legal consequences and the associated social and professional consequences of a felony conviction. Scholars considering the effects of legalized selective conscientious objection might consider comparative rates of service personnel reporting sexual harassment or refusing illegal orders, given that these processes once were unclear and laden with stigma and social pressures, and now are increasingly formalized and normalized for personnel. Selective conscientious objection invocation rates might be very different in a culture where selective conscientious objection is legal. We can expect a lack of legal sanctions to lessen the social stigma of objecting and even make possible the celebration of at least some instances of objecting. We can expect an even more changed environment if legal selective conscientious objection makes possible what some revisionists think would be ideal: punishing combatants post-bellum for service in unjust wars. We can imagine selective conscientious objection invocation even in just wars increasing markedly if uncertain personnel could choose selective conscientious objection instead of risking punishment for service in an unjust war.

178 *The moral equality of combatants*

Regarding the suggestion that military contractors could fill gaps created by selective conscientious objection invocation, it is dubious under current geo-political arrangements that private military contractors could be relied on to supply replacements in any great number for non-infantry-, administrative-, or analysis-type personnel because of the market forces guiding the private military contractors. First, the difficulty of private military contractors supplying replacement pilots would appear to be particularly acute since pilots must engage in regular training to stay operationally fit. The muscle memory and mental habits necessary for the difficult task of flying military aircraft is so fine, and degrades so quickly, that combat aviators are considered unfit to fly after less than two weeks out of the cockpit. Therefore, private military contractors would need significant complements of military aircraft in order for their pilots to stay fit (to say nothing of other kinds of military vehicles). This would be cost-prohibitive for many outfits, even if it were legal for them to purchase this equipment. Due to the expense and time needed for training, mega-contractors able to afford strike aircraft would need to have small standing armies of contractually bound employees to maintain and operate the equipment. Yet the contractors' contractual obligations would obviate the moral advantage of hiring them instead of fielding citizen-soldiers. Corporations would probably refuse to extend a selective conscientious objection exemption to their employees lest they lose the chance to replace *military* conscientious objectors. Thus the military's potential selective conscientious objection retention problem would be solved only by replicating it in the private sector. (No doubt, private military contractors can find unscrupulous people to meet even dubious contracts, but do selective conscientious objection advocates really want such people being sent into unjust wars?)

Second, while well-capitalized private military contractors could conceivably buy the sufficient materiel, it is difficult to imagine corporations doing so prior to winning service contracts, which could not be awarded until a military knew its numbers of conscientious objectors. It would seem difficult to estimate this even for the purpose of signing contracts based on probable future needs since the numbers of objectors will presumably vary widely based on the nature of a conflict. Private military contractors might amass fleets of military vehicles to assist small militaries or insurgent movements in ordinary operations, instead of relying on service to large militaries with selective conscientious objection shortfalls. Yet states probably do not want to allow or encourage private companies to maintain so much military materiel that they can serve as proxy armies to other states. Third, and relatedly, for security reasons, states would presumably demand exclusive, long-term contracts with well-equipped private military contractors, a move which would be at odds with the free-market principles animating the contractors.

I will now address the argument that it would actually be for the best if so many service members invoked selective conscientious objection that they weakened a military bent on making unjust war. While such principled disabling would be satisfying, it seems the wrong way to frame the issue. Due to the

The moral equality of combatants 179

ambiguity of wars' justice and service members' epistemic limits, it is not the case that a right of selective conscientious objection would entail a certain number of personnel refusing to deploy to objectively unjust wars. Rather, a right of selective conscientious objection would amount to a right to petition to refuse deployment to any operation the objector *considered* unjust. From the perspective of policymakers, then, a right of selective conscientious objection would mean a right to petition to refuse deployment to any operation. Some selective conscientious objection advocates suggest that a review board akin to a conscientious objection board could convene to distinguish genuine from spurious claims of selective conscientious objection (Wing 1999: 38). Yet a selective conscientious objection board presumably could not rule on the substantive matter of whether an operation was unjust any more than a conscientious objection board judges whether all war is really immoral. Instead, such a board could only endeavor to determine if the objector believed the operation to be unjust. What could the board say if a pilot argues that she believes the long-term effects of targeted killing show the practice to be disproportionate or that the impending war is unjust for not having met the last resort criterion of *jus ad bellum*?[5] It seems, then, that a right of selective conscientious objection would have to privilege service members' subjective assessments of impending operations and so would likely be invoked, to varying degrees, for every sort of operation, both objectively just and unjust. Remembering how controversial the humanitarian interventions in the Balkans were in the 1990s, we have to consider that legalized selective conscientious objection could mean that the military might be just as likely hampered in fighting just wars as unjust wars.[6]

As we consider how a putative right of selective conscientious objection would fare according to the security standard, we have to consider longer-term effects on the military's functionality after a certain operation sees significant numbers of selective conscientious objection invocations, regardless of the objective nature of that operation. Fighting an unjust war one year does not mean that a state should be unable to fight a just war the next year. What would be the long-term effects of fairly significant selective conscientious objection invocation on unit cohesion and morale? Would the military's legitimate functions be negatively impacted even if, in the arguably best scenario, selective conscientious objection invocation reduced the effectiveness of the military's ability to fight an unjust war? Would significant selective conscientious objection invocation introduce the sort of corrosive political or moral divisions in the military present in many civil societies? At present, officers in militaries with strong traditions of civilian control tend to pride themselves on isolating their political or religious views from their professional duties. An officer in such a military can be confident that his unit-mate will perform her job even if she does not share the same political or moral views. I wonder, though, if the political and moral differences manifesting in a refusal to perform one's job—which might literally mean leaving a pilot without a wingman—can so readily be bracketed when the objector returns from his non-war-fighting billet. Will the willing participant in the putatively unjust war easily reconcile with the unit-mate who left

180 *The moral equality of combatants*

him unable to do his job, or left the military unable to do its job properly? How easy is it to reconcile with a unit-mate whose decision might be taken by the willing participants as an implicit condemnation of him?

iii *Assessing the tenability of selective conscientious objection*

Let us use the practical elements of the security standard to judge the practical tenability of a rule permitting selective conscientious objection. Given all the foregoing considerations, we have to consider the possibility that legalization of selective conscientious objection could lead a military to being less effective and efficient than the *status quo*—ultimately, an unreliable instrument. It strikes me as too complicated to non-superficially judge proportionality since we would have to weigh the positives of respecting combatants' autonomy and making unjust wars harder to fight, against the negatives of perhaps making just wars harder to fight, endangering allies and domestic noncombatants, and perhaps weakening discipline, along with secondary effects of that weakening. Failure to meet the practical elements of the security standard would obviate the need to consider the deontological elements of the standard.

Selective conscientious objection would be untenable if the military could not meet the goals it is morally obliged to carry out. There are stricter standards for this threshold when the military directly defends the homeland than when it operates abroad. Abroad, selective conscientious objection would be untenable if the military was unable to meet a national security goal like winning a war, carrying out a punitive raid, patrolling sea lanes, etc. Domestically, the standards of success would be stricter since the failure to protect even a few civilians from enemy attack or the loss of even a small chunk of territory would fall short of the standard inhabitants reasonably expect their militaries to meet.

It takes a larger failure abroad to run afoul of the consent standard since the connections between one failed skirmish abroad and homeland security are tenuous. Granting a right of selective conscientious objection could still comply with the security standard if combatants' invocation of the right created some inefficiencies that did not lead to defeat. This is the case even if the inefficiency of combat operations led to more combatant casualties since combatants can be expected to endure more casualties in order to meet the demands of morality. The greater the inefficiency, though, the worse legalized selective conscientious objection scores according to the security standard. The greater number of personnel invoking selective conscientious objection, the less reliable a national security tool the military would be, even if it proved effective and not grossly inefficient in a given operation.

The considerations in the previous two sections suggest to me that selective conscientious objection is not practically tenable given the current structure of conventional militaries. Significant technological changes could change that calculation by radically reducing the training time for different specializations (though in the case of autonomous lethal robotics, at the cost of creating new

The moral equality of combatants 181

moral problems). The question of selective conscientious objection is an empirically informed ethical one. Since a philosopher is not in the position to make definitive judgments about the empirical aspect, I will continue to couch selective conscientious objection-linked claims about moral equality in the conditional mood despite the evidence pointing to the untenability of selective conscientious objection.

I will now answer the two questions highlighted at the beginning of the section. Why is the norm of obedience not void in the case of unjust war? Why is the permission for enemy troops to obey their lawful orders not restricted to just wars? Assuming that selective conscientious objection is untenable, it would then follow that the norm of obedience extends to all deployment orders, even when a combatant thinks the relevant operation is unjust. A military cannot efficiently, efficaciously, and reliably function to accomplish its morally important ends while also honoring a right of selective conscientious objection. Necessary components of the military profession are universally consent-worthy for facilitating militaries' legitimate functions in basically just states. If a caveat-free norm of obedience to lawful orders is a necessary component of the military profession, a duty to support just institutions means ceding claim-rights to adversary service personnel to obey all their deployment orders, including orders to possibly unjust wars. Service personnel then have permission from all affected to obey all deployment orders, even to objectively unjust operations.

III Obligations and justifications

i Objective justification

Yet one need not, and perhaps should not, act simply because one has permission. In addition to having permission to deploy from affected parties and a duty to obey their orders, combatants also have an obligation to obey their lawful orders since they voluntarily entered into a profession with these role obligations. An obligation is an agent-relative positive moral reason to act, a reason applying to the agent but not necessarily to others. Like other group-based obligations, the moral force of this obligation is based on members' promises, the benefits they receive from other service members, and the special attachment they have formed with their colleagues. The obligation is heightened for service personnel, as opposed to other kinds of group members, because of the importance of the service they provide, the uniqueness of the skill set they have acquired, and the opportunity cost the state incurred by training them as opposed to others.

Military role obligations only have agent-relative moral weight if the military is a good institution, which is to say, an institution for which there are positive agent-neutral reasons for joining. If the institution is not a generically good one for anyone to join (whereby they will then incur agent-relative reasons for acting a certain way), the promises entrants make to serve are not necessarily binding, fellow group members' support should perhaps not be

182 *The moral equality of combatants*

accepted, and a member should not necessarily form special attachments with comrades.[7] Entrants have no moral reason to privilege their agent-relative reasons for actions over agent-neutral reasons to refrain from the same actions (e.g., consequent to moral duties). These concerns do not apply if my argument in Chapter 5, sub-section III.iv was successful, where I argued that military service in a basically just state is good.

To be clear, all conventional combatants and privileged irregulars have *duties* to adhere to military norms no matter what political entity they serve, including the norm of obedience.[8] Their *obligation* of obedience indicates which chain of command they obey and which state they serve. This overlap of the object of the duty and obligation is not unusual. Duties apply to all (mentally competent, adult) people by virtue of natural properties and are enforceable by strangers. The breach of a duty usually violates a right. Obligations depend on special relationships or agreements; the partner in the relationship has a special authority to complain and enforce the agreement. For example, everyone has a duty to respect others' private property. A moving company has a special obligation to handle its clients' goods with care. A third party (who knew the facts of the case) could admonish the movers for burning the clients' goods in the street, but only the client would have standing to sue the movers for damages. The presence of both duties and obligations of obedience can explain why a combatant might respect his enemy's faithful service to her country, even when it comes at the expense of the first combatant's safety. Each conventional combatant can reason that a combatant *qua* combatant should be obeying her lawful orders and particularly the orders of her command (rather than those of another state). Duties can trump obligations, for example, combatants' duties to adhere to military norms could lead them to refuse orders violating *jus in bello* (such an order would also conflict with the norm of obedience to lawful orders).

One can be acting permissibly, or meeting a duty and/or an obligation, and still not be engaged in a justified action. For example, the only way for Smith and Jones to make money to support their families might be to engage in a duel where the survivor wins money. The duelists both have obligations to their families and each cedes claim-rights to the other, giving the other permission to duel. Yet dueling is not justified. Similarly, acting on a duty may not be justified since one duty can be overridden by another duty, such as when a duty to respect someone's autonomy overrides the duty to aid the person (e.g., the person who refuses a blood transfusion for religious reasons).

This is McMahan's bottom line: even if combatants are serving in a just institution, even if they combatants give each other permission to fight (which McMahan would deny),[9] and even if both sides have legitimate obligations to their states, the actions of personnel on the unjust side are still objectively unjustified if they advance the unjust ends of the war (McMahan 2008: 26, 2009: 56). Following McMahan's line, one who is merely permitted to do something has no particular reason to do it, whereas one engaged in justified action has agent-neutral positive moral reasons for acting. Thus, the mutual permission combatants have to obey all their lawful orders is not sufficient to justify their service in

The moral equality of combatants 183

an unjust war. The positive moral reasons generating obligations are not sufficient to generate justifications since the agent-relative reasons behind obligations are usually trumped by the agent-neutral reasons behind general negative duties (e.g., one cannot murder to save one's child). A positive duty to protect people (such as one's own citizens, who may be legitimately endangered when the just side counter-attacks) usually is outweighed by negative duties not to wrongly harm people. So a combatant's obligation to his state and his permission to act, granted by affected combatants and noncombatants, still does not justify his service in an unjust war.[10]

In order for the moral equality thesis to be defended, military norms, including obedience, must have the weight of general moral duties and must outweigh any countervailing duties that would be triggered by the advent of an unjust war. I already argued that security-standard-compliant norms are institutionally mediated moral duties. I have to show military norms have sufficient weight to be definitively action-guiding for both sides' combatants in areas where different duties are action-guiding for laypeople (and where a revisionist might say that non-professional duty supersedes the unjust side's professional duty and obligation). This argument will show that both sides are justified in deploying to war regardless of the justice or injustice of their state's cause.

My view is that service personnel in basically just states have overriding positive moral reasons for deploying to war whether their state has a just or unjust cause because obedient service to all lawful orders, including deployment orders, is consent-worthy to all affected parties as an expression of military duty (assuming the untenability of selective conscientious objection). Since the norm of obedience to all lawful orders is caveat-free (i.e., it is not contingent on the justice of the prospective war), it overrules potential countervailing duties to refrain from contributing to unjust collective actions. The norm of obedience has this caveat-free form because adherence to this norm is the only way to protect any political entity over time in the event that selective conscientious objection is practically untenable and no just and effective global government exists to keep the peace. The regular institutional practice of military service and just warfighting could not endure if the norm of obedience had a caveat against service in an unjust war and so the consent-based justification only accrued to the just side of a conflict. Unilateral justification from one side in the conflict would require a norm of obedience contingent on objectively just outcomes. Professional duty is instead expressed in proceduralist norms because professional norms have to be action-guiding and fact-relative standards geared toward correct outcomes are not action-guiding. Bilateral justification is then possible because consent accrues to the results of consent-worthy procedures. These are procedures that both sets of service personnel in basically just states can meet.

Service in an unjust war is not consent-worthy *per se*. Instead, hypothetical consent extends to a fallible system of governance and military protection that sometimes involves launching unjust wars, either because of miscalculation, error, or the efforts of malign policymakers. So the consent accruing to a fallible system of governance and military protection indirectly legitimates an anarchic

184   *The moral equality of combatants*

international system in which different states attempt to protect their own inhabitants, replicating the same risk of errors and corruption. This fallible system is consent-worthy because no better alternative making just warfighting possible exists in the absence of a just global government. The justification the contractualist model extends to norm-compliant military service does not withdraw when the fallible system fails, because fallibility is an inherent part of the consent-worthy system.

I will not be arguing that military service in an unjust war is morally required in the sense that service in all or certain unjust wars is the all-things-considered best action for all or for certain combatants. Such an argument would require showing that all other moral considerations are defeated by a service member's permission, obligation, and general justification. I am also not arguing that a combatant's justification for service in an unjust war ought to trump his own conscience if he feels that he cannot participate in the war. Rather, by arguing for combatant moral equality between some political entities, I hold that both sides have positive moral reasons for deploying and fighting that are stronger than countervailing reasons for disobedience, but not necessarily so strong that they are morally required to act.[11]

ii Procedural consent

I need to clarify some terminology before defending these claims. As McMahan uses the term, justification for an action means a positive moral reason for performing the action. By contrast, permission to do X means one is violating no duty in doing X. Permission does not amount to a positive reason for committing the action. An agent is subjectively justified in acting if she acts based on false beliefs that would justify the action if the beliefs were true. Objective justification for an action means there are positive moral reasons to act explained by facts independent of the agent's belief. McMahan denies the moral equality of combatants even in the unlikely event that all service personnel were subjectively justified in believing their cause was just since only those actors objectively justified in posing threats are non-liable for those threats (2009: 43).

For McMahan, objectively justified actors are right in what Derek Parfit calls a fact-relative sense. They perform actions that would be right to perform if the actors knew all the morally relevant facts. By contrast, performing the action that is only right in an evidence-relative sense is not objectively justified. Evidence-relative rightness is when the action would be right if the actors believed what the evidence before them gave them decisive reasons to believe and these beliefs were true (Parfit 2013: 143).

I will argue that state agents are objectively justified when they do the right thing in the fact-relative sense relevant to their professional norms. These are moments when they hew to their professional procedures and take into account all the available information relevant to that procedure. It is not the case that they are justified only when they act rightly in a (total) fact-relative sense. Their norm-compliant professional procedures and heuristics may only admit certain

The moral equality of combatants 185

kinds of information. I am not arguing that they are objectively justified when they act on right evidence-related grounds since the evidence they take into account or that is presented to them may be less than the total extant amount of evidence relevant to their professional procedures and heuristics.[12] To anticipate the military application of this argument in the next section, combatants are justified when they obey authentic deployment orders issued from their basically just states' leader(s), faithfully transmitted down the chain of command, regardless of the nature of the conflict to which they are deployed.

The plausibility of my claims about combatants will be aided if we first apply the contractualist model to more familiar cases of domestic state agents. A fairly detailed account developed on familiar terrain will enable more rapid application to the contested and unfamiliar military context in the following section. My view is that the same model of professional ethics can be applied to all state agents.

A judge might be subjectively justified (right in Parfit's belief-relative sense) in convicting a defendant if the judge wrongly believes prosecutors have proved the defendant's guilt beyond a reasonable doubt. Being right in a belief-relative sense, of course, is not the same thing as being objectively justified. The judge can be criticized if she failed to take into account all the exculpatory evidence defense counsel presented or failed to interpret the reasonable doubt threshold as it had been construed by precedent. Note, however, that the ground for critique is not the fact that the defendant is innocent, but something else: that the judge did not follow her role-appointed procedure, that less than the total amount of admissible evidence was considered, or that judicial or relevant key criminal justice norms were not obeyed.

Imagine a case where the admissible evidence points to a defendant's innocence despite the fact that he committed the crime in question. The admissible evidence excludes evidence the judge quashed because it was gathered through police misconduct. There are two facts in this case independent of the judge's beliefs generating positive moral reasons for her ultimate decision about the defendant's innocence or guilt: the defendant committed the crime and there is sufficient admissible exculpatory evidence to acquit him. The second fact regarding available, admissible evidence creates grounds for actors in the criminal justice system to be right or wrong in a *fact-relative sense relevant to their professional norms* (call this FRPN) in performing role-specified actions such as arresting, indicting, and convicting the defendant (or those actions' opposites). The FRPN standard often amounts to a professional's evidence-relative standard but there could be cases when a judge, for example, makes an evidence-relative right ruling based on the admissible evidence brought before her that is still FRPN-wrong. This discrepancy could occur, for example, if attorneys forgot to introduce admissible evidence into trial. Unlike the evidence excluded because of police misconduct, the judge has grounds to say, upon learning of the forgotten evidence, "the correct verdict that *any judge* should have reached (given all the extant admissible evidence) would have been different to the one I made." She would not question her ruling in this way years later if the exonerated

186 *The moral equality of combatants*

defendant later admitted his crimes or if someone protested that the rightly quashed evidence indicated the defendant's guilt. So, unlike an evidence-relative standard, the FRPN standard is not restricted to the agent's subjective point of view, but rather, to the evidential and epistemic standards for certain types of professional action and the *potentially* available information.

I will contend that the judge is objectively justified if she performs the action that is FRPN correct, and so is justified in acquitting the defendant if there is not sufficient admissible inculpating evidence *even if he is guilty*. I will first argue that the judge has a moral reason for adhering to a FRPN standard, and, second, that the FRPN-related reason is stronger than the reason to adhere to a total fact-relative standard in this case.

There are at least five reasons why the judge must adhere to her professional norms in this case instead of using her personal, nonprofessional, judgment— five reasons the judge has a positive moral reason to acquit someone who is actually guilty and who she may subjectively believe is guilty.[13] Since four of the five are moral reasons themselves, the positive moral reason for acquittal can be considered a composite, or summary, reason. The judge's reason for acquittal is not merely a legal or pragmatic (ends-justified) reason since derogation from proper professional norms in a basically just state would have serious negative consequences regarding people's rights and welfare. We will see that most of these reasons also argue for combatants obeying lawful deployment orders rather than relying on their personal judgment.

First, allowing evidence garnered through misconduct—even if the evidence accurately indicates guilt—may encourage further misconduct, violating more suspects' rights and falsely convicting innocents (call this reason "misconduct"). Second, there is no legally sound way for the judge to convict a defendant benefitted by the amount of exculpatory evidence presented in her court. The resulting impression of unfairness if the judge blatantly disregarded legal precedent and procedures in order to convict could contribute to the degradation of a vital institution. Perceptions of a corrupt legal system could lead witnesses or victims to refuse to testify, police to manufacture evidence, vigilantes to take justice into their own hands, etc. (call this reason "bias"). Third, the judge's ruling could have bad downstream effects by creating a bad precedent in case law ("precedent").

Fourth (the non-moral reason), a judge's legitimate scope of discretion would not cover ignoring a preponderance of exculpatory evidence if hypothetical consent determines the boundaries of discretion, along with other judicial norms ("discretion"). All potentially affected by a judicial decision could not be modeled as consenting to a discretionary rule like "act according to the evidence— except when you know it does not accurately indicate the defendant's guilt or innocence" because there is no reliable, accountable way to act on the caveat. Ordinarily, the judge has no epistemically respectable way to know the defendant's status apart from the presented evidence. The excluded evidence may not have been perused by the judge prior to its dismissal for cause; even if the judge excluded it after a defense challenge and so is familiar with its content, the judge

The moral equality of combatants   187

still cannot assume it is more authentic than the exculpatory evidence. Fifth, if the judge has extra-procedural knowledge of the case (for example, the judge herself witnessed the crime) and did not recuse herself, the judge could only act on her fallible knowledge by violating judicial procedure or giving the appearance of unfairness (call this reason "personal knowledge").

The judge's positive five-part moral rationale for acquittal connected to the FRPN standard just described is stronger than the moral reason attached to the total fact-relative standard for conviction. Indeed, all state agents have stronger reasons for heeding moral reasons connected to FRPN standards over moral reasons connected to total fact-relative standards. First, a total fact-relative standard cannot form the basis of an agent-guiding norm. Professional norms for state agents must be agent-guiding since they are effectively instructions from the agents' principals. Consent-worthy instructions cannot direct police officers to only arrest suspects if they are in fact guilty or judges to convict when defendants are in fact guilty because of state agents' epistemic limits (Parfit 2013: 150). State agents must act because of their professional obligations and the moral importance of their actions. They do not have the luxury of omitting interventions to avoid the risk of committing fact-relative wrongs. They have positive moral reasons for acting even when laypeople should perhaps omit the risks involved with intervention.

Second, the level of passivity on the part of state agents expected to *approximate* fact-relative accuracy in action, for example, only arresting people observed performing the *actus rea* of a crime, or only convicting people implicated by DNA evidence, video recording, and several eye-witnesses, etc., would likely fail the security standard for not adequately contributing to a secure environment.

Third, the only alternative to state agents adhering to their professional norms in determining how to act would be to rely on their personal moral judgment and personal epistemic faculties. It would fail the security standard to mandate state agents' action without providing them morally approved procedures for achieving these ends. Investing each actor with the prerogative to make decisions based on her own moral compass and reasoning without any kind of publicly tested professional procedure will likely lead to worse practical and moral consequences than a rule-governed alternative. Further, investing each actor with the prerogative to make decisions will lead to irregular and apparently capricious behavior that is objectionable on its own for inhibiting inhabitants' abilities to plan for the future.

Chapter 6 explained how state agents could harm people without wronging them since the affected parties could be modeled as ceding claim-rights against state agents where demanding those rights would inhibit the agents from acting in the affected parties' interests or the interests of other people whose rights the affected party has a duty to respect. This section clarifies that the ceded claim-rights are to state agents acting with respect to FRPN standards. State inhabitants can demand that state agents take proactive steps in conditions of uncertainty to meet their institutionally mediated collective responsibilities in

188 *The moral equality of combatants*

accordance with agent-guiding norms articulated with the security standard. For example, it is not reckless for combatants to launch an attack based on a probabilistic, rather than certain, proportionality calculation.

One might object that all I have shown with this argument for privileging a FRPN-related moral reason over a total fact-relative-related moral reason is that professional norms cannot be oriented toward right fact-relative outcomes, such that we cannot say a good judge is a judge who only convicts people who are actually guilty and acquits people who are actually innocent. The objection might continue that I have failed to show that state agents cannot be criticized from a moral point of view outside their profession. Maybe state agents are tragic figures who must make decisions that will be unjustified in a percentage of cases.[14] Perhaps we can excuse them since they are required to make important decisions on behalf of others. Or perhaps state agents should subvert their systems or resign when professional norms contradict ordinary moral expectations.[15] I will address this excuse-related objection before turning to the fourth reason for thinking there are stronger reasons for a state agent to adhere to a FRPN-, rather than a total fact-relative standard.

State agents acting rightly in a FRPN sense are not merely excused when they arrest, detain, penalize, prosecute, convict, and otherwise harm innocent people (Coady 1990: 163). They meet none of the markers for excuse. The state agents were not overcome by powerful, but understandable, emotions; they were not under duress; and they did not err, according to the standards of their profession. It is not the case that other professionals should not imitate their behavior. Police should arrest knife-wielding, blood-spattered people found near corpses with stab wounds 100 times out of 100 and judges should convict people if an overwhelming amount of evidence points to their guilt (there are procedures in both cases for innocent people to appeal). We do not want state agents sitting on their hands and we do not want them deviating from security-standard-approved procedures to make idiosyncratic decisions in these cases.

Further, given a reasonably effective and functional criminal justice system, even if a layperson knew the state agent was wrong in a fact-relative sense, we do not want that person interfering with the agent or the affected party fighting back against the state agent. These are both permissible reactions to an excused, but objectively wrong, lay agent. Instead, the criminal justice procedure provides formal means of redress to wrongly detained or convicted persons.

On the topic of excuse, it is worth saying more about why state agents must be judged by the lights of their professional norms in order to see if they have erred. Laypeople might be excused in an instance when a state agent would be justified for committing an action that is fact-relative wrong. Regarding the kind of reasonable mistakes that can lead to excuses, laypeople's typical mistakes come from using normal decision-making or risk assessment heuristics in a novel situation when those procedures will not yield the appropriate action. The layperson did not abandon a particular, formalized heuristic he was obliged to use in such a case. For example, a mistaken attacker might be in his predicament when he sees someone rushing at him with a knife or sees a notorious serial

The moral equality of combatants 189

killer coming his way. Normally, he has met the evidential threshold for a layperson to engage in defensive action. However, in these cases, the knife turns out to be rubber and the killer turns out to be the innocent twin. Had the mistaken attacker known all the relevant information, he would have realized his normal decision-making heuristic was not to be trusted.

In contrast, state agents have security-standard-compliant norms laying out society's expectations for their behavior. A judge should still use her normal professional decision-making procedure if she had all the relevant information regarding a crime; she now merely has more evidence to take into account according to the rules of the court than compared to a case where, say, a witness did not come forward. If the judge knew something exculpatory about the defendant defense counsel did not know, the judge should recuse herself and serve as a witness on behalf of the defendant. She cannot use her own unique knowledge about the case if the relevant information was not entered into evidence. So the layperson is excused for acting wrongly in a fact-relative sense because it is a reasonable mistake to use normal decision-making procedures when one has no reason to believe one is in an abnormal context. The state agent made no mistake in using her normal decision-making procedure. A judge is always in the same decision-making context. She is doing what her (hypothetical consent-contoured) professional duty has given her positive moral reasons to do.

The fourth reason state agents should adhere to their FRPN rather than a total fact-relative standard follows. Actions performed by laypeople that are only right in evidence- and belief-relative senses can be criticized from a fact-relative point of view. These actions are not ones that someone with all the relevant facts should perform. Yet no broader scope exists for criticizing norm-compliant state agents who hew to a FRPN standard. Most professional behavior by state agents (arresting, taxing, fining, searching with a warrant, convicting, waging war, etc.) only occur (properly) in governmental contexts according to definite, security-standard-compliant heuristics. They do not occur in a state of nature. It then does not make sense to say that a person's arrest, conviction, etc., is not right in a fact-relative sense since the relevant state actions are only triggered by definite heuristics with specific evidentiary requirements. They can only occur with respect to grounds for FRPN-relative right or wrong actions. There is no way for an "arrest" or a "conviction," etc. to be triggered by all the total facts.

The contractualist model is a moral theory dividing moral responsibilities between certain professionals and laypeople. Since professional ethics, on this view, is an institutionally mediated expression of collective moral responsibilities, there is no broader perspective from which to criticize state agents in security-standard-compliant institutions when they hew to their properly constituted professional norms. By this, I mean there are no reasonable grounds to criticize norm-compliant action when the norms are properly constituted. (People may argue over the proper constitution of professional norms, and therefore object that the extant norms local authorities assiduously observe are wrongly constituted.) The contractualist model shows how there can be different norms state agents and laypeople should follow in similar situations. For

190 *The moral equality of combatants*

example, judges and laypeople have different duties with regard to justice. All have duties to seek that justice is done. Laypeople usually have the opportunity to act on this duty in *ad hoc* situations affecting a limited number of people, but judges have an obligation to act justly in their professional capacity in an institutional setting designed to deliver just outcomes reliably and consistently to an unlimited number of people over time. The mediation of the criminal justice institution may direct judges to act differently than laypeople in the pursuit of justice. Consider *Crime*.

Crime

Archer knows Baker is guilty of murder. Archer is reluctant to tell the police, but a detective procures a truthful statement after threatening Archer. The judge throws out the inculpatory statement because of the detective's misconduct.

Archer would have been right to have voluntarily testified and is right to tell the press or the victim's family his story now in an attempt to see justice done. However, the judge would fail in her institutionally mediated duty to pursue justice if she ignored the police misconduct and took Archer's statement into account. Archer's duty to pursue justice directs him to act on the information about Baker while the judge's institutionally mediated duty to pursue justice directs her to ignore the information. Archer has no grounds for criticizing the judge's action. While it frustrates justice in the immediate term, as argued above, the expunging of the tainted evidence is an expression of a procedure that more reliably than not delivers justice to the majority of defendants the judge sees.

So if the judge's security-standard-compliant procedures and associated heuristics with specific evidence requirements are consent-worthy, her FRPN-related reason is stronger than a total fact-relative-related reason. She could be objectively justified in acquitting a guilty defendant. She does not deserve moral criticism; she should not feel shame for having failed to do the "right thing" if the true perpetrator later admits his guilt. The precedent of her decision should be followed.

There may be rare cases when it is morally required for a state agent like a judge to breach her professional norms and not adhere to the FRPN standard. The reasons arguing for privileging the FRPN-relative moral reason depend on the judge participating in a just institution in a basically just state. The hypothetical consent of the affected parties can be modeled to a fallible system of criminal justice in a state with mostly just laws and fair law enforcement since this creates a consent-worthy environment relatively free of rights violations. The justification of a state agent's hewing to her institutional duties breaks down if these duties are not security-standard-compliant institutional expressions of collective moral responsibilities. So if the judge is working in a tyrannical state or

The moral equality of combatants 191

the judicial system is terribly corrupt, it may be morally required to privilege the total fact-relative moral reason in a situation where the judge believes the evidence does not point to the fact-relative right outcome and derogate from the judicial norms (that corrupt colleagues do not follow anyway) in order to try to roughly affect some justice.

iii Military application of procedural consent

We are now in the position to see why service personnel can be justified in obeying orders to contribute to wars that are fact-relative wrong collective actions. Due process and the other judicial norms actors in the criminal justice system follow are fallible but consent-worthy procedures for securing justice. Service members' adherence to military norms, including obedience to all lawful orders (if selective conscientious objection is untenable), is the consent-worthy but fallible procedure for delivering national security to a state. Like police and judges, it is service members' hewing to professional norms and associated heuristics, rather than contributing to fact-relative just actions, that wins the hypothetical consent of all affected. Again, hypothetical consent works out the details of the professional duty that is an institutionally mediated expression of the collective responsibility to deliver security to one's community. If a right of selective conscientious objection is untenable, then there is no way for service personnel to meet their duties to contribute to their state's security without obeying all their (*in bello*) lawful orders, including deployment orders. As with judicial norms, military norms narrow the epistemic scope required for decisions by service members so they are called on to make correct decisions in the FRPN sense relevant to military norms. A judge's professional epistemic scope is broader than a service member's, but is also artificially narrowed by norms facilitating the profession's end. Service personnel need only assure themselves that their orders are genuine ones passed down from their legitimate commanders, that the orders are substantively lawful (in the *in bello* terrain), and that subsequent actions are compliant with military norms. Service personnel can be objectively justified in serving in an unjust war if they meet these requirements. Deployment is not justified if their deployment orders are not genuine, either because they do not issue from their legitimate political leader or they are not faithfully transmitted down the chain of command. A service member deploying will likely be evidence-relative-justified if he receives the order from his usual superior officer in the usual way or receives a properly formatted and coded transmission over the secure network normally transmitting certain orders, but is not FRPN-justified if these orders are actually forged or emanating from a rogue commander. There are two facts independent of the service member's beliefs relevant to the rightness of his deployment: facts related to the justice of the war and facts related to the genuineness of his order. The service member is objectively justified in obeying his deployment orders if his orders are genuine ones passed faithfully down his chain of command.

192 *The moral equality of combatants*

Let us compare a service member and a judge in more detail to better make the case. The introduction of these matters in the section on selective conscientious objection will allow me to make these comparisons fairly rapidly.[16] The service member receiving genuine deployment orders through his chain of command to a conflict that is actually unjust has a total fact-relative-related reason to refuse deployment and a FRPN-related moral reason to deploy. The latter reason trumps the former reason for the "bias," "precedent," "discretion," and "personal knowledge" reasons mentioned in sub-section III.ii.

Bias. Service members' principled refusal to deploy can have grave implications for civil-military relations, leading civilians to lose trust in their military. If the military loses the support of the public it may lose the budgetary, manpower, and rhetorical support necessary to meet legitimate national security goals. It seems naïve to think the public would be buoyed by a "principled" military composed of troops willing to refuse to deploy to unjust wars. The public is never unanimous regarding the justice of military conflicts, so a portion of the public will feel alienated from the military given any significant invocation of selective conscientious objection. It may well be that a significant portion of the military refuses to deploy to a conflict that the majority of the public thinks is just. Principled invocation of selective conscientious objection will no doubt be deemed by critics as shirking or politically motivated obstruction, further alienating the public.

Precedent. As also discussed in section II, the precedent of selective conscientious objection invocation even in the face of an objectively unjust war (which many will nonetheless believe is a just war) may increase the rate of invocation in the face of a just war. Further, deterrence and diplomacy will likely be complicated due to the precedent of selective conscientious objection invocation and the associated perception of the military's unreliability.

Discretion. Affected parties cannot be modeled as extending to service personnel a legitimate scope of discretion such that they are duty-bound to obey all lawful orders except deployment orders to putatively unjust conflicts because there is no reliable, accountable way of implementing the caveat. While service personnel can consult non-military authorities to gather views about the impending conflict, they ultimately would have to make a personal judgment about the conflict's justice, according to the caveat under discussion. There is a relevant difference between service personnel and judges in that the former do have means of getting information outside their professional channels, but they are similarly limited in access to information that is legitimately action-guiding. There are systemic problems with judges acting on extra-judicial knowledge even in the rare case when a judge might have personal knowledge of a case. There are some of the same systemic problems with service personnel acting on information contradicting their orders: their epistemic fallibility and the systemic problems involved with role actors acting on their own *ad doc* initiative instead of hewing to role-appointed procedures. Discretion also creates the opportunity for shirking and the temptation for shirking would be high when it comes to deployment.

The moral equality of combatants 193

Personal knowledge. A judge could readily create the impression of unfairness if she departs from judicial norms because of personal knowledge about the case. A principled invoker of selective conscientious objection, acting on her personal study of the impending conflict, could readily be characterized as a shirker or political partisan. Permitting this apparent shirking might degrade the military's discipline and morale, damaging the effectiveness that is morally relevant in order to fight just wars.

So a service member has moral and not just legal or pragmatic (e.g., avoiding punishment) reason for hewing to a FRPN standard when it comes to deployment. Erosion of the military's ability to efficiently accomplish its missions can degrade its ability to protect its state's security, or that of allies and the beneficiaries of humanitarian intervention. A service member lacks an FRPN-related reason to deploy if he did not receive deployment orders, did not receive them from his commanding officer, if the order was not faithfully passed down the chain of command, or if the order did not originate from his political entity's legitimate authority. Note, FRPN- and evidence-relative right actions may diverge with respect to the latter three eventualities.

Once deployed, a combatant does the FRPN-relative right thing if his actions are substantively consistent with military norms, regardless of whether he thinks they are consistent or inconsistent with such norms. He may perform the evidence-relative right action if he approves an airstrike based on a sound proportionality calculation that is wrong by a FRPN-relative standard because it was possible to know that there were more noncombatants in the blast radius than presented to him (perhaps the targeteer was negligent in evaluating the target). Yet if the collateral damage estimate is state-of-the-art based on available information and technology—such that no military actor could have discerned the presence of extra noncombatants—then the attack is objectively justified even if it is a wrong fact-relative action.

Under most circumstances, a service member's FRPN-related moral reason for obedience trumps his total fact-relative-related reason to disobey deployment orders. As with other state agents, total fact-relative standards are not consent-worthy. Consent-worthy norms have to be action-guiding and the putative rule "deploy only to wars that are actually just" is not action-guiding. The level of passivity required to even approximate fact-relative right actions (waiting until one was subjectively certain) would not be consent-worthy as there will be at least some occasions when national security depends on combatants deploying promptly when ordered.

Further, according to the contractualist model, there is no external moral standpoint from which to criticize norm-compliant military personnel for their actions since military norms are an institutionally mediated expression of the collective moral responsibility to deliver security.[17] War does not occur in the state of nature or in civilian life. It is inherently the function of political entities to prosecute. If selective conscientious objection is untenable, there is no other way for political entities to prosecute just wars over time but with militaries demanding obedience of its members to all lawful orders. To be clear, service

194 *The moral equality of combatants*

personnel *can* be criticized for derogating from military norms and the norms themselves can be criticized for not being compliant with the security standard.

One might object that a service member's negative duty to refrain from killing innocents in an unjust war trumps his positive FRPN-related duty to serve his state (McMahan 2009: 71–72). Generally, killing innocents is worse than failing to protect innocents. Given that political leaders and their national security advisers are fallible, the objection continues, service personnel should defer to their possible negative duty when there is any doubt about a war's justice (McMahan 2011: 145). If most wars are unjust, the doubtful service member has a greater chance of avoiding violations of a negative moral duty if he errs on the side of not deploying. If his odds are even or better to deploy to a just war, refusing to deploy in doubtful cases will mean that he has breached a lesser duty if indeed the dubious war was unjust.

We have already seen in Chapter 4 that non-culpable combatants are not unjustified in participating in unjust wars or operations. So non-culpable combatants on the unjust side lack strong moral reasons to refrain from deploying or fighting. The above argument, related to the *possibility* that a combatant is fighting in an unjust war, could constitute a weaker moral reason for refraining to fight. By analogy, I have a strong moral reason not to take something I know belongs to someone else. I have a weaker moral reason not to take something if I think it is mine, but have some doubt.

All affected parties—combatants *and* noncombatants in all the basically just political entities in the world—can be modeled as hypothetically consenting to a delineation of military norms including an (*ad bellum*) caveat-free norm of obedience if selective conscientious objection is untenable and there is no just global government. Actual or potential *combatants* can be modeled as consenting to this arrangement for the additional reason that they do not want to be exposed to *post-bellum* prosecutions for fighting in a war that turns out to be unjust. If selective conscientious objection is untenable, there can be no exception for deployment orders to putatively unjust wars built into a consent-worthy norm of obedience. Norms have to be agent-guiding and fact-relative prescriptions linked to outcomes like "disobey orders to objectively unjust wars" are not agent-guiding. This fallible proceduralist regime will be consent-worthy so long as the international order is composed of independent states and selective conscientious objection is untenable. Since the norm is (*ad bellum*) caveat-free it cannot be overridden by a putative *ad bellum*-related duty not to participate in unjust wars or any other kind of general, other-oriented duty not already incorporated into *in bello* prohibitions. The positive moral reason associated with military duty is stronger for service personnel than a relatively weak moral reason not to participate in wars one suspects might be unjust.

A second reason combatants' positive moral reason associated with military duty outweighs moral reasons associated with general, other-oriented duties is that the most potent relevant rival potentially applicable, the duty not to kill innocent people, is not operative in this case. Combatants and noncombatants on the just side are relevantly non-culpable, but they are also duty-bound to

The moral equality of combatants   195

support just institutions and to ceding claim-rights against being exposed to just lethal collateral risk or to being directly targeted, depending on the role (noncombatant or combatant) they choose to play. So people in the just state are not "innocent" in the sense of being wronged if harmed by norm-compliant enemy service personnel.

Finally, to say service in a given war is justified is not to say it is required. The foregoing argument about justification for service even in unjust wars depends on the service personnel in question serving a basically just political entity. Adhering to fallible procedural professional norms related to state service is only justifiable if the norms are in service of a just institution in a basically just state. The "norms" facilitating the signal ends of unjust institutions like mafias or unjust political entities carry little moral weight. Affected parties cannot be modeled as ceding claim-rights giving permission to agents of such unjust institutions since the agent behavior is not in service of their rights. Combatants in unjust states do not have duties to protect their states and are not objectively justified in hewing to the FRPN-related reason to deploy instead of the total fact-relative-related reason to disobey. They may be morally required to disobey deployment orders to a dubious war. Service personnel may be morally required to disobey deployment orders in a situation where their once basically just political entity has fundamentally changed for the worse during their terms of service in terms of its basic laws, its political system, or its constitution.

iv Summary

The benefit of protection by state institutions is that it provides regular, enduring, broad-scale, impartial, expert protection. However, there are also inherent imperfections with institutional protection in a quasi-anarchic international system. The institutions involved are fallible and vulnerable to over-reaction, corruption, and political manipulation. If a ban on selective conscientious objection is necessary for efficient and effective military protection, then all combatants in a conflict are objectively justified in obeying their lawful orders and fighting regardless of whether they fight for the just or unjust side. Non-culpable combatants lack strong moral reasons against deploying or fighting because structural features of military action mean the strong moral reasons applying to the collective action do not necessarily apply to individual contributory actions. They are permitted to fight by foreigners granting them liberty-rights to wield and manage violence according to properly constituted military norms. Noncombatants grant liberty-rights to combatants to pursue their tactical goals while also subjecting noncombatants to a degree of risk and to calculating their projected deaths in a proportionality calculation to be weighed against their tactical goals. By enlisting, combatants grant liberty-rights to enemy combatants to directly target them. The enlistees give up claim rights to their enemies, but get liberty-rights from their enemies to fight in return.

Combatants must take advantage of these liberty-rights in war because they have institutionally mediated duties to create secure environments and

196 *The moral equality of combatants*

obligations to do so for the benefit of their states. Failure to fight endangers domestic noncombatants in a war, whether it is initially defensive or offensive (in the case of counter-attacks). If selective conscientious objection is untenable, the state is vulnerable over the medium and long term because of the precedent service members' refusal to fight creates. Service personnel may act on their duties and obligations even if they suspect the war is unjust because all potentially affected foreigners can be modeled as giving them permission to serve in a fallible institution dependent on obedience to function, arrayed against other fallible institutions in an adversarial system. They can be modeled as giving their adversaries permission because they hypothetically consent to their own service personnel serving them in the same system. Service personnel are justified in deploying to any war their legitimate superiors order them to join because the self-help by institutional proxy arrangement in which they participate serves all *ex ante* better than alternatives. So even if combatants and noncombatants in an unjustly attacked state are harmed by this particular war, they are benefited by the arrangement making the unjust war possible. If selective conscientious objection is untenable, there is no way to have the beneficial arrangement without tolerating the errors—the unjust wars—the system makes possible.

IV Conclusion

Revisionist just war theory is the most significant contribution to the Western just war tradition since the 1977 publication of Michael Walzer's *Just and Unjust Wars*. The work of revisionist scholars is paradigm-changing to the extent that one must either ally with or be against them. In this book, I argued that most revisionists—specifically, reductive individualists—are unable to defend the asymmetry thesis at the heart of their arguments. Further, I argued that the thesis is unsupportable because it is not necessarily the case that actions contributing to the main strategic thrust of unjust collective actions or outcomes are unjustified. It follows, then, that *in bello*-compliant combatants contributing to the main strategic thrust of an unjust operation or war are not unilaterally liable to the defensive violence of the just side. Combatants on rival sides of a war, performing the same physical behaviors, are performing normatively identical actions, distinct from the outcomes to which they contribute. Combatants have permission from all those affected to engage in those *in bello*-compliant actions without attention to the justice of the war or operation. These actions are objectively justified since they are in response to a duty to obey lawful orders as an expression of their collective moral responsibility to contribute to the security of their states. The duty to obey lawful orders does not admit of a caveat related to serving in unjust wars. Thus, despite the differing nature of the collective actions they further, combatants on either side of a war are both objectively justified to deploy and to fight.

The elimination of the asymmetry thesis undercuts the revisionist rejection of separate moral domains for *jus in bello* and *jus ad bellum*, the requirement

The moral equality of combatants 197

of combatants to refuse deployment to wars they think unjust, the potential permissible targeting of noncombatants, and the potential exposure of *in bello*-compliant combatants on the unjust side to *post-bellum* prosecution. Finally, I have defended the traditional collectivist and exceptionalist approach to just war theory, over an approach that attempts to link military norms to the same norms applying to individuals in civilian contexts.

Notes

1 Australia will recognize selective conscientious objection in the event that conscription is re-introduced.
2 McMahan (2009: 99) (in the context of a just war). Stephen Coleman, personal communication; David Garren, personal communication.
3 This limits, and improves, on the argument in Skerker (2014).
4 These statistics were communicated to me by the Director of the US Naval Academy's Internal Research Department, CAPT (ret.) Glenn Gottschalk.
5 It is instructive that the 1971 US Supreme Court ruling upholding conscientious objection rejected selective conscientious objection over concerns that selective conscientious objection could not be administered with sufficient uniformity and fairness.
6 McMahan acknowledges this might be the case for non-defensive wars and humanitarian interventions, but thinks selective conscientious objection and the promotion of combatants' moral responsibility for assessing *ad bellum* would be justified by a reduction in unjust wars (2011: 139, 146). He also rejects Ryan's historical examples of combatants refusing to fight in just wars (Ryan 2011: 140).
7 McMahan rightly argues against Kutz's contention that the internal relations of a group can justify attacking another group (2009: 82; cf. Kutz 2005: 176).
8 Unprivileged irregulars have moral duties not to murder, rape, etc., but do not have role-based martial duties.
9 McMahan correctly argues against Hurka that combatants' ceding a right against being attacked to their enemies cannot justify those actors' performing objectively unjust actions (2006: 199–218, 210–212). While Hurka and I share the same basic idea about reciprocal permission, I think my formulation is better than one stating that combatants cede a claim-right against being attacked but retain one of defending themselves. The latter formulation would seem to preclude offensive operations on a tactical construal of what self-defense means and support the asymmetry thesis on a moral reading of self-defense wherein only the just side may engage in offensive operations.
10 The difference between service members' positive moral reasons and permissions accounts for how service personnel from a basically just state can act justifiably in targeting terrorists in a failed state, even while wronging noncombatants who are killed as a side effect of the raids. The noncombatants are wronged because, lacking a military of their own, they cannot be modeled as extending reciprocal permissions to other militaries to pursue their legitimate activities while posing a proportionate risk to noncombatants. Nonetheless, the agent combatants are adhering to their institutionally mediated moral duty in acting. In general, the harmed noncombatant, *qua* autonomous person, has grounds to find a foreign combatant's service to her basically just state consent-worthy in the same manner she does a foreign police officer's arresting someone in the officer's country. However, the harmed noncombatant does not have grounds to consent to a foreign combatant's attack on her or foreign police officer's arrest of her *qua* the target of these actions because she is not benefited by the governance regime indirectly or directly justifying the combatant's, and police officer's, actions, respectively.

198 *The moral equality of combatants*

11 There are similarities between my view and that of Vitoria. Vitoria argues that it is permissible for soldiers to deploy in all cases where the injustice of a looming war is not obvious, because it would be impractical for the prince to explain the rationales to every soldier and because commoners do not have formal influence on matters of state anyway (2010: Q2.2.3). Soldiers are duty-bound to deploy even to dubious defensive wars due to the risk to their people if they wrongly refuse deployment (2010: Q2.3.5). Finally, Vitoria argues that both sides can be justified in a war in the sense that one side is objectively justified and the other is subjectively justified (e.g., all the evidence suggests their cause is just) (2010: Q2.4.2). Apart from methodological and foundational differences, my conclusions are different than Vitoria's in that I argue both sets of combatants can be objectively justified by acting in the FRPN right manner. Second, I focus on the difficulties associated with granting selective conscientious objection rather than the difficulties in explaining *cause belli* to service personnel as an element justifying obedience.
12 Renzo has a similar idea; Renzo, M. "Duties of Citizenship and Just War" (unpublished manuscript), section 5.
13 Estlund argues that judges cannot substitute personal judgment if the system is just (2007: 221).
14 For discussion of this possibility, see Weber (1958: 126) and Coady (1990: 260–262).
15 Revisionists would seem to be committed to this position.
16 McMahan rightly rejects Estlund's view that suitably arranged democratic processes are like a jury's decisions and so service members can accept a democratic leader's order to go to war as being procedurally just even if it is factually wrong (2009: 68–69; cf. Estlund 2007: 224). While I share with Estlund the idea that it is generally wrong for a service member to rely on his own judgment regarding *ad bellum* issues, my argument is not linked to democratic processes but instead the basically just institutions of both democratic and non-democratic states.
17 Collaterally harmed noncombatants in failed or unjust states are wronged, but blame is not properly directed at the agent personnel, assuming they have carefully observed *in bello* restrictions. Rather, blame should be directed at the militants in the failed state or leaders of the unjust state whose activities have goaded the agents' just response. Benbaji makes a similar argument about the shifting of blame in reference to conventional inter-state wars (2011: 64).

References

Benbaji, Y. (2011) "The Moral Power of Soldiers to Undertake the Duty of Obedience," *Ethics*, 122: 50–52.

Benbaji, Y. and Statman, D. (2019) *War by Agreement*, Oxford: Oxford University Press.

Coady, C. (1990) "Messy Morality and the Art of the Possible," *Proceedings of the Aristotelian Society*, 64: 259–279.

Dill, J. and Shue, H. (2012) "Limiting the Killing in War," *Ethics and International Affairs*, 26(3): 311–333.

Garren, D. (2007) "Soldiers, Slaves, and the Liberal State," *Philosophy and Public Policy Quarterly*, 27(1–2): 8–11.

Gross, M. (2010) *Moral Dilemmas of Modern War*, Cambridge: Cambridge University Press.

Estlund, D. (2007) "On Following Orders in an Unjust War," *Journal of Political Philosophy*, 15(2): 213–234.

Hurka, T. (2005) "Proportionality in the Morality of War," *Philosophy and Public Affairs*, 33(1): 34–66.

The moral equality of combatants 199

Hunt, J. (2008) "Creating a MarSOF MOS," *Marine Corps Gazette*: 42–47.

Kolb, L. (2008) "Reagan and the Draft," *Washington Times*. www.washingtontimes.com/news/2008/may/16/reagan-and-the-draft/.

Kutz, C. (2005) "The Difference Uniforms Make," *Philosophy & Public Affairs*, 33(2): 148–180.

Lazar, S. (2017) "Just War Theory: Revisionists vs. Traditionalists," *Annual Review of Political Science*, 20: 37–54.

McMahan, J. (2006) "On the Moral Equality of Combatants," *Journal of Political Philosophy*, 14(4): 377–393.

McMahan, J. (2008) "The Morality of War and the Law of War," in Rodin, D. and Shue, H. (eds), *Just and Unjust Warriors*, Oxford: Oxford University Press.

McMahan, J. (2009) *Killing in War*, Oxford: Oxford University Press.

McMahan, J. (2011) "Duty, Obedience, Desert, and Proportionality in War," *Ethics*, 122(1): 135–167.

Parfit, D. (2013) *On What Matters*, Oxford: Oxford University Press.

Robinson, P. (2009) "Integrity and Selective Conscientious Objection," *Journal of Military Ethics*, 8(1): 34–47.

Ryan, C. (2011) "Democratic Duty and the Moral Dilemma of Soldiers," *Ethics*, 122(1): 10–42.

Shanker, T. (2006) "Young Officers Leaving the Army at a High Rate," *New York Times*, www.nytimes.com/2006/04/10/washington/10army.html?_r=1.

Skerker, M. (2014) "An Empirical Defense of the Moral Equality of Combatants," in Ellner, A., Robinson, P., and Whetham, D. (eds), *When Soldiers Say No*, Surrey: Ashgate.

Steinhoff, U. (2008) "Debate: Jeff McMahan on the Moral Inequality of Combatants," *Journal of Political Philosophy*, 16(2): 220–226.

Vitoria, F. de (2010) *On the Laws of War and Peace* in Pagden, A. and Lawrence, J. (eds), *Political Writings*, Cambridge: Cambridge University Press.

Weber, M. (1958) "Politics as a Vocation," in Gerth, H. and Mills, C. (eds), *From Max Weber*, Oxford: Oxford University Press.

Wing, I. (1999) "Selective Conscientious Objection and the Australian Defence Force," *Australian Defence Force Journal*, 137: 31–40.

Index

agent-relative preferences 168n15
Anscombe, G.E.M. 28
asymmetry thesis 7, 15–16, 24–5, 74, 97, 196

basically just state 119, 133
Bazargan, S. 50n17, 51n22, 97
Benbaji, Y. 135n11, 168n10, 169n22, 198n17
Bomann-Larsen, L. 27

chevauchée 149
collective action 11–12, 24, 35; contributions toward 36, 77–82; justifications of 76; in war 14
collective moral responsibility 121–3, 125, 127, 159, 164
collectivism 8
conscience 184
consent: hypothetical 42–3, 127–8, 135n7, 143, 161, 173; tacit 42–3
contractualist model 124, 127, 129
corporate intention 36, 86, 103, 110; in the military 102–5
culpability 16, 54–5, 64, 70, 78, 81, 93, 96, 98, 101, 107; attacker 61; for collective action 17; epistemic element in the military 98–102; intentional component in the military 102–5; motivational element in the military 106–11

defensive rights *see* rights
discrimination 5, 145–9
duty: joint 122; professional 122–3, 125–6, 132; to support just institutions 159, 195

eliminative killing 68
exceptionalism 9
excuse 188–9
Estlund, D. 198n16

Fabre, C. 48n3, 48n6
fact-relative sense relevant to professional norms 185–94
failed states 197n10
Ferzan, K. 51n23
Frowe, H. 11–13, 31–4, 48n5, 71n15, 72n23, 112n11

global government 124
goal-oriented collective 35, 54, 77, 80–2; liability for 78

Hurka, T. 169n22, 170n26, 197

individualism 94–6, 111; descriptive 8–9, 54; evaluative 8–9
innocent projectile 64–9
institutions 120–5, 129, 159, 164
irreducibly corporate action 11, 75–6, 80–2, 85–93, 98; agents behind 88; contributions toward 85–93, 106; culpability for 96–112; justification of 89–93; liability for 78; objections to concept 93–5
Isaacs, T. 35

joint mechanism 87
jus ad bellum 3, 5, 91, 111; responsibility for 175
jus in bello 5, 75, 102, 111, 138–9, 144, 156, 161–2, 173
justification 16; for collective action 17, 85–93; evidence-relative 191, 193; fact-relative 183–5, 188, 190; in military context 191, 193
just war theory 9, 17, 75, 83, 94, 96, 111

Lazar, S. 49n15
liability 4, 6–7, 14–16, 47, 55, 62, 64, 70, 78, 98; for actions in war 35–7;

Index 201

agent-responsibility 37–42; definition 29; hybrid model 31; objectively unjust proceeding 28–30; strict 38–9; theories of 26; unjust threat 28–9

McMahan, J. 11–13, 28, 31, 37–42, 50n19, 112n3n11, 113n22, 119, 138–9, 182; regarding combatants' consent 169n21, 170n23, 170n24; objective justification 184
McPherson, L. 35, 47n2
military: enlistment 133; role of 123; service 132–4
Miller, S. 120
mistaken attacker 56–8
moral equality of combatants 3, 6–7, 92, 120, 156, 172–3, 183–4
moral division of labor 111
moral luck 40–2; consent-based 42; external imposition of 43–7
motives 107; professional 107–10

necessity 145
negligence 102
non-culpable attacks 55–7, 60, 63–4
non-culpable threats 30, 38
norms: military 164–7, 183; professional 125, 129, 156

obedience, norm of 154–6, 172, 183
obligations, military 182
opportunistic killing 68
orders, in the military 105
organization 35, 54, 76, 87
other-oriented action 50n20
over-determined actions 82

participatory intention 97
police ethics 160
private military contractors 178
professional morality 135n5

proportionality: *in bello* 146, 149–54; in security standard 145
psychotic attacker 56–7, 62

reductive individualism 16, 38, 93–5, 196; critique of 25–6, 77; defined 10; differences among scholars 11–14; methodology 83, 113; role responsibilities 122; theories of liability 27
reductive traditionalists 173
reductivism 8, 24–5, 54, 70, 94–6, 111
reflective equilibrium 26, 112n11
regular war 19n1
responsibility: causal 38, 41, 58; moral 37
responsible action 16, 28, 35
revisionist just war theory 54, 74, 111, 134, 147, 149, 173, 196; differences among 8; method 6–7; thesis 4–6, 138, 153
Rodin, D. 35
rights: defensive 60, 63; institutional 145; joint 121, 125, 159; negative 121; positive 121

security standard 129–31, 139–41, 143
selective conscientious objection 119, 172–81
self-defense 3, 5
Statman, D. 135n11, 168n11
Steinhoff, U. 47n3, 170n24

tactics 129
Tadros, V. 47n1, 48n10
targeting: collectivized 138–42, 144; individualized 140–2
Thomson, J.J. 28–9
thought experiments 83, 100

Walzer, M. 170n23
waiver: hypothetical 59–63; to right to life 165

Zohar, N. 135n2

Printed in the United States
by Baker & Taylor Publisher Services